DIRECT
PUBLIC OFFERINGS

DIRECT
PUBLIC OFFERINGS

THE NEW METHOD FOR TAKING
YOUR COMPANY PUBLIC

DREW FIELD

SOURCEBOOKS
NAPERVILLE, IL

Published by: Sourcebooks, Inc.
P.O. Box 372, Naperville, Illinois 60566
(630) 961-3900
FAX: 630-961-2168

This publication is designed to provide accurate and authoritative information in regard to the subject matter covered. It is sold with the understanding that the publisher is not engaged in rendering legal, accounting, or other professional service. If legal advice or other expert assistance is required, the services of a competent professional person should be sought.
From a Declaration of Principles Jointly Adopted by a Committee of the American Bar Association and a Committee of Publishers and Associations

Library of Congress Cataloging-in-Publication Data
Field, Drew.
    Direct public offerings : the new method for taking your company
public / Drew Field.   p. cm.
    Includes index.
    ISBN 1-57071-146-1 (pbk.)
    1. Going public (Securities) 2. Securities--Marketing. 3. Direct marketing. I. Title.
HG4028.S7F538 1997
658.15'224--dc21   97-5297
                                                    CIP

Printed and bound in the United States of America.

Paperback — 10 9 8 7 6 5 4 3 2

TABLE OF CONTENTS

Chapter 2   *19*

The Time Is Right to Market Corporate Shares

To Gwendolyn

INTRODUCTION

Money for your company's growth is available from the largest pool of capital in the world. It can be had at zero interest and need never be repaid. It comes free of restrictions on how you run your business.

American households are ready, willing, and able to invest billions of dollars into direct shareownership of businesses but they have not been doing that. This book explains why. Then it shows how to get that money, on those terms, through Direct Public Offerings of corporate shares.

The reason we are not buying corporate shares is that we are not being sold corporate shares. We are not being sold corporate shares because that role has been left exclusively to the securities industry, which no longer appears to have either the interest or the ability to market corporate shares to American households.

This is the first revision of the original book on Direct Public Offerings. It is substantially expanded to include the last five years' experience with DPOs, as well as changes in the regulatory environment which make it easier to do DPOs. First published in 1991 as *Take Your Company Public!* (Simon and Schuster/New York Institute of Finance), it introduced the term "Direct Public Offering," or "DPO," as a way for businesses to raise capital by marketing their shares directly to individuals. It explained that the traditional underwritten IPO is not working to let most people invest in new issues. It showed how the tools of direct marketing could be used to offer shareownership directly to a company's "affinity groups," such as its customers and people in its community.

The original four chapters have been retained, with a few new facts inserted into the original text. Chapter Five, the "How to Do a Direct Public Offering" part of the book, has been substantially rewritten, based upon the author's experience and observation of the many Direct Public Offerings that have been done since the first edition. Three new chapters have been added to this edition and the Glossary, which many readers said was the most useful part of the book, has been expanded.

Chapter One of this book tells how Wall Street has changed, how it is no longer a readily accessible channel through which money can flow from individuals to businesses through shareownership.

Chapter Two shows that the money is really there and—just as important—that we "consumers" are ready to be sold on putting our money into shareownership.

Not every business is a candidate for a public share offering. Chapter Three helps you decide whether it is right for your business. Chapter Four explains how the securities industry does an underwritten public offering and when that may still be the way to go.

The how-to of a Direct Public Offering is discussed in Chapter Five. You are led through each step from the day you decide to go forward to the day when all of the money is in and you have hundreds, or thousands, of fellow shareowners.

New Chapter Six is called "The Regulatory Framework," and it carries the good news of positive changes at the federal and state regulatory level for encouraging Direct Public Offerings.

Chapter Seven is about a phenomenon that has only come of age since the first edition: "Selling Shares on the Internet." The impact of electronic share marketing is just beginning to be felt. We have already accumulated experience with DPOs announced, sold, and completed by using the Internet. This embryonic new medium is already improving communication with prospective investors, reducing cost, and making the entire potential of DPOs more realizable than ever.

We introduced "DPOs" in the first edition of this book. Now we have been able to add "Case Studies of Direct Public Offerings" as Chapter Eight. It tells the stories of specific successful Direct Public Offerings and also recounts some efforts that failed, with suggestions as to what went wrong.

In the extensive Glossary, you can find out what you need to know about corporate shares, public offerings, and direct share marketing.

The message is this: The money is there for your business, on the best possible terms. But the old ways of getting it are not working any more. A new way—Direct Public Offerings—will work. Here is how.

You can use this book in several different ways. If you are fairly new to the subject of public shareownership, then a front-to-back reading is recommended. Perhaps you know a fair amount about corporations and securities markets, but you doubt this book's premises—that individuals would like to invest in corporate shares but the mechanism is not currently accessible to them. If so, then Chapters One and Two may help you to believe these premises really are true.

You may own a business now and wonder if going public is the right objective. Perhaps you dream of becoming an entrepreneur but are blocked by the thought of being choked by a shortage of equity capital. Or you may be a lawyer of other advisor to these entrepreneurs or would-be entrepreneurs. Chapter Three provides the tools for deciding whether public shareownership is the right path for you or your client.

If an underwritten public offering is in the cards for your business, or if you have always wondered what the mystery of going public was all about, Chapter Four should cast light on the process. For those of you who are ready to get started, Chapter Five can guide you through a Direct Public Offering.

Marketing shareownership brings into play all of the federal and state laws that were intended to protect investors from unscrupulous or reckless perpetrators of scams and failures. There may not seem to be much of a relationship between the regulatory hurdles and the real frauds that occur, but compliance with the rules of the game is essential. Chapter Six, "The Regulatory Framework," is a beginning guide to choosing the right course and making the right decisions to stay within the law.

Direct Public Offerings and the Internet seem to have been meant for each other. They both are about direct access by individuals, without interpreters or gatekeepers. Chapter Seven describes the beginnings of this relationship between DPOs and the Internet.

You can dip into the subject at any point by turning to the Glossary. Virtually everyone, from complete novices in the world of business to corporate securities or direct marketing professionals, will find the Glossary useful. It joins the inside terms of these two specialties and defines them in the context of Direct Public Offerings.

The following sections summarize the book's chapters a little more fully.

Why So Few Corporations Do Underwritten Public Offerings

Shares of more than ten thousand corporations are being bought and sold in the public trading markets. Nearly every one got there through an underwritten initial public offering, an "IPO." Entrepreneurs once came to the securities industry because it had the customers, the stockbrokers, and the experience in selling shares to individual investors.

Today, only a token few entrepreneurs make it through the underwritten IPO process. Those who do go public find that they then share ownership in their corporations with a few institutions and speculators. Why? The supply of money from individuals is there, and entrepreneurs have a strong demand for equity capital. What keeps supply and demand from matching? The reason so few corporations do underwritten IPOs is that the old mechanism—the underwriting syndicate—is not functioning the way it used to. Investment bankers currently find more profit in re-arranging and dismantling, and those brokers who specialize in selling stock to individuals are a vanishing breed. Institutional money managers have displaced individual investors as the Street's most significant customers. Complex new financial instruments, such as options and asset securitizations, now compete powerfully with common stock as the basic product of the securities industry.

More undermining to underwritten IPOs than changes in customers and products has been the shrinking of the securities industry. Brokerage firms have been disappearing steadily, through liquidations and mergers, since the early 1970s. Among those hardest hit have been the firms that once sold IPOs to individual investors.

The Time Is Right to Market Corporate Shares

Now is actually a very good time to be going public. Aside from the pre-occupation of institutional money managers with short-term results, most investment decisions are not made based on the current stage of the business cycle. A basic truth is that, when held for several years, corporate shares have consistently been the best investment. Direct Public Offerings are all about finding the individuals who will see the long-term potential of a company and reaching them with an effective marketing program.

Owning shares in an entrepreneurial corporation fits with some of the major trends that will likely be with us for the next several years. Chapter Two looks at the changes taking place in six major areas—people's personal values, politics, economics, finance, technology and work ethic. Together, these changes will encourage individual shareownership of entrepreneurial corporations.

Chapter Two examines each of these six trends. Much of this chapter is opinion. You may disagree. It is presented as food for thought and as a rationale for making the decision that you can successfully market your company's shares directly to individuals who will invest their own money.

In Chapter Two you can find the themes for your own direct share marketing programs. Wall Street has perennially given us credit for only two motivations: fear and greed. But now, marketing of consumer goods and services has gone well beyond fear and greed into the hierarchy of human needs and unconscious desires.

Honest, fair and effective Direct Public Offerings have only to draw on this ready knowledge and developed art.

Is Public Ownership Right for You?

The balance of the book is directed to the entrepreneur who has a business, or an idea for a business. Chapter Three is presented to help an entrepreneur decide if public ownership fits both the corporation and the objectives and personality of the entrepreneur. We begin with 20 questions intended to help the entrepreneur (as well as corporate directors, lawyers, and advisors) face some facts about the business and some issues of personal motivation. Beyond the numbers analysis come the twin issues: "Is my company an attractive investment proposition?" and "Am I suited to sharing ownership of my business with the public?"

Reasons for choosing a DPO have been gathered from entrepreneurs who have taken their companies public. Then a "Screen Test for a Direct Public Offering" is provided to help you decide if your business is a DPO candidate.

Pathways are provided that help to answer the questions: "How much money can I raise?" and "What percentage of my company do I have to sell?" Sometimes the answer is that more time and development is needed before going public makes sense.

How an Underwritten IPO Is Done

There are some instances when an underwritten IPO may be available and may still be the best alternative. Chapter Four explains how an underwritten IPO is done, where this method began, and when it may work today. The risks and costs of an underwritten IPO are described — those that come with success as well as those that come with failure.

The mechanics of an underwritten initial public offering are explained, including how to shop for a managing underwriter. What the "letter of intent" means—and what it does not mean—is made clear. You will see how the shares are sold and to whom. The process and its ritual are demystified. Some situations are described for which an underwritten initial public offering may be the right choice, when it may work better than a Direct Public Offering.

How to Do a Direct Public Offering

Chapter Five is a how to description, drawn from my experience in the direct marketing of more than $100 million in corporate shares in over 20

DPOs. You will be led step by step through the entire Direct Public Offering, beginning with how to prepare your corporation to go public. You will learn how to price your shares fairly and design a successful direct share marketing program, including how to do the necessary market research. There are sections on preparing a schedule and budget, as well as on proposals and contracts.

Chapter Five shows how to manage the process, how to bring allies into the marketing campaign, and how to select target markets and media. A big part of the process is selecting the right team, including the project manager, the lawyer, the marketing people, a systems manager, and the exchange specialist or over-the-counter market makers for the new shares. There are suggestions about preparing the prospectus, fulfilling responses, and closing sales.

New responsibilities come with the opportunity to raise capital through going public. Chapter Five concludes with how to comply with ongoing securities law requirements, maintain a fair market price for your shares, and get the most from your status as a public company.

The Regulatory Framework

Most of us are accustomed to viewing regulations and regulatory officials as the enemy, or maybe just a necessary evil. In securities marketing, it is easy to drop into that perspective, since rules about securities are usually in the way of our getting the money we need right now.

However, securities regulations only exist because so many people have abused the public's trust, to extract money for promises and pieces of paper. Chapter Six takes a position of acceptance that these are the rules, however out-of-date or ineffectual they may be in our opinion.

This overview of the securities regulatory framework also acknowledges that the officials who administer the federal and state securities laws have, in my experience, been working hard and fairly to balance the objectives of business with the interests of the individual investors they are charged with protecting.

Particular regulatory assistance has been created for small business. Much of it is described in this chapter, such as the Small Business Initiatives adopted by the Securities and Exchange Commission. There is a brief introduction to the Small Corporate Offering Registration (SCOR), a fast and inexpensive way to do direct public offerings of $1 million or less. This is a new and rapidly expanding tool, ideal for a Direct Public Offering.

Selling Shares on the Internet

Whatever you may find in this Chapter Seven that you are ready to use, a warning: it's probably already out of date. Just like the hardware and software of computer communications, any moment's state-of-the-art is the next moment's obsolescence.

It is in this contemporary medium that the securities regulators have been especially industrious and helpful. Much of the chapter describes and comments upon new guidelines for marketing securities through electronic delivery.

Doing Direct Public Offerings on the Internet is the frontier of corporate finance. We have only begun to offer ways in which you can develop your own opportunities for raising equity capital through electronic communication.

Case Studies of Direct Public Offerings

For the first time ever, this book can bring together a set of DPO case studies, with enough diversity to begin disclosing some general principles. You will find the similarities, the trends, and the common problems.

There have been occasional Direct Public Offerings as long as there have been corporations issuing shares—that is the only way capital was raised in the beginnings of public shareownership. Each time, however, a company had to "reinvent the wheel." There was no passing on of experience from one to the other.

It is the purpose of this book to help entrepreneurs decide whether the DPO alternative is for them and, if so, how to do one successfully. Learning from others who have been there is the goal of these case studies.

Glossary

The Glossary is much more than short definitions of a few standard terms. It comprises nearly a third of the book and explains the meaning of many strange and colorful phrases that populate both the worlds of corporate finance and direct marketing. But the Glossary goes further, putting those meanings in the context of this book's theme: Underwritten public offerings are not happening much anymore, and you can do better through a Direct Public Offering.

Marketing shares directly to the public may seem new to you and filled with risk, but it is really just a return to basics. Shareownership in your company is something of real value, created through inspiration, startup capital, and hard work. You who created that value are best able to select the people who will now wish to share it. No one can tell them your story more effectively and fairly.

It has been nearly 40 years since I first helped a company go public, through an underwritten IPO. My experiences as a securities lawyer for entrepreneurs convinced me there had to be a better way. The DPO is that better way. For most entrepreneurs today, it is the only way. I hope this book will convince you of that and help guide you through a Direct Public Offering.

CHAPTER 1

WHY SO FEW CORPORATIONS DO UNDERWRITTEN PUBLIC OFFERINGS

Of all the roller coaster rides on Wall Street, few can match the ups and downs of initial public offerings, the underwritten IPOs put together by investment bankers and sold through syndicates of securities brokerage firms.

At the peak in 1961, more than 1,000 entrepreneurs saw their company's shares sold to the public. The next year, there were fewer than 700 and then half that many by 1964.

The next high, one not equaled since, was in 1969, when there were again just over 1,000 IPOs. And then the drop was almost to ground zero. There were never more than 50 IPOs in any year from 1974 through 1979.

The pace has been in the 150 to 500 range since 1980, except for the miniboom of 1983 when there were nearly 900. [These numbers have only moved up a little since this book was first published in 1991, despite a widely-acclaimed "hot IPO market." There were 608 IPOs in 1994 and 579 in 1995, while the dollar amounts totaled nearly $30 billion each year.] An average of fewer than 300 first-time stock offerings a year does not even replace the loss of public companies through merger, liquidation, and stock repurchase programs.

Even these numbers are deceptively large. In the last few years, many IPOs have been new closed-end mutual funds. They are publicly traded pools of money that have been invested in municipal bonds or other securities. In 1985, four out of the largest five IPOs were funds for investment in securities or real estate.

[Several major IPOs have resulted from the spinoff, or restructuring of large public companies. Of the ten largest IPOs (all of which were in the last decade), most resulted from repackaging companies like Sears, Pacific Telephone, AT&T, Coca-Cola Enterprises, and Nabisco.]

Another distortion resulted from the hundreds of mutual savings and loan associations which have converted to the stock form since 1982. They had technically been owned by their depositors and borrowers. When they sold shares for the first time, some of them were among the largest IPOs ever.

IPOs Are Way Behind Supply and Demand

Those numbers really start speaking to us in the context of what has been happening to entrepreneurs and to investors in areas other than IPOs.

United States' gross national product, adjusted for inflation, had tripled from the 1961 peak in IPOs to 1990. But the number of corporations making first time share offerings dribbled into the last half of the 1970s at only a tenth of the previous decade's level and has never recovered its pace of the 1950s.

A more realistic comparison is the level of initial public stock offerings with measures of supply and demand—the supply of cash in the hands of individuals who could invest and the demand shown by the number of entrepreneurial corporations which could go public.

[According to the Securities and Exchange Commission's *Report of the Advisory Committee on the Capital Formation and Regulatory Processes*, issued July 24, 1996, "The fact that the primary equity markets have not demonstrated any long-term upward trend as a source of capital since 1933, despite the fact that real Gross Domestic Product has tripled during that period, amply justifies an inquiry into possible regulatory inefficiencies." This book takes the position that it is the traditional marketing structure, more than regulatory inefficiencies, that is stifling the sale of corporate shares to individuals, and that direct public offerings by businesses to their affinity groups will open up the flow of capital.]

The Supply of Money in American Households

From 1961 through 1988, the insured deposits in savings and loans grew from about $60 billion to nearly $900 billion. Then there was the growth in bank savings, and the $300 billion that has gone into money market mutual funds, a creature not even around in the 1960s. [By 1996, there was some $3.1 trillion in over 6,000 mutual funds.] Total assets of households increased from $1 trillion to nearly $10 trillion. Increases in household assets and deposits do not necessarily translate into money that could be invested in corporate shares. There is risk to consider. Savings accounts will always give back what we deposit. Stocks may return more or less. What do we know about the supply of money for risk investment in new issues of corporate shares?

Individuals Have the Money to Buy Corporate Shares

One indication of what is available for shareownership is the level of so-called discretionary income, the amount left over after paying for a "comfortable living," as defined by the U.S. Census Bureau. Since the early 1960s, the number of American households with significant discretionary income has doubled. By 1987, these people had $320 billion of annual income they did not need just to live well. How much of that money is really available for taking risks? One indicator is the $210 billion that Americans put into legalized gambling in 1988. Another $40 billion or so is estimated to have been bet illegally, mostly on sports. True, gambling money gets recycled quickly, while cash put into stock investments is used in the business. But gambling activity increased in the 1980s at the rate of 10 percent a year.

Individuals Have Been Cashed Out of Corporate Shares

Since the late 1950s, individuals have consistently received more cash out of the stock market than they have put into the direct ownership of shares. [That trend is still continuing. As a 1996 Securities and Exchange Commission study put it: "The data also show that, for equity securities, redemptions have substantially outweighed issuances since the 1980s."] In the four years through 1988, household investment in corporate shares declined at the rate of $100 billion each year. Much of this money was returned to investors because of cash takeovers or management buyouts. More came from management use of corporate funds to repurchase shares, as a way to increase earnings per share by decreasing the number of shares. When investors received all this cash, they did not recommit it to shareownership. In 1988, when nearly $100 billion came out of stocks, there was a $200 billion increase in savings accounts. Amounts invested in debt securities grew by $450 billion. [A study by Harvard economist, Benjamin M. Friedman, based on Federal Reserve Board data, showed that the percentage of U.S. corporate shares owned by individuals went from over 90 percent in 1950 to about 70 percent in 1980, to 50 percent in 1994. According to the Securities Industry Association, households held 82 percent of U.S. corporate shares in 1968, and 58 percent in 1988. The proportion of total investments by individuals which was in corporate shares dropped from 44 percent in 1965 to 27 percent in 1975.]

Entrepreneurial Corporations Are Ready to Go Public

The low level of IPOs was not for lack of entrepreneurs. The rate of new corporations being formed had gone from around 100,000 a year in 1950 to over 700,000 in 1986. It more than doubled from 1975. Most incorporated businesses will never be candidates for public shareownership. But seven times as many new corporations are being formed, while the number of IPOs has gone down. Entrepreneurs have become a major market for services. Magazines have been built around them. Major accounting firms have created separate units to serve them. Banks have developed "middle market" strategies for lending to entrepreneurs. [In 1996, an estimated 20 million businesses have fewer than 100 employees, while accounting for half the nation's employment and more than a third of gross domestic product.]

Why Supply and Demand Are Not Being Matched

Individuals have a plentiful supply of money available to risk in growing corporations. More and more entrepreneurs have been starting their own businesses, creating an increasing need for shareowner capital. If only one in a hundred of the companies incorporated in the 1980s were to go public in their tenth year, the annual rate of IPOs would be over 6,000. If individuals could be persuaded to part with just ten cents of every dollar of discretionary income, there would be $30 billion for investment in shareownership. That could provide each of those 6,000 businesses with $5 million in new capital.

So why is that not happening? If you believe the supply is there, in the accumulated assets and discretionary income of individual Americans; if you believe that entrepreneurs are being held back by a lack of shareowner capital; then what is keeping the entrepreneurs and individual investors from getting together? The reason supply and demand are not meeting is because the old market mechanism is not up to the job. Underwriting syndicates do not have the capacity to match supply and demand. A new market is needed.

Let us take a look at how an underwritten IPO is done and then see why it is not working anymore.

Changes in Investment Banking

The structure of an underwritten IPO has not changed much since the 1920s. An entrepreneur signs a letter of intent with investment bankers, who are in the corporate finance department of a securities broker-dealer firm. That firm becomes the managing underwriter and organizes an underwriting syndicate with other securities firms. They all employ stockbrokers, who sell the shares by telephoning their customers and prospects.

An underwriting syndicate is a pyramid sales structure, organized around a single transaction. You can see it reflected in the "tombstone" newspaper announcements of completed underwritings. At the top is the managing underwriter, with any co-managers placed off to its right. Next down the pyramid are members of the underwriting syndicate, arranged in tiers, from major to submajor Wall Street firms, followed by regional brokerages and then local ones.

The power of an underwritten IPO has been this pyramid, the underwriting syndicate. With a syndicate of 50 firms, the strength of 20,000 brokers can be made available. If one in ten of these brokers completed just one $10,000 sale, an underwriting of $20 million could be sold to 2,000 individual shareowners.

Erosion has damaged the underwriting syndicate at all of its levels. It no longer commands the attention of investment bankers at the top of the pyramid; the middle has been mostly wiped out as securities firms have disappeared and, at the pyramid's base, brokers are busy selling products other than stocks. In the 1970s, the head of a leading IPO underwriting firm testified before the SEC about why so few corporations were going public:

~The public was burned by promotional issues in the 1960s

~Institutions dominate today's market

~The small broker has almost disappeared, and the large investment banking firms are not interested in small issues

To these reasons we can add three more: (1) Products promoted by the securities industry have changed, away from stock to futures, options and other new financial instruments. (2) Wall Street makes money today from businesses that are very different from being the intermediary between entrepreneurs and individual investors. (3) Most important, individuals are no longer customers of the securities industry, in the way we once were. What all of these changes get down to is that *we are not buying corporate shares because they are not being sold to us.* The reasons why so few corporations go public begin with the general shrinking and concentration of the securities industry.

The Street Gets Narrower

During the boom times for IPOs, hundreds of securities broker-dealer firms had corporate finance departments, staffed with investment bankers. They went searching for product, by calling on private companies in the industries that were popular with investors. Keith Funsten was president of the New York Stock Exchange, leading a large and successful advertising and promotion campaign for individuals to "Own Your Share of America."

Since the 1960s, underwritten IPOs have become an ever tighter bottleneck for the flow of capital from individuals to entrepreneurs. The securities firms which once filled out underwriting syndicates have largely disappeared. Those remaining have increasingly moved into different businesses. At all levels of the pyramid, from investment bankers through underwriting syndicates, down to stockbrokers and their individual customers, the infrastructure for underwritten IPOs is critically weakened. And there is no sign that the securities industry will ever recommit to marketing corporate shareownership between entrepreneurs and individual investors.

Always a cyclical business, the securities industry has suffered waves of mergers and liquidations every three years or so since the early 1960s. In 1961, member firms of the New York Stock Exchange reached a peak number, 681. They were "the Club," the firms with the size and stature to participate in underwriting syndicates. Rules of the Exchange fixed the rates for trading stocks, prohibiting any price competition. As ways were found to get around fixed trading rates, exchange membership began to decline, to 505 by 1975, when fixed commissions on the Exchange were deregulated into the free market. Three years later, there were 465 member firms.

Smaller brokerages, who were not Exchange members, could once have been counted on to fill the "selling groups" sold shares to local customers. In 1961, there were 4,700 nonmember firms. By 1977, only 2,800 remained in business. The effect of this narrowing of Wall Street was described by three chairmen of the Securities Industry Association. David Hunter, chairman in 1977: "Looking at it from the standpoint of the nation as a whole, I'm concerned that the industry is shrinking to a point where it may not perform one of its major functions—capital raising for business." Mr. Hunter's successor, Robert Baldwin, head of Morgan Stanley & Co.: "We are letting America's capital-raising mechanism deteriorate. Sometimes the destruction seems deliberate." I.W. Burnham II, a founder of Drexel Burnham Lambert: "We're shrinking. Our ability to finance corporate America is being weakened."

Waves of consolidation have continued. The end was prematurely described by Chris Welles in his 1975 book, *The Last Days of the Club* and 1981 gave rise to a book titled *The Year They Sold Wall Street* by Tim Carrington. After the October 1987 stock market crash, another cycle of mergers and liquidations began.

Syndicate Brains Versus Brawn

Investment bankers bring in the corporate clients and manage the stock offering for the underwriting syndicate. Investment bankers needed the brokers and traders to sell shares, while the brokers and traders needed the investment bankers to manufacture new product. This relationship of the investment banker "brains" and the retail broker "brawn" has largely come undone.

Status and power among Wall Street investment bankers is signified by the tombstone ads which announce a completed underwriting. Copies of the ads are imbedded in acrylic for display on desks and conference tables. They are made into wall plaques. Tombstone reprints on slick paper appear in packets given to prospective investment banking clients.

At the top of the underwriting syndicate pyramid in these tombstones are the managing underwriters. In the next layer are syndicate members from the 20 or so "major" firms. Over 70 percent of the underwriting volume is usually managed by just seven of these majors. None of the investment bankers consistently in this small group of the brains has a significant retail sales force, except Merrill Lynch. What they do have is a reputation for being able to design and manage corporate finance transactions.

If the brawn, the big retail firms like Smith Barney, Dean Witter and Prudential, can ever convince corporate management that they also have the investment banking brains, then they could muscle their way to the top of the pyramid. Instead, the brains developed a method to assert their dominance, without adding a sales force. They could put together a small group of institutional buyers for a new issue of securities, then go to the corporation with a pre-packaged underwriting. It was a technique used in Europe and called the "bought deal."

"Bought Deals" Replace the Syndicate

Underwritings have been the last of the old fixed fee business to go. One of the ways to remain in everyone else's syndicate is to maintain the industry standard for underwriting fees—6 to 7 percent for IPOs, depending on the offering size. When there is no syndicate, the investment banker who originated the deal keeps all the fee—rather than giving 60 percent of it to the selling brokerage firm. Since virtually all of the stock is bought by institutions, who do business with all the major firms, the only reason to form a syndicate is reciprocity. The originating firm includes other brokers in the selling portion of the fee, so that they will, in turn, be included when those other brokers originate a deal.

Beginning in 1982, the SEC let large corporations register an offering before picking an underwriter. That let them put it on the "shelf" until an underwriter came to them with a price for the entire issue—a bought deal. These shelf offerings did not allow time for an underwriting syndicate to be put together. The investment banker either presold all the securities to institutional money managers, or took some risk by using its own money to buy for resale.

Back in 1981, the year before the SEC rule was adopted, all but 2 percent of new common stock issues were sold through syndicates. The next year, more than 30 percent of the dollar volume was handled entirely by managing underwriters, without an underwriting. Even an AT&T common stock issue, over $100 million, was all sold by Morgan Stanley to institutional money managers in 1982. This was a dramatic example of how bought deals have replaced syndicated sales to individuals. Ma Bell was the symbol of individual shareownership in America—the favorite stock investment of more than two million households. With its huge capital needs, AT&T had been a sustaining source of syndicate fees for retail brokerage firms.

Bought deals have helped the brains do without the brawn. One result has been a drastic reduction in the ranks of brokerage houses with a retail sales force but no corps of investment bankers on staff.

"Soft Dollar" Orders Replace Syndicate Sales

Just as the issuers of corporate shares chipped away at underwriting fees through inviting bought deals, the institutional money managers attacked Wall Street's profits with their tool—"soft dollars." This device rebates a portion of the underwriting fees, by providing research reports and other services "free" to the money manager who places an order for shares.

The mechanics work like this: (1) A money manager decides to invest in shares being sold through an underwriting syndicate, (2) A "research" securities firm has furnished the money manager with research reports, without charge, (3) the money manager orders the shares from the managing underwriter, directing that credit for the sale go to the research firm, and (4) the research firm gets paid 60 percent of the underwriting fees on those shares. Soft dollars have become big business, with some brokers acting as an exchange—purchasing services for cash from non-broker vendors and trading them to money managers for commission business.

Now that institutional trading commissions are negotiated, there is little need for soft dollars on stock market transactions. Volume discounts are out in the open. Where the soft dollar business really flourishes is in underwritten new issues. That is the last part of the securities business where commissions are the same percentage on large orders as on small ones.

Soft dollar deals are a major reason that investment bankers would rather not form a syndicate. If the new issue will be popular with institutions, then make them buy it from the managing underwriter, who can keep the 60 percent selling portion of the underwriting fee. Forming a syndicate only siphons off commissions through directed orders used to repay soft dollar arrangements.

Investment Banking Profit Is Not in Syndicated IPOs

One of the reasons so few corporations are going public is that syndicated IPOs are no longer where the money is in investment banking. On a $10 million IPO, with a seven percent commission, 60 percent of that goes to the selling brokers and 20 percent to cover expenses. The managing underwriter stands to collect only $140,000 for investment banking services. Corporate finance departments of Wall Street firms are expected to pay their investment bankers an average of nearly $1 million a year. With the cost of support staff and overhead, they need to generate annual fees of at least $2 million each. In order to make ends meet, the IPOs that Wall Street takes on are the ones that will be likely to bring additional income, from previous venture capital investing, and from trading activities, merger and acquisitions, and a series of future financings.

IPOs are very time intensive. A lot of handholding is required since an IPO involves the financial security and personal dreams of an entrepreneur, who is probably going through this for the first time. Regulatory compliance is often difficult the first time, so is educating the sales department. A new product has to be introduced to the market. Not every IPO gets done. Some fall out near the end of the process, after most of the time and money has been spent. The successful ones have to carry the cost of the failures.

Most important today is the "opportunity cost" of committing investment bankers to syndicated IPOs. Even a smooth underwriting can use 20 percent of an investment banker's time over the six-month process. If people are off doing an IPO, they are lost to far more profitable opportunities.

The Profit Is in Merchant Banking

Underwriters arrange for money to flow from those who want to invest it to those who want to use it. In merchant banking, the people who do the arranging also put up the money. In addition to a commission, they are in for whatever gain or loss comes from the investment. Morgan Stanley's chairman put it bluntly: "We're becoming a merchant bank, with the whole range of principal activities much more important to us in terms of profits."

The Profit Is in Financial Engineering

Designing a new security allows a firm to charge fees without any direct competition—until the innovation gets copied. Examples have included "stripping" bonds into separate interest and principal segments and naming them TIGRS and LIONS; packaging auto loans like bonds and calling them CARS; even attempting an Unbundled Stock Unit to replace common stock.

The Profit Is in Program Trading

Using proprietary computer software, developed by its in-house "rocket scientists," firms take advantage of momentary price discrepancies between such markets as the stock exchange and stock options. This is seen as a far more profitable use of brains and capital than selling advice for a percentage fee. [According to the Securities and Exchange Commission's July 24, 1996 *Report of the Advisory Committee on the Capital Formation and Regulatory Processes*, the "U.S. capital markets have shifted —on a relative basis—from a primary role as a source of capital to a venue predominantly for secondary trading. The secondary trading markets for common equity have grown exponentially in comparison to the primary issuance market, with over $5,500 billion in secondary trading versus $155 billion in primary issuances in 1995. The registered primary issuance market for common stock has remained relatively stagnant as a source of capital since 1933."]

Hollowing Out the Middle of the Syndicate

Transformation at the top of the syndicate has drawn away the brains, the investment bankers who brought in the corporate clients and put the stock underwriting together. At the same time, the brawn of underwriting syndicates has been hollowed out—brokerage firms which that individuals have mostly disappeared.

The Vanishing Submajors

Below the 20 or so majors in an IPO tombstone ad, there was once a layer of smaller Wall Street brokerages, the submajors. Many of them had investment bankers who could manage IPOs, as well as a staff of retail stockbrokers who brought distribution power to underwriting syndicates.

Samuel Hayes, investment banking professor at Harvard, counted 23 submajor bracket firms in 1971. These were all important Wall Street presences in the industry and many had national retail networks. By 1978, his list had only two submajors. Five had moved up the pyramid and the other 16 were gone. Professor Hayes observed that: "The submajor bracket, which historically provided the vital retail distribution capacity for an underwriting syndicate,…has virtually disappeared as a result of the waves of mergers and liquidations in the industry."

Regional Syndicate Members Are Mostly Gone

Brokerage firms with headquarters off Wall Street often had the best retail distribution. They did very little business with institutions and concentrated on using local offices and hometown brokers to serve individuals. The fate of regional firms is illustrated by a 1955 tombstone ad, showing syndicate members for a General Motors stock offering. By 1977, every one of the eight Boston members had gone out of business, as well as 17 of the 24 California firms and 23 of the 33 in Pennsylvania.

Most of the industry's contraction continues to be off Wall Street, as regional brokerage firms are acquired or liquidated. At least 15 succumbed during 1988. Many of those remaining have been acquired by financial conglomerates looking for distribution of their life insurance and mutual fund products.

Crumbling at the Base of the Syndicate

Underwriting syndicates cannot sell a stock issue to individual investors without a broad base of sales people—ones who have customers interested in buying IPOs. The entire marketing effort is done in two weeks of telephone calls, with no advertising or other supporting communications. So many shares have to be sold, within such a short time, that it is rare for any single firm to do retail stock offerings in-house.

Most damaging to the IPO distribution pyramid has been shrinkage in the sales force. From over 100,000 brokers in the 1960s, licensed registered representatives at securities firms had dropped below 40,000 by 1977. While that number worked its way back up to 70,000 ten years later, more of the licenses were used to sell products other than corporate shares.

Fewer Securities Analysts Cover Fewer Stocks

The loss of stockbrokers dealing with individuals was not the only damage to the troops needed to sustain underwritten IPOs. Also important at the base of the syndicate are the securities analysts who issue reports on industries and individual companies. They generate trading activity in stocks the syndicate has brought to market.

Membership in the New York Society of Security Analysts began a steep decline in the 1970s. Because of the demise of regional firms, the New York Society includes nearly all the brokerage firm analysts. More important than the decline in the number of analysts is the fact that almost none of them follow corporations that have recently gone public. Why? Because that is not where the money is. Although there are over 10,000 stocks being actively traded, these analysts mostly cover only about 400 of them. Those are the ones bought and sold by institutional money managers. They are also the stocks for which speculation in stock options is available. At the "micro-capitalization" end (companies with a total market value of their shares at less than $100 million), there are over 3,600 stocks. Only 23 percent of these receive any analyst coverage at all, and less than one percent of the analyst earning estimates are for micro-caps.

One of Wall Street's rules is that everyone's salary and bonus must be covered by the customers or by the market. High-priced general overhead is not acceptable. That goes for analysts, whose work is either for institutional customers, who will pay soft dollars to document their investment decisions, or for the firm's traders, who try to make money by knowing something before others do. Neither institutional investors nor the firm's traders have an interest in the shares of recent IPOs.

"The Old-time Stockbroker Is a Dying Breed"

The broker who said that, to a *Wall Street Journal* reporter, went on: "We're becoming an industry of tax shelters and packaged products." Not many tax shelters anymore, but certainly packaged products. And packaged relationships are replacing the one-to-one dialogue of stockbroker and customer.

In the days when syndicates worked, the power came from thousands of individual brokers, each with a book of customers. Brokers knew their customers' financial situation and personal objectives. When a new offering was announced, they could éach call a few likely buyers, talk about the company, and help make a decision.

The retail brokerage house was once a provider of "back office" services to a confederation of independent brokers. These confederations stopped making sense when brokers no longer owned the place where they worked. In the 1970s, securities firms took themselves public. Others have since been acquired by huge conglomerates, like Sears and GE, Prudential, and American Express. When a brokerage is a public company, or a corporate division, the objective is net profit and cash flow for the owners. How well the sales force is serviced, or how much the brokers make, is incidental to the bottom line.

The old-time brokers represent a threat to the firm. If they leave, with their book of customers, there is that much less commission business to cover office rent, telecommunications, computers, and support services. Profit for the house is not in being the back office to a group of primadonnas, who can storm out the door with their revenue base at any time.

Profit is in capturing customer money and putting it into securities which are manufactured and maintained in-house. Profit is in customers who have turned their money over to the firm for management, without any ties to a particular broker. As Professor Hayes put it: "The intent is to make individual accounts more proprietary to the firm and less of an individual entrepreneurial activity."

Profit Is Not in Selling Stocks for Commissions

Commissions on selling stocks and bonds were once nearly the sole source of revenue for the securities industry. More recently, commissions have been less than 20 percent of total revenues. And a large portion of those commissions comes from selling futures, options, and other new financial instruments.

As the securities industry shifts away from commissions on stock and bond sales, there are fewer brokers and analysts paying attention to individual corporate shares. Less dialogue takes place with customers about company operations, products and management. Brokers stop using IPOs as the subject for cold calling prospects. There is not enough profit for the brokerage firm in selling stocks for commissions. Brokers are expected to produce more revenue than they can generate by selling a product that will be held for several years before it is resold. They need the faster turnover provided by futures and options. Brokers are also pushed away from selling individual stocks and toward products that make more money for their employer.

Evergreen Income Is Replacing Commissions

Wall Street is dismantling its commissioned intermediary business, turning to more profitable activities. Today's game plan for individual investors calls for converting them into sources of "evergreen income," a term which describes the year-round flow of fees from the customer, without any repeated selling efforts. Emphasis is away from commissions on transactions and toward getting an annual percentage of the household's assets. These fees come in on a regular basis, so long as the customer's money stays with the firm.

Fees based on assets under management are predictable. They get spread evenly over all four quarters of the year. They do not depend upon market cycles nor upon the personality of particular brokers. Compared with commissions on sales, asset-based fees are ideal for managers. The retail securities business can be made to fit within the financial conglomerates that have replaced Wall Street's producer/partnerships.

To implement the evergreen income strategy, sales people are encouraged to gather assets, through CDs, money market funds, or whatever "bridge" products will attract a customer to do business with the firm. Then the job is to convert that money into something that generates income for the firm just by being there, such as an in-house mutual fund. A major tactic is the "wrap account," which wraps in a management fee and brokerage commissions for a flat 3 percent per year on the customer's assets.

Initial commissions may be unprofitable, as they usually are with brokered CDs or money market funds. But the broker shares in the annual fees from mutual funds or other management by the firm. Gathering assets can provide a stream of future income, with little or no future servicing of the customer. Brokers become new business developers, rather than ongoing advisers.

At a big retailer like Shearson (now Smith Barney), evergreen fees accounted for a fourth to a third of total earnings. The firm became much less dependent upon commissions generated by a broker's book of customers. And, if the broker leaves, the customers will probably stay.

John Steffens, president of Consumer Markets for Merrill Lynch, described the change from a commission business to evergreen income: "It's called asset gathering. We asked ourselves, 'Where are the biggest pools of assets?' The answers were the $2 trillion held in certificates of deposit, several trillion in cash values in insurance policies, a trillion in trusts and a trillion in employee benefit plans. We decided we wanted to gather and manage those assets over a period of time."

One of the more subtle effects of the evergreen strategy is to transfer the judgment and trust relationship from the personal broker to the impersonal firm. Stockbrokers who generate commissions by advising customers to buy or sell are disappearing. That leaves no one who can call a few close customers and place shares in an IPO.

Shareowners Are Switched to Other Products

The New York Stock Exchange found, in one of its surveys of U.S. shareownership, that most people acquiring stock for the first time had gotten shares directly, from employers, rather than through brokers. These newcomers were viewed as prospects for other products. As the Exchange Chairman told the 1983 convention of the Securities Industry Association:

> The essential news, quite obviously, is that the securities industry's customer base has expanded by a whopping ten million individuals, including seven million relatively affluent, mostly younger people who have never owned stocks before.

> It is probably safe to assume, too, that most of these new customers and prospective customers still do not know very much about such relatively new components of securities firms' product mixes as options and futures.

The logical consequence of this view is for the securities industry to encourage individuals to sell their employer's shares, in order to put the money into products generating evergreen fee income.

Individuals Fear Wall Street, Stocks, and IPOs

Even if the syndicate could be resurrected somehow, there is another, larger obstacle. Individuals are afraid to do business with Wall Street, afraid to own corporate shares and afraid of underwritten IPOs. Some facts: The number of individual shareowners in the United States grew rapidly, from six million in 1952 to thirty million in 1970. Then it dropped, to twenty-five million by 1975. When it began to grow again, it was mostly through employee stock plans and direct sales of mutual funds, not brokerage accounts. Trades of less than 900 shares, typical of individuals, comprised over 40 percent of New York Stock Exchange volume in

1974. Their share was less than 10 percent ten years later. The volume represented by 100-share orders, a sign of the small investor, fell from 10 percent to less than 2 percent in the same decade. Only seven out of every hundred U.S. households had an account with a securities firm. A 1989 Roper Organization poll reported that only 11 percent of American households said they would trust a stockbroker to give good advice on investing a $10,000 windfall, while 35 percent would trust a commercial bank and 25 percent would trust a savings and loan. Only 1 in 7 households had dealt with a stockbroker in the past year.

Individuals Have Gone to Discount Brokers and No-load Funds

Individuals who do buy stocks, based on their own information and judgment, more often use discount brokers—not the firms who are in underwriting syndicates. The discount business concept is a no-frills order execution service: "You call us, we don't call you." It is the opposite extreme from telephone selling of underwritten IPOs.

Discount brokers have grown rapidly since they became legitimate in 1975. Estimates of their share of all retail commissions run from only 8 to 10 percent. However, retail commissions include fees paid for all kinds of brokered transactions: CDs, mutual funds, futures, options, bonds, as well as stocks. Most of the activity is in securities other than corporate shares, especially at full-service firms, where customers are paying for management and advice.

Measured by retail accounts opened, discount brokers pick up about 40 percent of the new individual investor business each year. These people are choosing to connect with the stock market through brokers who never get invited into underwriting syndicates. [The percentage of mutual fund sales in 1988 was 70 percent for funds with a brokers' commission. By 1994, the share was down to 55 percent, with no-load funds moving up to nearly half of all mutual funds sold.]

Individuals Are Afraid to Buy Stocks from Brokers

Then there are the individuals who just do not want to do business with a telephone sales broker, because of their past experience or stories they have heard. In a 1986 Harris Poll, 83 percent of those surveyed said they believe the stock market is driven by "unmitigated greed."

Wall Street insiders often confirm this perception. According to Donald Regan, former head of Merrill Lynch, as well as former Secretary of the Treasury and Chief of the White House staff:

> "The public has every reason to believe that the present game is rigged. It is."

George Ball, chairman of Prudential-Bache, told Congress:

> "Institutions, corporations and individuals no longer view the equities markets as viable places to raise capital. The October crash, compounded by insider trading, scandals, Boeskyism and a repugnance of corporate raiderism, has made people very chary of Wall Street."

A warning of these consequences came from the president of the New York Stock Exchange back in 1970:

> "Bluntly stated, the securities industry, more than any other industry in America, engages in mazes of blatant gimmickry...tending to undermine the entire moral fabric."

As the 1990s began, Wall Street was increasingly being portrayed in news, books and films as dangerous to one's financial health. [In a 1995 survey of 2,000 salespeople in the insurance, used and new cars, real estate, appliances, and securities businesses, the question was asked, "Is honesty important in your job?" Securities salespeople came in last in answering "yes," at 52 percent, compared to 88 percent in insurance and 82 percent in used cars.]

Underwritten IPOs Have Mostly Been Poor Investments

1987 was a bad year for most stocks, and only one in five of the IPOs that year was selling at year-end above its offering price. It was worse at the end of 1973, when year-end prices were higher for only 36 of the 417 stocks brought public in the preceding 18 months. Taking a longer period still shows dismal results.

Some 2,800 IPOs were followed by *Forbes* magazine over the period from 1975 to 1984. Only four in ten showed a higher trading market in late 1985 than the original offering price. Someone buying shares in each offering would have had an overall return of only 3 percent a year. Forbes asked:

> "But wasn't the game worth playing on the chance that you might end up with one of a handful of big winners? Not necessarily. It is unlikely that the average investor could buy 100 shares on the offering of a so-called hot issue because the allocations usually go to favored customers, which often include hedge funds and other institutional investors. So, even if you bought a big winner, chances are you didn't get much of it. Not enough to compensate for the inevitable losers. "

University of Illinois Professor of Finance Jay Ritter did a similar study of 1,526 IPOs during the same decade. The total return on those stocks, including dividends and price changes, was ten percentage points behind the S&P 500.

Professor Ritter also found that favored institutional money managers did much better than the general public. The average IPO stock jumped up

14 percent on the day of the offering, then went back down. Those big investors who "flipped" their new issue allotment on the first day did very well. Long-term investors did poorly.

Why is the record so poor? According to Alexander Schwartz, former co-manager of corporate finance for Prudential-Bache: "Our industry is totally to blame for encouraging companies to go public that have yet to show profits or have small profits but no real history." Each boom in underwritten IPOs since 1961 has gone bust, driving away thousands of individual investors.

Penny Stockbrokers Are Not the Answer

Going back to the 1920s, there have always been the penny stockbrokers. They are the securities firms dealing in corporate shares that come to market for less than a dollar per share. At that price, customers can invest ten thousand dollars and imagine becoming a millionaire when the share price goes from ten cents to ten dollars.

Some of these brokers run "boiler rooms" or "bucket shops," with hundreds of licensed representatives making cold calls to prospect lists all over the country. There are wild stories about self-dealing, market manipulation and other forms of stock fraud. State securities administrators run highly publicized crackdowns, and the games float to a new location. Penny stockbrokers will probably always be there. They advertise to entrepreneurs, as the way to go public and achieve the American Dream. There may be some who are legitimate. The record of seven decades is against them.

The Consequence: Few Corporations Are Doing IPOs

The reason why so few corporations are going public is because Wall Street is not making a priority of selling IPOs. At the top of the underwriting syndicate, many investment banking "brains" have deserted IPOs to go into the businesses of merchant banking, program trading, and M&A dealmaking. To protect their position as "majors," they go around the syndicate, arranging bought deals between large corporations and institutional money managers. They are not creating stock offerings for sale to individuals.

The big retail securities houses, the "brawn," are paying salespeople to put individuals into packaged products, ones that generate evergreen income through management fees and rapid turnover. Entrepreneurial stockbrokers, who advise their individual customers on stock selections, are on their way out. Smaller Wall Street firms, the "submajors," are gone, as are most of the regional brokerage houses.

There are scarcely any suggestions that Wall Street intends to reverse these trends and use syndicated IPOs to sell shares to individuals. Everything points to private funding through institutional venture capital firms and a few very wealthy individuals, followed by "public" offerings sold exclusively to institutional money managers and a few very wealthy individuals. Even if the securities industry tried to recapture the new issues booms of the 1960s, Wall Street is no longer the route to household capital. Most of us are afraid to trust our money to a broker's stock recommendation. New investors are choosing discount brokers, whose way of doing business does not fit the underwriting syndicate. Nor is there indication that the securities industry has any other program for matching the supply of household funds with the need for entrepreneurial capital. There will have to be a new market mechanism, a way around Wall Street.

CHAPTER 2

THE TIME IS RIGHT TO MARKET CORPORATE SHARES

The reason why so few entrepreneurs are selling shares in public offerings, and so few individuals are able to buy shares in IPOs, is because the traditional marketing mechanism is not working very well. The problem is with the intermediary system, not with individuals' supply of money or their motivation to own shares.

Right now is actually a very good time to be going public. Owning shares in an entrepreneurial corporation fits with some of the major trends that will be with us for the next several years.

Values of today's Americans favor entrepreneurs over bureaucracies. We do not trust government or big business. We believe in our personal potential and we want a sense of community and participation in decisions affecting our lives.

Politics is moving away from geographical boundaries and toward specific issues. One way individuals will regain political power is through corporate shareownership. Control of corporations will pass from management bureaucracies to shareowners' parliaments.

Economics will shift from spending and debt toward savings and investment. Inflation will continue to subside and interest rates will stabilize at their historic averages. The economic climate will encourage shareownership.

Finance will break away from Wall Street's control and into direct relationships between corporations and investors. Institutional money managers will fade, as will the casino games they support. Corporate shares will return as the favorite financial instrument.

Technology will make direct communication between individuals and corporations quick and effective. Electronic media will permit buying and selling stock to be easy and fair. Through their corporate shares, individuals will own the technology that replaces their labor.

Work will lose its class consciousness, as workers become owners. People will work to follow their own interests, rather than become servants to managers. Shareownership will free many from dependence upon a weekly paycheck.

While some structures are adjusting to meet these changes in attitude and behavior, Wall Street is choosing to concentrate on the past, as the intermediary in rearranging and dismantling. The future will be in direct relationships between entrepreneurial corporations and individual investors.

We are coming to the end of bureaucracy as the way to cope with economic realities. Government regulation of business and redistribution of income has not worked very well. Outright government ownership of business has become a rejected failure. What is working are enterprises meeting specific needs and responding quickly to change. In many countries, this occurs in an underground economy. In ours, it is out in the open but burdened by a structure that still accommodates bureaucracies. Change is coming first in the United States. Just as we led the way 200 years ago in political freedom, our country is forging the paradigm for economic freedom.

The Paradigm

Businesses which are patched together around anything but a single objective will lose customers, employees and access to capital. Corporations will be as large or small as the particular job they are trying to do. Entrepreneurs who lead them will become heroes and role models, right up there with sports and entertainment stars.

Successful corporations will be owned by groups of individuals who have an interest in the business, beyond just making money on their investment. These affinity groups will include employees, customers, suppliers, and neighbors. They can also come from a shared interest in the technology or concept at the core of the corporate purpose. Affinity groups will unite as shareowners across country borders and corporations will lose national identities. Coalitions will be formed among shareowners of different affinity groups. Corporate parliaments will enable individuals to carry out their ideas and values, as an alternative to governmental entities.

Shareowners will nominate and campaign for corporate directors with an enthusiasm seldom seen in government elections. Directors will select and monitor chief executive officers for the single purpose of serving the long-term best interests of the shareowners.

Concentration on long-term self interest will lead to less conflict with values of the surrounding society. This will allow governments to reduce their role as regulators of business behavior. The politics that most affects our lives will take place in the corporate arena.

Corporations will be an even more important influence on our material world than they are now. But they will be out in the open and subject to the control of vigilant individual shareowners. Corporate behavior will then reflect our current cultural values.

These are some of our emerging values, ones which will help entrepreneurs market shareownership in their corporations:

We Want to Participate in Our Own Issues

Our structures of business and government have been shaped by cycles of war and economic shocks. Those crises called for mobilization of the whole country under one management. People had to trust in big hierarchies as the only way to restore peace and prosperity. Few of us today actually experienced the feelings of panic from the Great Depression, when one in four could not get a job, or from World War II, when it was really possible that we could be invaded and conquered. Without those fears, we are not about to turn our lives over to big government or big business.

Most of our issues today are specific and can best be handled through small organizations, independent from large bureaucracies. And we want to participate in those organizations, to feel we have an influence over their direction and will get our fair share of their results.

In the direct marketing of corporate shares, an entrepreneur is offering a chance to participate—as an owner and a voting member. The corporation will have a specific goal—a human need to meet, a problem to be solved. Shareownership will be offered directly to individuals who have an interest in that goal and want to participate in its achievement.

We Want Better Games to Play

The logical prospects for shareownership are those of us with some money we do not need to cover basic needs. We can afford to play games. Our old games were owning things and looking good. But now we are ready for something more than the creature comforts and the appearance of having made it. We want games that count, that are played out in the real world, not in a casino or stadium or television studio. And we do not want zero-sum games, where the losses have to match the gains. We are looking for win/win arenas. Personal growth, not beating an enemy, is our challenge.

Investing in corporate shares is a game of skill, as well as chance. It is immensely complex, with variables that can never be foreseen. We participate, not only in choosing to buy shares, but also in electing directors and deciding when to sell. We can even be of service, by investing in corporations that meet human needs.

We Want to Be More Than Consumers

Consumer spending reached two-thirds of gross national product in 1986, in an almost steady rise since 1950. New consumer products and heavy marketing have worked to soak up our income. Then easy consumer credit got us to spend our future earnings.

Today, after a few years of declining inflation, we have lost the "buy now before it costs more" fever. We are looking for different ways to feel good. Values from earlier times and other cultures are coming in from the fringe, especially with the increasing power of women and the "60s generation." These post-consumer values open the door to marketing share-ownership in entrepreneurial corporations. For instance, some corporate objectives will advance the concept expressed as "right livelihood" or "follow your bliss." The business may provide ways to free workers from time-consuming chores, or offer opportunities for new careers.

Or take the idea that each generation should consume only the renewable resources of our earth, that we must preserve or replace all that was here. A corporation's products may be directed toward restoration or preservation. An entrepreneur may have included this value in the way the corporation manufactures its products.

We still want to have things and to look good. Investment in corporate shares will have to pass a rational analysis of risk and reward. It may help if owning particular shares will impress our peers. But corporate share-ownership can also be marketed as a way for us to be more than what we consume.

We Want to Do It Ourselves

We do not trust others to know what is best for us. So we become informed and use our own judgment. We read the labels for ingredients and warnings. We ask others with experience. Many of us who are already investors use discount brokers. We may belong to one of the 7,000 investment clubs or to an individual investor association. [Investment club members of the National Association of Investors Corp. have grown from 7,000 when this book was first published, in 1991, to over 25,000 by late 1996, with new clubs forming at the rate of 1,000 a month.] Our sources of information include a business news media that has vastly expanded in the last few years. Scores of investment newsletters and data bases have become available through our PCs. We are smart shoppers—educated and hungry to learn. High pressure, fear-and-greed pitches will not work with us. What will work is a direct communication from an entrepreneur, telling us what the corporation has done and where it is headed. We can then figure out what is in it for us.

We Want Advertising to Inform Us

Advertising and promotion have become our first source of knowledge. Sure, we know it is intended to convince us to buy. But we can separate the facts from the puffery. Advertising is efficient. We skim the newspaper or magazine. A radio or television message only gets us for 30 or 60 seconds. With our mail, we can stop at the envelope, the peek inside, the first sentence. We know about public relations, the way advertising comes out looking like news. We take it with the same understanding that we are being sold.

Advertising is entertainment. It is art. We get humor, music, and stimulation of our basic drives. Advertising has worked well in leading us to spend on something we use or consume. Advertising will be just as effective in persuading us to invest in corporate shares.

Politics

Governments are not working very well. Most of us feel our participation in them will not make any difference in what gets done. Corporate shares can provide us with a place to put our time and money where we can hope it will make a difference.

Corporations are Replacing Governments

For a while, we left all our social problems to the governments. Assign the issue to the public schools, create a new department, or put another line in the budget. We have learned that governments are limited in what they can do. They only seem to work when the issues are ones which affect us all in about the same way. One giant lesson has been that government-owned business does not work. Nor does protection of business through regulated prices or territories. Nations which combined business and government are having to restructure their economies.

Privatization has been underway since 1979 in Great Britain, where government-owned industry has declined from 10 percent of gross domestic product to 6 percent. Over 50 countries have joined in selling government-owned businesses. Sales prices totaled $43 billion in 1988 alone. In the United States, the trend is to cut business loose from government support, through deregulation and tax reform. Competition among corporations is replacing government in determining how economic needs will be met. Corporations are becoming more global and less identified with a particular nation. This happened through worldwide marketing, then in foreign manufacturing operations. Now, globalized stock markets are adding international ownership.

National governments will continue to decline as the instruments for meeting our needs. They worked best when war was the ultimate power.

We are now in a world where business and money determine who gets what, not armies and weapons. Corporations will be the vehicles for getting things done. Ownership of corporate shares will be the way to participate in the process of meeting human needs.

Corporate Parliaments Are Replacing CEO Kingdoms

Owning stock in a big corporation has not provided individuals with any sense of influence or participation. The corporation has been the domain of one person, the chief executive officer, who selects a board of directors and a line of succession. Many CEOs claim to serve "multiple constituencies" of suppliers, bank lenders, employees, customers and the general public, as well as shareowners. Dividends, as a percentage of earnings, are at their lowest level in nine years. Legislative proposals to reduce the double tax on dividends were defeated by lobbyists for big corporate managements, who would rather keep those earnings to increase their realm.

Institutional investors have been forced to break the "Wall Street Rule," which says: "If you do not like what the CEO is doing, vote with your feet—sell the stock." But the managers of huge public pension funds found they could not do this without taking losses because of their size and the limited number of blue chip corporations in which to invest. These big investors have begun acting like owners—voting against management and making their own proposals, meeting with CEOs to express their sentiments. This is helping to shift power in corporate governance from CEOs to shareowners.

There is an opportunity to market participatory shareownership, in contrast to a managerial class which reduces shareowners to the status of depositors. Shareowners can vote by secret ballot. Cumulative voting will allow any substantial coalition of owners to be heard. Directors can be nominated by shareowners and the entrepreneur/CEO can be the only employee allowed to be a director. The board chairman can be a significant shareowner who really runs the board on behalf of the shareowners.

Entrepreneurs Are Replacing Bureaucrats

Americans have always preferred small organizations to large ones. We distrust concentrations of power. These feelings have come to be centered on bureaucratic corporations that seem to be responsible only to the person at the top, who is responsible to no one. We admire the individual who ventures out with a small band of followers.

The biggest movement in business is the tearing apart of large corporations. It is as if the question had been asked: "How can we have corporations that are the right size, run by people motivated to serve the shareowners?" And the answer was: "By starting with big bureaucracies, breaking them into rational units and turning them over to people with an owner's motivation." The era of takeover and breakup will run its course as the supply of bargains declines. Besides, this is a game for only a few big players. The rest of us will get our chance to play a more constructive game, backing entrepreneurs who will replace bureaucrats.

Individual Shareowners Are Replacing Custodians

For a while in the 1970s, it seemed as if all the corporate stock would be owned by pension funds and insurance companies. Their rate of growth, if continued, would soak up most of the available shares. Individuals were in the midst of their 30 years of selling corporate shares. The trend has turned around. The percentage of institutional ownership has stopped growing, even as the total amount of stock outstanding has decreased through takeovers and repurchases. Individuals are again becoming direct owners of shares, through employee stock purchase programs.

Executives came to realize what payments into pension plans were doing to corporate earnings and cash flow, especially as institutional money managers continued to underperform market averages. The reason was given in the *Financial Analysts Journal* in 1977:

> Unfortunately, institutional investors do not behave like rational capitalists. Too often their objective is neither to create wealth nor to keep it, but rather to avoid losing their sinecures. In short, they act like what they are, which is bureaucrats.

CEOs retreated from defined benefit programs to the more predictable defined contribution method. Many substituted programs where the employee has to make some of the investment decisions. Others turned to plans which invested in the employer's own stock.

There has been encouragement from Washington for the concept of more individual shareownership. From the 1976 majority section of the Report of the Joint Economic Committee of Congress:

> To begin to diffuse the ownership of capital and to provide an opportunity for citizens of moderate incomes to become owners of capital rather than relying solely on their labor as a source of income and security, the Committee recommends the adoption of a national policy to foster the goal of broadened ownership.

Pension Reform Is Happening in Congress

We have begun to see some restoration of tax incentives for individual ownership of corporate shares. Individual Retirement Accounts are making a comeback. [In 1993, half of the profit from sale of shares in a "qualified small business" were freed from capital gains tax. The increasingly popular "401(k) plans" are beginning to allow employees to choose their own individual corporate shares to buy.] The political winds are right for marketing corporate shares to individual investors.

Economics

Most economic factors seem to come and go, and come back again. Individual investing in corporate shares has been that way. It was big in the 1920s and 1950s but has not come around since. There are three economic cycles that will propel individual shareownership in the next few years:

We are moving from inflation to stable prices.

We are displacing jobs with technology.

We are starting to spend less and save more.

There are volumes of data and theory to support the presence of these trends—and volumes to refute them. All we can do here is suggest why they help make this the right time to market corporate shares.

From Inflation to Stable Prices

Inflation has happened over many centuries in different civilizations. It has always ended. And it is during the periods of price stability that individuals have most often purchased corporate shares.

There is good news for those who believe that prices increase because there is more money available to spend. "Too much money chasing too few goods." The supply of money has recently been growing at below Federal Reserve target levels. Individuals have less money to spend, because inflation-adjusted wages have gone down in most of the last 15 years and are 8 percent below 1972 levels. A slowdown in business spending is suggested by the two-year decline in the index of leading indicators.

Government spending, as a percentage of gross national product, is going down and the annual deficit has been decreasing in most years since 1983. If interest payments on existing debt are excluded, government outlays and revenues are in balance. This means that a continuing decline in interest rates will substantially reduce the deficit, since most debt comes due within five years and will be repriced at lower rates.

The interest rate reduction which began in 1982 has survived some relapses and will continue, until we reach the levels which have existed in most of the last few hundred years—2 percent to 4 percent for long-term government bonds. Lower interest rates shift money away from fixed-income investments and into corporate shares.

From Jobs to Technology

Unemployment has been a great fear ever since families began migrating from farms to the cities in the 1500s. It has been the theme of religious reformation, political revolution, literature and the arts. We went through our last round of that awful fear in the Great Depression. World War II put people back to work. It seemed to prove that the answer was to create a demand for goods and services that were quickly used up.

In peacetime, the consumption of war materiel was replaced by the consumption of household goods and services. We invented consumer products, our advertising told us about them and our retailers sold them. Jobs were created, incomes rose, we spent more—which meant more jobs and income and spending. There were plenty of jobs available to absorb our increasing population. More money for consumer spending was created by increasing the proportion of women working, from about a third in the 1950s to well over half in 1988.

But the spending/jobs/income system developed problems. Inflation sent prices up faster than wages. What we produced, per hour worked, stopped increasing fast enough to let our employers pay us more for doing the same work. Now we have to use technology to extend what humans can do. According to the 1996 study "The State of Working America," by the Economic Policy Institute, the annual income of a median family fell 5.2 percent, or $2,200, between 1989 and 1994.

Productivity—output per worker—will be to the next few years what the goal of full employment was to the past. The United States still leads the world in output per worker, but our rate of growth has fallen way behind other industrialized nations, especially in the service-producing industries, which now provide 70 percent of our jobs. We spend less than any other major industrialized country on research and development related to industrial growth. Our production of machine tools and other capital goods has just turned up for the first time in ten years.

We have been making more jobs, rather than better workplace technology, because it has seemed cheaper. The cost of capital—interest rates— has been much higher than before the 60s, and the cost of labor has been stable to lower. Those days are over. Demographics predict a decline in the supply of new workers, particularly fewer women coming to work at lower pay than men and the aging of the baby boomers.

The future will be for those who can finance new production technology by marketing shares, rather than by borrowing money. Financing new tools through borrowed money, the route big corporations would likely take, means paying interest and setting aside cash for repayment. Shareowner capital is the natural way to match the risk and reward potential of investing in tools.

Entrepreneurs have a huge advantage over bureaucratic corporations in their cost of shareowner capital. Big corporations will have to sell stock at the price of their shares in the trading market, usually in the range of 10 to 15 times current earnings. Entrepreneurs can generally offer shares at higher multiples of current earnings. Investors see a greater chance of rapid growth and increased earnings from young companies than from mature corporations. But this advantage is academic with underwritten stock offerings. Institutions are the stock buyers in an underwriting and they mostly want big companies. To get long-term investors, ones willing to take the risk of delay and failure, shares must be marketed to individuals.

From Spending to Investing

Spending was our national policy for over 50 years. Spending brought production and production meant jobs. So we taxed away savings, gave tax deductions for borrowings, and encouraged spending on things that were quickly used up and left a demand for more.

But what if we spent on things produced outside the United States? What if foreign producers invested in tools that would increase production without having to hire more people? What happened to this policy when other countries caught up with our ability to produce? What happened was those countries increased wages, improved quality, and reduced costs—all at once. They had policies that discouraged spending and funneled money into building tools for production. We were stuck with tax laws and government programs that made it difficult to keep markets or increase incomes.

Change at the talk level began more than ten years ago. There has been consistent growth in the acceptance of the need to spend less and invest more. Change at the action level in government is finally underway. Deductions for interest on consumer debt have largely been eliminated. Investment income is less heavily taxed. Direct government spending programs are continuing to shrink. Even the defense budget will decline, following reductions in other countries.

Government spending has not been the culprit in the last few years. It increased by just one percent of national income, from 22.8 percent to 23.8 percent, between the 1970s and the 1985-87 period. But individual consumption was up five points in the same period, from 69.3 percent to 74.1 percent of national income. Savings—the percentage of our national income left over after spending—was 7 to 8 percent in the 1970s and 2 to 4 percent in the mid-1980s. Since investment comes from savings, net investment in business fell from 7 percent of gross national product in the 1970s to under 5 percent in the mid-1980s.

So, if we start spending less, we save more and there is more money for investing in corporate shares. Can we spend less? Will we choose to spend rather than save, or do we need to use 98 percent of our national income just to get by?

There are both signs and reasons showing that the spending/saving cycle has reached its spending apogee and is on the way back toward an increase in money available for buying corporate shares. They include: The personal savings share of after-tax income went from 3.2 percent in 1987 to 4.2 percent in 1988 and 5.5 percent in the first half of 1989. That translates into $100 billion more per year available for investing in shares. Of the 3.6 percent increase in the consumption-to-income ratio between 1981 and 1987, 3.5 percent was for discretionary purchases, not necessities. Consumer installment credit, which went from 7 percent of disposable income in 1950 to 19 percent in 1987, has been level for the last two years. Car loans, which make up 40 percent of consumer credit, now have an average maturity of 4.7 years. Many have balances of more than the car's trade-in value, slowing new car sales.

As a national average, we have started to spend less and many of us can afford to spend a lot less. Nearly 30 percent of American households have "discretionary income," which the Census Bureau defines as money left over after taxes and the necessities of life. That translates into 26 million households in the United States who have an average discretionary income of $12,300—a total of $319 billion a year.

It is true that our spending is still a huge percentage of our national income. But the statistics average out all American households. Some of us spend all of this year's income and part of next, using five-year car loans and increasing credit card balances. Since some of us are spending more than 100 percent of our income, that means that others of us are saving at way beyond the income-minus-spending average. Even within the same household, it is not inconsistent for us to borrow at cheap car loan rates and also invest in corporate shares. While consumer debt is high, households receive far more interest income, on deposits and other lender instruments, than they pay in interest expense.

Individuals have an immense amount of money already set aside, available for buying shares. Our deposits just in savings institutions have grown from $11 billion in 1950 to nearly $900 billion today. Bank deposits, real estate equities, mutual funds—all reflect our decisions to save and invest.

Finance

Values, politics, and economics have created the right time for entrepreneurs to raise capital. The right financial technique is the direct marketing of corporate shares to individual investors.

Corporate Shares Are the Best Financial Instrument

We have come through a period in which earning interest looked better than owning shares. It was also a time when tax laws, inflation, and institutional investors combined to chill individuals' interest in stocks. That cycle has turned. Before 1958, dividends on corporate shares provided a better current income than interest on deposits or bonds. Since then, there has been a "reverse yield." Dividends, as a percentage of stock prices, have been less than interest, as a percentage of bond prices. That explains very simply why the number of shareowners increased by 250 percent in the 15 years through 1958 and why individuals have been selling stocks ever since.

Throughout history, stock yields have been lower than bond yields only 2 percent of the time. Yet, a reverse yield has been the norm for the last 30 years. Stock yields have been relatively steady—in the 3 percent to 5.5 percent range. The reverse yield phenomenon has been a function of interest rates, which historically are from 2 percent to 4 percent on deposits and top quality bonds.

As interest rates continue to decline, individuals will return to buying corporate shares, the way they did in the 1950s.

Deposits. Interest rates on insured deposits are likely to decrease even faster than on bonds. Capital ratio regulations encourage banks to reduce assets and deposits. Instead of holding on to the loans they make, banks are packaging them as securities, for sale to institutional investors. They can then let deposits flow out by cutting the rates they pay individuals.

Government Bonds. These public debt obligations will soak up far less money in the future. Britain has been running a budget surplus since fiscal 1987. Japan's deficits peaked in 1983 and surpluses are expected by 1991. United States' deficits have been falling as a percentage of gross national product since 1985 and could be gone by the mid-1990s.

Corporate Bonds. Long-term corporate debt instruments are not likely to attract more money from individuals, for they are very different from the simple IOUs issued by the government. There are indentures and covenants and trustees. An investor needs to research the fine print of 100-page legal documents, as well as the credit of the company. Directors and managers have a legal duty to shareowners—to do everything to protect and enrich them that they would do for themselves. Their duties to bondholders are limited to what is in the legal documents.

Junk Bonds. Disillusionment with corporate bonds will increase with the junk bond experiences. There are $200 billion of these high-yield, high-risk debt instruments outstanding, compared with only $2 billion ten years ago. They do not carry investment grade credit ratings from Moody's or Standard & Poor's, so most investors have had to trust the investment bank that sold them the bonds.

Junk bonds became acceptable because investors bought two assumptions: (1) the investment bank that sold them the bonds would always make a market—there would always be an offer to buy them back—and (2) if the bond issuer got in trouble, the investment bank would find a way to refinance and prevent a default. Both of the assumptions were proved mistaken in 1989. In the first nine months of the year, 14 companies had defaulted on $3.4 billion in junk bonds. Several major junk bond investment bankers refused to make offers, at any price, to buy back bonds they had initially sold.

Options and Futures. At the riskier end of the investment spectrum, the options and futures market scandals have generated plenty of publicity for the fact that individuals nearly always come out behind. These are zero-sum games, where there is an equal loss for every gain. Commissions on the frequent turnover can quickly eat up any profits.

Limited Partnerships. We can expect less money to flow into limited partnerships. They are a cumbersome alternative to corporate shares, used to pass through tax losses and avoid the corporate double tax on dividend income. Congress has wiped out most of that advantage.

Miserable performance should help end the era of limited partnership investing. Some 12 million individuals put $100 billion into limited partnerships over the last decade. Their losses are estimated at $24 billion. Now they are learning that getting out of limited partnership investments is nothing like the trading market for corporate shares. Selling can be slow, difficult and costly.

Sales of real estate limited partnerships have gone down from $8.4 billion in 1986 to a $2.3 billion annual rate in 1989. That drop comes despite rich incentives for the securities industry—selling commissions of 8 percent, as well as other fees which bring total front-end costs to 15 percent—plus annual management charges.

Mutual Funds. There are over 1,000 stock mutual funds today, four times as many as ten years ago. [In 1996, there were an astounding 6,000 mutual funds of all types.] As they have grown, their performance has gotten worse. In the five years through 1989, only 37 percent of all diversified U.S. stock funds did as well as the Standard and Poor's 500-stock index, down from 52 percent in the previous five years. [According to Lipper Analytical Services, diversified U.S. stock funds gained an average of 12.1 percent a year over the ten years through 1995, compared with 13.8 percent for the Standard & Poor's 500-stock index. "Growth" stock funds in 1995 had a 20 percent return, compared with 37.5 percent for the Standard & Poor's 500-stock index and a 45.5 percent return reported for members of the National Association of Individual Investors Corp.] These results are not encouraging more individuals to invest in funds. [Maybe not, but the effect must have been delayed. Individuals have more than doubled the amount in equity mutual fund investments since this book was first published. Perhaps because they have been given so little opportunity to invest directly in new issues, through Direct Public Offerings.]

These managed investment pools will probably always have their place. But they do not work for those of us who want to participate in selecting particular businesses and in voting shares or communicating with management. If professional managers do worse than a dart board or other random selection, it does not really cost us to play the game ourselves. [One of the reasons for using mutual funds to invest was the high cost of commissions to buy shares, especially in the small investment amounts that most of us could afford. This has changed dramatically in the last five years. Discount brokers' prices were beaten by "deep" discount brokers and now, for those of us willing to use our computers, commissions are under $15 per transaction. In the last few years, more than 100 large corporations have adopted "Direct Stock Purchase Plans," so that individuals can purchase shares directly from the company's stock transfer agent, often with no transaction cost at all. Mutual funds also carry a hidden cost of the income taxation from frequent sales of shares that show a gain, which fund owners end up paying, even while their own investment in the fund stays the same.]

The Supply of Shares Has Been Decreasing

Individuals have been receiving cash in the redemption or takeover of shares in amounts far in excess of their new share purchases. According to the Federal Reserve, the supply of shares decreased by $287 billion in the period 1985-88. The ownership of corporate shares by households was reduced even more, by $401 billion during those four years, as mutual funds and foreigners increased their shareholdings.

Most of this shift out of corporate shares was not because individuals chose to sell. Buyouts by private groups and repurchases ordered by management forced investors to exchange shares for cash. Harvard professor Jay Light has figured that, if the trend continues, "the last share of common stock owned by an individual will be sold in the year 2003." Experience shows that the trend will not continue that long, that the cycle will come around and individuals will buy corporate shares.

Meanwhile, there is a plentiful supply of money going into other financial instruments. In 1988, when a net $96 million of corporate shares were removed from public ownership, the amount of deposits increased by $198 million, while net purchases of government and corporate bonds totaled $457 billion. The Federal Reserve's Flow of Funds data for 1995 showed individuals selling a net $168 billion of individual shares that year, while buying a net $88 billion of equity mutual funds.

When corporate shares are once again marketed to individuals, the supply of money will be there. Historically, the only channel for marketing new shares has been underwritten IPOs through investment bankers.

They have abandoned that activity in the last few years, largely to earn fees in the takeovers and restructurings that have reduced the supply of shares. Direct marketing will enable entrepreneurs to reverse this flow and recapture the billions that have come out of individual share-ownership.

"Deleveraging" Has Already Begun

While corporations have been taking shares out of investors' hands, they have had to increase corporate debt. Total corporate liabilities have gone from 45 percent of gross national product in 1980 to 54 percent in 1989. There are signs that the tide has turned, that stock will now begin replacing debt. Some of the biggest corporate users of junk bonds and other debt are beginning the process of "deleveraging," paying off those liabilities from money obtained through issuing shares.

There are many explanations for the reversal. Junk bonds now cost a 7 percent premium over Treasury bonds, compared with just 2 percent a few years ago. The stock market has become more favorable, with higher price-earnings ratios. Maybe it is simply the cycle that swings between net stock redemptions and net stock issuances.

Selling Shares Is an Entrepreneur's Best Alternative

Entrepreneurs with big-league dreams will reach a point where growth outstrips available capital. Selling shares to the public allows an entrepreneur to get the necessary money and still keep control of the business. With the underwritten IPO market largely unavailable to them, what have entrepreneurs been doing as they reach the going public stage? Thousands of them have been selling out.

Selling Out. The number of companies merged or acquired in the $3 to $100 million price range has gradually increased from 13,500 in 1985 to an estimated 18,500 in 1989. Their large competitors bought them to increase market share. Foreign buyers used them to enter U.S. markets. Many an entrepreneur has cashed out well but no longer had a business to build.

Venture Capital. An alternative to selling the whole business is to negotiate a private investment. The traditional source, venture capital firms, have gotten most of their money the last few years from institutional investors. As a result, many of them have become bureaucracies, protecting jobs by avoiding risk and by tying up entrepreneurs in a maze of restrictions.

When there is no functioning IPO market, it changes the character of the venture capital market as well. Any investor has to have an exit plan or two. Going public was the best one for successful venture investments. Now, the plan has to contemplate forcing the entrepreneur to sell out.

Institutional Investors. Institutions have lots of money. But very little of it has flowed directly into shares of entrepreneurial corporations. Institutional structures only seem to accommodate corporate investments that are channeled through managers and brokers. Insurance companies and some pension funds can put billions into office buildings and shopping centers, using their own in-house staff to evaluate and monitor. No similar process has ever worked well for buying shares of private corporations.

Besides, the great migration of money into pension funds is about over. The 100 largest money managers saw their pension accounts nearly double between 1984 and 1988, to a total of $2 trillion. The private sector side of that growth reversed in 1988 when corporate pension funds paid out $10 billion more in benefits than they received in new money. Funds for government employees are still growing, but about 80 percent of U.S. pension plans are overfunded, with $300 billion more than they are expected to need to pay benefits. This trend will accelerate as employers move away from defined benefit plans, install employee stock purchase programs, allow employees to direct their own pension investments, and shift from having employees to contracting jobs.

Institutions will increasingly invest only in the stocks of very large companies. But it will be less and less through professional managers, who are paid a fee to pick individual stocks. Their results have been worse than the stock market averages. So those responsible for the funds will shift to indexing, a computer-based program for investing throughout the entire market for acceptable stocks. Indexing keeps a weighted dollar amount in each corporation's shares. As the stock market averages move, so goes the fund's portfolio.

Indexing will soak up shares in the 200 to 1,000 major corporations. They will become the "institutional market." Any employer who still tries management of a pension fund through stock picking will be playing with money that is there for employees and retirees.

As institutions take over the big corporation stock market, entrepreneurs and individuals will be free to develop their own markets.

Individual Shareownership Is a Worldwide Trend

An announced motive for privatization—selling shares of government-owned businesses to individuals—has been to create "a nation of share-owners." England's Prime Minister has said: "It should be as natural for people to own shares as to own their own home or car." French government television commercials promote: "Shares—Today's Way to Save." Factories in Russia are selling shares to their workers. Managers want to sell stock to the public, to soak up some of the money earned in the black market. Russian co-ops, which are like limited partnerships, may soon be permitted to become corporations. They have increased 600 percent in number in the last year, to 100,000, and their revenues have grown much faster. Stock exchanges are blossoming in many European and Southeast Asian nations, attracting investment from local residents and from all around the world.

Worldwide, the privatization trend continues into the 1990s. Sales of state-owned telephone companies in Britain, France, and even Germany have been directed toward creating millions of new shareowners among their citizens. Another part of this individual ownership trend is the "microlending" that began with Muhammad Yunus and the Grameen Bank in Bangladesh. Beginning in 1977 with loans of $21 each, the Grameen Bank now lends more than $1.5 million to poor entrepreneurs every working day. The two million borrowers now own 90 percent of Grameen Bank's shares. Microlending has begun to work effectively in other developing countries, such as Peru and Bolivia, and in the United States.

Direct Share Marketing Is an Established Method

Corporate shares have been marketed directly for many years. The applications have been in special ways, to particular markets, but the direct share marketing method is well established.

Employee Stock Purchase Plans. A majority of the individuals who are investing in stock for the first time are being offered ownership in the shares of their employer. Most of the publicity has concerned employee stock ownership plans, or ESOPs, where a bank or other trustee is the legal shareowner and management is motivated by tax benefits or takeover protection. But the trend of legal rules for ESOPs is to pass real ownership on to the employees.

Stock options—the right to buy stock at a favorable price—are being issued to many more employees. In the past, options were for top management only. When the options are exercised, the sale of stock occurs directly between the employer and the employee, without a broker.

Sales to Existing Shareowners. Through rights offerings, new shares are made available to current shareowners. Corporations are often able to meet all their new equity capital needs through rights offerings. Individuals welcome the chance to increase their investment without paying any brokerage fees.

Dividend reinvestment programs allow shareowners to apply their dividends to buying more shares. First started in 1969, they came to be offered by more than 1,200 corporations, with 6 million shareowners participating. In some years, a quarter of all equity capital raised by public corporations has been through dividend reinvestment.

Corporations have been conscious of offending the securities industry. AT&T, which raised $1.1 billion through dividend reinvestment in 1980, made a survey of securities brokers when it started its program. According to the company's investor relations manager: "A great majority [of brokers] said that they were happy we are doing this because we are taking business that is a thorn in their side. They don't make a heck of a lot of money on small orders such as this."

Dividend reinvestment plans were extended gradually. Some companies give discounts of 5 percent or so from the current market price. Many let shareowners add new cash to the dividend amount. Next came "optional cash investing" programs, where anyone owning at least one share can buy more directly from the corporation, up to as much as $60,000 at a time. Directories are available that describe the features of each program. There is a service which will funnel an individual's cash into particular plans on a monthly basis.

Sales to People Who Are Not Already Shareowners. Now there are programs open to people who are not shareowners at all. Several corporations will allow someone to first become a shareowner through a direct investment. These programs are passive—an investor needs to take the initiative to discover where they are available and how to buy shares.

Citicorp took the last step in the logical progression by actively marketing shares directly to people who are not already shareowners. Its Citibank subsidiary included with 5 million credit card bills the pitch: "Investors: Now you can buy Citicorp stock directly, no fees, no commissions." In its initial phase, over 12,500 cardholders bought Citicorp shares by mail. Average investment was $1,200.

This method of direct share marketing has really caught on since this book was first published. More than 130 companies had "Direct Stock Purchase Plans" in effect by late 1996, compared with just 52 only two years earlier. These included companies like Sears, McDonalds, and Wal-Mart. Enrollment fees in the program ranged from $5 to $15, annual account fees were between $3 and $5 and per-transaction fees from $1 to $10. Some companies offer discounts from the share's price in the trading markets.

"Informal Investing." Entrepreneurs are already marketing shares directly to individuals at an annual rate of $33 billion. This is the so-called "informal investing" that takes place through little networks all over the country. [The term "angel investing" seems to have caught on in the 1990s.] Individuals and entrepreneurs learn about each other through their accountants, their dentists, and through friends of friends.

According to researchers at the Small Business Administration, "informal investment appears to be the largest source of external equity capital for small businesses," more than banks and eight times as much as the amount raised from venture capital firms. The SBA studied the informal investments of 435 individuals. They averaged three or four corporate investments, of about $60,000 each. Total participation in the informal investing market was estimated by the SBA at 445,600 companies and 719,600 investors. This level of direct investment between entrepreneurs and individuals took place without any direct public marketing. It happened because there is a massive demand and an immense supply—and no marketing mechanism adequate to bring them together.

[In late 1996, the SBA announced its program for expanding an existing network of angels and entrepreneurs to allow each side to present its data and story to the other.]

Technology

Most corporate shares are still marketed and traded through technology unchanged since the 1920s: The media are the telephone and the trading floor. The methodology is collecting a percentage commission out of every transaction. Capital is being allocated by a trading technology and a trading mentality, a combination which tends to cause turnover in existing businesses, rather than bring life to new ones. [This technology is finally beginning to change. See Chapter 7, "Selling Shares on the Internet."]

The securities industry is a labor-intensive business, with an extremely high unit labor cost. Sustaining its low-tech nature requires big deals or rapid turnover. Wall Street is not the right mechanism for matching entrepreneurs and individuals in long-term shareownership.

New technology is ready. It has been tested. We are entering the stage where the techniques of direct marketing will create a flow of capital from individual investors to entrepreneurs, telecomputer trading markets will bring liquidity and a sense of fairness to individuals who invest in new shares, and the new capital will finance cybernetics, the technology that replaces human labor, freeing investors from dependence on wages.

The Techniques of Direct Marketing

Going public without an underwriter is a simple progression from the direct marketing of other financial instruments. There is plenty of recent experience in bypassing securities wholesalers and retailers.

Commercial Paper. Large corporations sell these IOUs, due in less than nine months, to companies with extra cash on hand. Most of the money exchanged directly between corporate treasurers, through commercial paper, would otherwise have gone into banks as deposits and back out as bank loans.

From less than $5 billion in 1961, commercial paper grew in 20 years to a $100 billion market. There are securities firms who act as commercial paper dealers, but most paper is placed directly between the issuer and the investor.

Treasury Bills, Notes and Bonds. The United States Treasury has built a very successful, low-key direct marketing program for individual investors. At its regular weekly auctions to the securities and banking industries, the Treasury also accepts "noncompetitive bids" of $10,000 or more. Individuals get their Treasury bills, notes, or bonds at the same price as the auction.

Treasury has chosen not to advertise its direct sales program. But it has used two other very important direct marketing tools—public relations and customer service.

When a news story mentions the results of a Treasury auction, it will usually refer to the amount of noncompetitive bids. There will often be a sentence or two that tells the reader to ask at any Federal Reserve Bank. Occasionally, there will be a feature story about the availability of direct purchases. These public relations seem to be carefully managed to get the word out, without telling people to short-circuit their bank or broker.

Once we have picked up the idea to buy Treasuries direct, the way has been made very easy. Telephone directories have a special listing under Federal Reserve Bank for direct sales. There is an efficient, friendly person to help us, at a clearly designated window in the Bank. The one-page form is simple, and we can do it all by mail. Interest can be credited directly to our checking account. U.S. savings bonds became available in 1988 through a 24-hour telephone service. Individuals can call 800-US BONDS and pay for investments on their credit cards.

Savings Deposits. Technology in the use of media to promote investment products has had as much inventing and testing as money could buy in the last few years. All the deregulation of financial services has launched a thousand major campaigns. When banks and S&Ls were allowed to compete with money market funds, they sold $100 billion of accounts within the first nine months. All the media were used. Every ad agency had its creative department pull out the stops.

Brokers. There have been piecemeal attempts to use some direct marketing techniques within the securities industry. Mailed invitations to seminars, interactive video presentations by satellite, pitches on VCR cassettes. They lead to a telephone or in-person closing, but much of the broker's prospecting and "qualifying" work has already been done.

Fundraisers. Direct marketing technology is startling in its ability to select target markets, suggest what motivates them, and find the media to reach them. Some of the most advanced techniques have come from fundraising for political and charitable causes.

Credit Bureaus. There are three major companies that verify the credit-worthiness of people who want to charge their purchases or borrow money. They have records on 160 million Americans. Banks, retailers, and others give the bureaus monthly computer tapes with the purchases and payments of nearly every household. Other information is added to personal files from driving records, employment histories, and bank balances. Magazines sell subscription lists, mail order firms and charitable fundraisers provide information. All of this is merged and can be sorted to fit a profile of the target market.

IPOs. Going public through direct marketing has been done for many years. Each time, entrepreneurs were largely reinventing the wheel. Control Data sold shares door-to-door in 1957. Two years earlier, James Ling took LTV public through a booth at the Texas State Fair. Ads in Vermont newspapers in 1984 gave local residents the chance to buy shares of Ben & Jerry's Homemade, Inc., the premium ice cream maker.

Except for the direct IPOs of savings institutions in the early 1980s, there has been no cumulative body of experience from which to design and manage a program. Direct marketing of shareownership is where hamburger stands were before McDonalds, where air courier services were before Federal Express. The market is there. The technology is ready. It only needs systems and commitment.

[In the six years since this book was first published, the "systems and commitment" have been built. See Chapter 8, "Case Studies of Direct Public Offerings."]

The Electronic Stock Exchange

With most stock trading, the only information we get comes from the person who is selling us shares, or buying them back. And the only way we can buy or sell is through that broker-dealer. Old, old technology still dominates trading in corporate shares. Investors can only have access to the market through brokers, who usually deal through specialists and market makers. As a result, it all seems very one-sided. The insiders taking advantage of the outsiders.

The laws are in place for us to get our information and complete our trades on far more equal footing. Congress mandated a national market system in the Securities Reform Act of 1975. Why does it not happen? Resistance to a fairer, cheaper market comes from those who make money the old way. The Securities and Exchange Commission considers that its mandate is to protect the securities industry, as well as police it. So the SEC has done virtually nothing to carry out the expressed will of

Congress, which would radically change the highly profitable specialist role. [Since this book was first published, a new SEC Chairman, Commissioners and staff have taken several big steps toward a fairer, cheaper trading market and the use of electronic technology.]

The ease of switching to electronic trading is shown by the path taken by insiders for their own trades. Rule 390 of the New York Stock Exchange requires all its member brokers to place orders for listed stocks through its specialists, who run around the trading floor with pad and pencil. Many members choose instead to go through a nonmember broker, which does trades of 3,000 shares or less all by computer. It takes 4 seconds and can save $30 on a 1,000 share order.

Extensions of existing software would permit anyone with a computer and modem to have access to all bid and ask quotes, trading history and published information on any public corporation. Buy and sell orders could be executed directly.

The SEC has also been dragging its feet on making information about public companies retrievable by PCs, so that individuals could readily get the information now funneled through stockbrokers and investment advisers. For years, it has been assigning low priority to EDGAR (Electronic Data Gathering, Analysis and Retrieval) and has set 1993 for requiring electronic filings from 11,000 publicly-traded companies. [By mid-1996, EDGAR filings were mandated for nearly every corporation selling its shares to the public. The SEC has an excellent website, easily accessible and usable by those of us who are barely Internet literate.]

[The SEC has also gone from an obstacle to a leader in encouraging electronic delivery of information about corporations and their securities. See Chapter 6, "The Regulatory Framework."]

Technology is already in place to take stock trading and investment analysis from the trading post to the computer terminal. There are 25 million personal computer users in the United States. That is just counting homes and small businesses. Over half of our affluent households have computers. Software is marketed, some by discount brokers, that allows information retrieval, investment analysis, and stock trading to be done entirely by telecomputing. No human voice necessary. Corporations can have the full text of their news releases available within 15 minutes to anyone with a terminal and modem. For $8 a month, a subscriber can have releases on companies and industries automatically put into a PC memory.

When trades and information go through a telecomputer system, monitoring for unlawful behavior becomes much more effective. Investors feel less dependent upon market professionals.

[In the six years since this book was first published, this forecast of electronic trading has seen the swiftest implementation. By 1996, entire brokerage firms exist to execute trades exclusively through Internet communications. Information about "the market" and about individual companies in abundantly available through electronic data bases.]

Cybernetics Is the New Economic Engine

Technological breakthroughs have catapulted us into long cycles of growth. We are entering a such a period now, one that will bring the economic activity that followed invention of the steam engine and the automobile. Something that will improve our standard of living the way it was changed by the electric motor and the transistor/microchip.

That technological breakthrough will come in cybernetics, the computer/communications/mechanical systems that will do the tasks we humans now perform. Tools will liberate our bodies and minds from having to produce and maintain. Ownership of those tools, through corporate shares, will be marketed to individuals. Dividends and trades in shares will replace some of the income we now receive in wages. The market for shares in entrepreneurial corporations will expand as individuals come to believe that they could achieve the American dream. For most of us, that will be doing what we want with our time, while still having enough income to meet our needs and primary wants.

Cybernetics is synthetic human energy and synthetic mental processing. It performs the basic recognition of our senses, the matching with patterns in our memories, and the instructing of body parts to move in certain ways. Synthetic human energy comes from electricity, which will become far more plentiful and less expensive as we make strides in such technologies as photovoltaics and superconductivity.

Synthetic mental processing will come from increasing speed and storage capacity in computer hardware, which allows for more complex programming. Simple, single-purpose computer chips, which replace many human functions, are already used in assembly line manufacturing. Entrepreneurs will bring forth applications beyond our imaginations.

With inexpensive and inexhaustible electrical energy, it will become feasible to desalinate water and move it anywhere. Combustible fuels can be produced from renewable resources through safe processes. We will remove the economic limits on using motors, heating, and cooling.

Capital for these entrepreneurs will come from individuals, from people who share the vision and have enough faith to take a risk. When a venture hits, it will bring its shareowners some economic freedom. They will have to work less for money, just as the technology they have financed is leaving less work to be done by human hands and minds.

[The greatest leap in cybernetics since this book was originally published has been, in one word, INTERNET. The mid-1996 numbers were 144 million PC users, of which 25 million are connected to the Internet. See Chapter 7, "Selling Shares on the Internet."]

Work

Direct marketing of shareownership is part of the way we will resolve two issues which are behind many of our current difficulties: How can we be happier in our work? How can we fairly share the wealth? This is not to say that entrepreneurs will go public, or individuals will buy shares in order to solve the world's problems. What it does mean is a more receptive market for shares, because people sense there is a way for them to become happier in their work and a way for them to share in business profits.

Some prospective investors will understand an entrepreneurial corporation's potential for fast growth and large profits. They see the chance to make enough money so that they are less dependent upon a paycheck. Other prospects—like employees, subcontractors, suppliers—envision how buying shares could help change the content of their own work, as new capital is invested in production technology. We are developing some different attitudes toward work, views that fit nicely with shareownership:

Work Can Make Us Feel Good

Our American work ethic came out of sixteenth–century Europe and the concepts of sin and redemption. From the English Statute of Artificers in 1563 to the U.S. Full Employment Act of 1948, it was accepted that everyone should work. We worked because that was our lot in life. Then we worked to consume. Reward in the afterlife was replaced with spending our way into heaven on earth. Work was still a means to an end, a necessary evil. Now we are learning that each of us can find a livelihood that will bring us a sense of purpose, a peace, our self-esteem. This belief that work can bring personal happiness fits with the new optimism that we can collectively find ways to improve life on our planet.

There is growing acceptance that the world will not soon end from war or pollution or the exhaustion of its resources. People can, through their work and capital, develop ways to survive and to improve the quality of life.

If our objective is to get away from working just for money, then we need to create other money sources. Saving and earning interest is too slow. Gambling gives such poor odds. Investing in shares holds out the possibility that we can eventually work to feel good about ourselves and not just work for the money.

Wealth Can Be Fairly Shared

It is not exactly that the rich get richer and the poor get poorer. From World War II until 1965, people at all income levels had big increases, on average. But the relative allocation remained about the same. The top fifth of American households got about 40 percent of the income and the bottom fifth got about 5 percent.

In the last ten years, the incomes of households in the bottom 40 percent have gone down, after inflation effect. Those in the top 20 percent continued to increase, most rapidly in the highest 5 percent. [This trend of the 1980s continues into the 1990s, according to several studies. Median family income continues to decline, in inflation-adjusted dollars, while the top 20 percent continue to increase their share of total income and business profitability reaches its highest level in 40 years. Increasingly greater returns for invested capital and lesser payment for work is demonstrated by the 25 percent gain in output per worker reported for the last 22 years.]

Ownership of wealth is much more concentrated. The Federal Reserve Board survey of 1983 consumer finances found that the 2 percent of households with incomes over $100,000 a year owned 28 percent of total household net worth, including 50 percent of corporate shares. The top 10 percent of households, by income, owned 57 percent of the net worth. [This concentration has continued to increase since this book was first published, as the wealthiest 1 percent of the people collected 60 to 70 percent of the total increase in U.S. wealth.] Justice Louis D. Brandeis predicted: "We can have democracy in this country or we can have great wealth concentrated in the hands of a few, but we can't have both." Discontent with this distribution comes in cycles. It will one day lead to a different allocation of wealth. The least disruptive way will be by helping workers become shareowners through direct marketing.

CHAPTER 3

IS PUBLIC OWNERSHIP RIGHT FOR YOU?

The first part of that question is why sell shares to the public, at all. There are the clear disadvantages that come from being a public company: having to remember that the former owners of a private business are now stewards of money entrusted to them by strangers; filing all those reports and issuing news releases to keep shareowners informed; wondering whether a sudden drop in the trading price will be followed by a lawsuit; and living in the "fishbowl," where anyone can find out how much money you make and the value of your company shares.

Obviously, few of us would take on these challenges unless we thought it was worth it. The reasons for choosing to go public usually include being able to have capital that never has to be paid back and doesn't require any interest or dividend payments; getting that capital without giving up control over the business decisions management can make; creating a liquid trading market for shares that the company's founders, management and major owners may use to begin cashing in on their investment; and having a security to use, instead of cash, for compensating key employees and acquiring other businesses.

Going public with your corporation can rank right up there with such major decisions as choosing your career or where you live. You may go through the same process—imagining what it might be like, listing the pros and the cons.

On the positive side:

Acceptance. This is the way that nearly every business goes, if it is to become significant.

Security. Having a large number of strangers owning shares means freedom from having a few lenders or investors looking over my shoulder.

Wealth. My best chance to build a really major estate, and to diversify my investments, is to go public.

Stardom. To become well-known for what I do, it is important to build a public company.

Altruism. Going public will benefit my employees and others who believe in the business.

Some of these may not be of interest or concern to you. But you will need some strong motivations to overcome the natural forces of inertia and such negatives as:

Denial. There are other ways to finance and direct my corporation. I don't need public shareownership.

Insecurity. I may not be ready to have public shareowners relying on my ideas and abilities.

Fear. What if my corporation is rejected by investors, or my shareowners sue me?

Procrastination. I can stay private for now and reconsider later.

Laziness. It involves too much hassle with the SEC and snoopy shareowners.

These negatives can be overcome with a good public offering program and a team of qualified people. This chapter will help you decide whether going public really makes sense for your corporation, whether it fits with your personal views and whether your corporation is really an attractive investment at this stage of its development.

Twenty Questions

Here are questions that can begin to guide your consideration of whether you and your corporation are right for public shareownership.

Does public shareownership fit your corporation? Is your corporation independent of ties to other corporations or family businesses? Can you have public shareownership without imposing serious limitations on the corporate business? Could the opportunities and problems of your business be explained openly and understandably to your target investors? Do your auditors and lawyers go along with the concept of public shareownership? Will public shareownership leave you free to comply with agencies that regulate your business?

Are you ready to share ownership of your corporation? Are you able to separate the corporation from your personal image and identity? Can you live with the possibility that you might one day be forced out of your job? Will you be able to keep from paying your personal expenses out of the corporation? Are you willing to have your compensation set by independent directors and disclosed in public documents? Can you put up with a board of directors that may outvote you?

Will your corporation appeal to individual investors? Can you explain the essence of the corporation in just a few words? Would an investor have a good chance of seeing the share value double or triple within three years? Are there people you know right now who could be counted on to buy at least 25 percent of the offering? Can you identify groups of several thousand people who should have the interest and money to own your shares? Are you willing to price your shares at a discount to their estimated market value?

Are you clear about the amount, purpose, and timing? How much money would you be going for and how much of your ownership would you be giving up? What do you propose to do with the proceeds from the offering? Is your corporation in the right stage of its development to be going public? Can you describe your plan for the business, going out five years? Do you know when you expect to need more capital and how you would raise it?

These are all big questions. You can reconsider and fine-tune the answers as you move toward the offering process. For now, they are just a modeling exercise, to see if you should really be on the path toward an initial public offering.

Reasons for Choosing a DPO

Once crossing the economic and psychological threshold toward becoming a public company, what are the reasons for choosing a DPO? The ones we hear most often mentioned are:

We're able to choose our fellow shareowners. By marketing directly to the company's existing affinity groups, the present owners generally attract like-minded people. This translates into long-term, friendly investors, who aren't demanding the time and attention that institutional money managers and brokerage securities analysts do. It means less focus on quarter-to-quarter results and more on long-term objectives and values beyond the financial bottom line.

We create "ambassadors of good will" who not only do more business with the company they own, but promote it to everyone they know. One catalog retailer measured sales per catalog and found that shareowners ordered twice the dollar amount that other regular customers did. Another entrepreneur can actually credit several product and service innovations to feedback from shareowners who are also customers.

We can control the pricing and know what it will be at the outset. Part of the traditional IPO is the "pricing dance." At the time underwriters are pitching for the business, they will suggest a percentage of the company that should be sold, for the capital to be raised from the public. But there is never a legally binding agreement on that pricing until the shares have actually all been spoken for by investors. Then a final price is negotiated and the underwriting agreement signed. With a DPO, the board of directors makes the pricing decision early in the preparation phase, relying upon analyses made by the company and its advisors. There isn't the risk that the offering will be called off at the last minute (after spending all that time and money) because the price is unacceptable, or that management will feel compelled to go forward with that price.

We'll have a more stable trading market for our shares. Many underwritten "public offerings" are really just extensions of venture capital financing, in that the shares are owned by a few hundred institutions, with decisions actually made by a much smaller number of money managers for those institutions. They tend to think and act much alike, creating the so-called "herd instinct" in buying and selling. It's not unusual to see a disappointing quarterly earnings release followed by an immediate price drop of 30 percent or more. By contrast, thousands of individuals, nearly all in for the long term, make more independent and personal decisions about when to buy and sell, smoothing out the stock price fluctuations. Because those individuals already have a relationship with the company, they will pay attention to regular communications that prepare them for the events—good and bad—of a business's life.

We can worry less about lawsuits. There is always something from which a plaintiffs' securities class-action lawyer can make a claim—something that happened, that could have caused the stock price to change and something you didn't tell the public about before it happened. The critical element is not whether a wrong can be claimed, it is whether the economics of bringing a lawsuit make sense: How much are the "damages," measured by the drop in price times the amount of shares held by the public? How many members of the class (shareowners with losses) are there, how many of them will choose to be part of the class, and how much will it cost to communicate with them? With most IPOs, the "class" consists of a relatively few managers who have lost a lot of other people's money and can either admit to their bosses and clients that they made a bad decision or claim somebody deceived them. On the other hand, DPOs have more stable prices (thus, smaller losses) and they are owned by thousands of individuals who are interested in long-term performance and don't need to find a scapegoat for short-term "paper" losses.

There will be less interference with how we run the business. As institutions have become dominant owners of many corporations, some of their managers have taken on the crusade of "corporate governance" and "executive and director compensation." Because they own so many shares, and because they know each other, institutional money managers can make "suggestions" to management, with the unspoken (or spoken) threat of mass selloffs of the shares or motions to be presented at the next shareowners' meeting. Even when there are no management issues raised, just dealing with telephone calls and e-mail from securities analysts and money managers can be time-consuming. One executive, considering the DPO/IPO choice, conducted an informal poll of similar companies and found that counterparts who had done DPOs spent about 10 percent of their year on shareowner communications and issues. Those who had gone the underwritten IPO route were spending 30 percent to 40 percent of their time on those matters.

The DPO will cost less. Costs of a completed public offering are subtracted from the offering proceeds, rather than going through the company's income statement as operating expenses (although they do get charged in the period in which an offering project is abandoned.) They are still important, since they reduce the amount of offering proceeds the company can use. Our history with DPOs has consistently been that they cost about half that of a similar-sized underwritten IPO. In part, this is because direct marketing costs are substantially less than brokers' commissions. But it is also because the process is managed by the person spending the money and things become considerably more cost-effective. A body of knowledge is being built up about DPOs, their regulatory, marketing, and process management steps. That can be passed on to companies and their lawyers and other service providers, rather than "reinventing the wheel" with each offering. The competitive nature of underwritings prevents there being any central data source, or spirit of companies helping each other.

Which Companies Can Do a Direct Public Offering?

DPOs are not for every business. There are some companies that don't lend themselves to any form of public participation, that really need to be operated in private. There are some entrepreneurs, too, who are not likely to adapt to having hundreds or thousands of investors in an operation they have considered to be their private domain. Perhaps the business or its current owners may not be able to accept that public investors, and the regulators who are charged with protecting them, need to know some basic things about what management has in mind for the company and whether it is being a good steward of the public's trust.

Even if a business is ready for public investors, it may still not be a candidate for a Direct Public Offering. Our twenty years of experience in helping companies do DPOs led to developing a "screen test" for deciding quickly which businesses could probably have a successful DPO.

Screen Test for a Direct Public Offering

One: *The business would excite prospective investors, making them want to share its future.*

The day will soon come when millions of Americans will become securities analysts, using computer-based tools for screening and selecting among thousands of companies. We will be creating and managing personalized "mutual funds" through our employer's retirement plans and our own savings. Our stock selections will be based upon our individual criteria and financial analysis programs. Until then, companies will have to attract us with a story close to our personal interests. We're not ready for the "dull but good" businesses yet.

Two: *There is a history of profitable operations under the company's present management.*

We have learned that excitement is not enough in a Direct Public Offering. The shoppers' "impulse purchase" phenomenon seldom happens when the amount involved is at least several hundred dollars. A compelling presentation may work for charitable donations, but people stop and analyze before buying a company's shares. So . . . what about all the traditional IPOs of companies that barely have revenues and are years away from their first profits? That's a very different market than the one for DPOs. The selling is done in an underwritten IPO by telephone calls and meetings with money managers for institutional investors. Promotional efforts are directed to individuals to create demand in the aftermarket, so those professional investors buying the IPO can realize an immediate profit. In a very different process, DPOs are sold when the prospectus is read by cautious individuals spending their own money. With some exceptions, they want proof that management can turn a profit.

Three: *The company and management meet standards of honesty, social responsibility and competency.*

The closer we feel to where our money is actually put to use, the more we need to feel comfortable with it. "It's 3:00 a.m. Do you know where your money is?" was the advertising theme of one of the first socially responsible mutual funds. When people invest directly in shareownership of a company, after making their own decision and using their own money, they feel a sense of identity with that company. Polls consistently show that an overwhelming percentage of consumers prefer products from companies that aren't causing harm. That carries over to buying shares as well.

Four: *The business can be understood by people who may have no experience investing in shares.*

Your business doesn't need to be understandable to all people—just to those in the affinity groups to which you will be marketing your shares. But those affinity groups need to be large enough to buy your entire offering. (We explain in Chapter 5 how to calculate whether your affinity groups are sufficient for your DPO to work.) Shares are sold in a DPO when someone reads the prospectus. If they are struggling to grasp the concept, or are lost in confusing details, they will lose interest. One exercise is to try describing your business in ten words or so. Another is to try telling your whole story—what your business is, what you're going to do with the public's money, and the particular risks of investing in your shares—in the equivalent of a one-page memorandum.

Five: *The company has natural affinity groups, with discretionary cash to risk for long-term gain.*

Our first DPOs, starting twenty years ago, were consumer banks, that marketed shares primarily to their depositors. These customers obviously had some money they didn't need for immediate living expenses, money they had already trusted to the bank. Most of the DPOs we have worked on since have been directed to large groups of retail customers, suppliers, and employees. But affinity groups can include people who don't have an existing relationship with the business. For instance, we have found that people in the same geographic community are likely investors, even if they aren't also customers. Other groups may be interested in the particular technology or corporate mission of a business. One of our clients appealed to a whole subculture of believers in homeopathy. Several wineries and breweries have attracted capital from people who like the idea of getting in early on a new brand of their favorite beverage. Just the numbers in your affinity groups is only part of the story. In looking at your demographics, it's also important to measure the strength of the affinity (how loyal do they feel toward your company), their ability to part with a significant amount of cash, and the likelihood that they would use that cash to own shares (rather than spend it on some consumer item or put it away in a savings-type, low-risk investment).

Six: ***Those affinity groups will recognize the company's name and consider its share offering materials.***

One of the advantages in marketing a bank's shares to its depositors was that they certainly would pay attention to any communication from their own bank, at least long enough to find out what it was about. Several other DPOs have been for companies with consumer branded products, and we've carried the logo, slogans and color identifications through into the share offering materials. We've had companies with names that were entirely different from their product names, where the marketing challenge was to transfer the feelings about the known name over to the new one. Creating recognition for a company with no identification among affinity groups is beyond the present state of the art.

Seven: ***Their names, addresses, telephone numbers, and some demographics are in the company's database.***

This is an ideal. For the banks and catalog retailers, having an up-to-date database was a welcome fact. Most businesses will need to find alternatives to database marketing, and we may one day drop this test entirely, as no longer so important. Recent share offerings have worked even without the database. Two of them, a beverage company and a clothing designer/manufacturer, sold over 80 percent of their products through distributors and retailers. We had only a very limited database of people who drank or wore those products. There are ways to "profile" those nameless customers and figure out how to reach them through selected media. It makes the process more difficult and less predictable. On the other hand, we've learned that having the database of affinity groups is not enough to assure a successful DPO—the other tests still need to be met.

Eight: ***A company employee is able to spend half time for six months as project manager, directed by the CEO.***

There needs to be one person for whom the DPO is the top business priority. Experience has shown that anything less than that will lead to slippages in the schedule and a decline in enthusiasm for getting the job done. Our advice has always been that the employee chosen should not be the CEO (although several successful ones have been run just that way). Nor should it be the CFO (although other successes have been managed that way, too). The ideal is someone earlier in their career who works directly under, and speaks with the authority of the CEO or CFO.

Nine: ***The company has, or can obtain, audited financial statements for at least the last two fiscal years.***

This is the requirement for the new securities law filing forms made available to small businesses (under $25 million annual revenue) by the federal Securities and Exchange Commission. There are other forms, for offerings of up to $5 million, which allow lower standards of review by outside auditors. Unless the company has been in business less than two years, we suggest that you not try to save accountants' fees by using unaudited (even "reviewed") numbers. There are situations when auditing prior years will be difficult and, rarely, impossible. That usually occurs when a company carries large inventories and did not have a year-end physical count, observed by a representative of the auditors or other independent professional. In those cases, or where the accounting records need to be put in auditable shape, it may be prudent for the company to arrange some private financing until it is ready for public scrutiny.

There are two tests that are not included in this list—probably the two most important ones. You'll see why they're not part of the screening and why they are so critical in the analysis of whether a company can do a Direct Public Offering.

One of the two big ones is that the offering will be a good investment prospect for the intended market. This test is not that difficult to apply. With a little information about the company, its history, prospects, market, and management, anyone with some interest in the particular industry will be able to sense the fairness of what is proposed to be offered. If the current owners have an unrealistic view of what they need to give up in exchange for invested capital, they had best not try a DPO. Our experience, with offerings that were successful, and a couple that were not, is that most people (even those who have never invested in a business before) can judge the fairness of an offering just as well as the experts.

The other big requirement, not a part of the "Screen Test," is that the company's management be truly committed to using a Direct Public Offering. This usually means some motivation beyond raising needed capital. A consumer branded product company may want to create more loyal customers, to spread the word to their friends, for instance. A utility may want the local political support of a broad base of customer/shareowners. A distributor of newly developed products may seek people with an economic interest in the company's benefit, who will supply ideas and comments. We have found that successful DPOs do not come from an attitude of: "Well, nothing else is working, so let's try this and see what happens." There will be a series of obstacles and some disappointments, as there is any time something new is being developed and introduced. The regulatory overlay to marketing securities ensures some frustrations. Commitment by top management will be necessary to keep the process on track.

Your Purpose for Bringing in Public Shareowners

Whenever we are offered possessions the sellers have used for themselves, we naturally want to know why they are selling. Is this car about to break down? Have home prices hit their peak around here?

It is the same thought process when you are suddenly willing to sell a part of your corporation. Of course, it is a lot less suspicious when you are keeping most of it for yourself. But you still need to express a clear answer to the question, "Why are you selling shares now?"

Your chance to tell that story will come in the prospectus—the legal document by which shares are sold. In the prospectus, one of the required sections is Use of Proceeds. This tells the prospective investor what the corporation intends to do with the money received from selling shares. That can be woven into a description of the business plan—made a part of the story told by the prospectus.

Raising capital is not the only motivation for most initial public offerings. You may want to have publicly traded shares in order to set up an employee stock ownership program. Some of your private investors, who helped you get the business started, may need a way to get some cash from their holding. Your bank may want to see some more equity capital as a cushion before it extends more credit. Customers may be more comfortable doing business with a public company, one they can expect to be around for a while.

Having a market may be part of your strategy for acquiring other businesses by issuing shares to their owners. All that makes sense and can help in marketing shares.

What will not work as a purpose for the offering is a motive that takes away the investor's hopes and dreams. For instance, there are corporations which reach their optimum size rather quickly. Perhaps one in a retail or service business. The owner is satisfied with the operation, except for paying the interest on bank borrowings to finance inventory and receivables. Since dividends are not required on shares of common stock, how about replacing borrowings with shareowner money?

It is clear what is in it for the owner, who can take out salary and benefits while plowing profits back into the business. But who wants to be an outside investor in a scheme for the sole benefit of the present owner? There has to be a basic element of "we're all in this together and we're shooting for the moon."

Where Public Shareownership Does Not Fit

There are corporations that should not even be considered for public shareownership.

Some corporations have a single, brief purpose. They may be organized around a business that is only temporary. Others may exist on the life cycle of a single product.

A few corporations are merely convenient forms for individuals to sell their personal services. Doctors and lawyers are not yet permitted to share ownership of their professional businesses. Most entertainers and athletes have not chosen to sell shares in their careers. But advertising agencies and stockbrokers have had public shareownership for years. It comes down to whether shares will sell and whether the corporate business can be operated fairly for both the shareowners and the producers. There are corporations in businesses that could not stand the publicity that would have to follow a public share offering. Others may be in regulated businesses that do not lend themselves to absentee ownership.

Sometimes the corporation and its business may be good for the founders, but still not be a fair proposition for public shareowners. The basic investment proposition must (a) make sense and (b) convey real hope for shareowners to achieve their own personal goals through the investment.

Good Businesses May Be Bad Investments

A strategy can make good sense and have big potential for corporate insiders, yet be a bum deal for outsiders who buy at the public offering.

Just as one example, here is a plan that is attractive to the founding group, but does not make sense for its new public shareowners:

> The corporation is formed to go into a business filled with hundreds of small competitors, just as that business is being entered by some big players. By growing quickly through a public share offering, the corporation can get to a size where a big corporation will buy it out to increase market share.

> If the plan is successful (a big if, based on the history of industry shakeouts), the corporation is sold at a price that reflects the cost of getting rid of a competitor and buying some lead time. For the founders, that may be several times what they paid to get the corporation started.

> The public shareowners, who took a big risk on a long-shot, are lucky if they break even.

> The founders can rest on their nest egg, with the prestige of having run a public company and sold out to a big corporation. The plan was a good one for them, but even the best scenario was a bad one for the investors.

Propositions that do not fit for public shareowners may do very well with other money sources. An example would be the grow-fast-and-sell-out strategy just described. That investment proposition could be just right for a debt financing, particularly if repayment were secured by corporate assets and personal guarantees from the founders. The lender might take some extra risk in return for rights to share in the gain from selling out.

Innovation Overload

The fact is that shareownership is a new concept for the majority of us. It will take some time getting used to it. Meanwhile, we are most likely to get our feet wet as shareowners if there is a lot of comfort with the corporation. Something simple and close to home.

Innovation overload makes us feel confused and even claustrophobic. Too many new things at one sitting. That is when we are not likely to overcome our inertia and part with our money.

If your corporation is at some cutting edge of technology or merchandising, perhaps it is better to wait a while before seeking public shareownership. Combining new ideas in business with new ideas in shareownership just may be too much.

This advice could also be completely wrong for you. Your intuition or market research (or, better yet, both) may tell you that your future shareowners would love a chance to be way out there in effecting change. Just be aware.

Another early warning signal can be some regulatory obstacle that may limit or close off public shareownership. One that comes up frequently is the need for audited financial statements. If you have changed auditors recently, or if you have missed some major auditing standard, such as year-end inventory observations, it may be impossible to go public when you would like.

If it is an auditing glitch, get a second and third opinion. There is ethical imagination to be found among CPAs, although it sometimes takes some looking.

Public Shareowners and the Lone Wolf Entrepreneur

Readiness for public shareownership begins with the values and attitudes of the entrepreneur. It takes a particular mix of personality traits to go from sole ownership to sharing "your" corporation with a thousand strangers, who expect you to take care of their investment as you do your own.

Some entrepreneurs know they want a public corporation from the very beginning. Others accept it as the only way to pay for their plans. It can be an intuitive feel that sharing ownership is right. Or it can come from quantifying all the pros and cons.

Then there are entrepreneurs who would rather live with the limitations of private ownership than involve outside investors. That is clearly their right to choose. Individuals who would really like to participate as investors in that business are going to have to find a competitor—or help start one.

Some entrepreneurs may kid themselves into thinking they can operate with public shareownership. In fact, they may be unable to separate their corporation from their own personality. There are egos that extend into the corporate business and could no more believe in sharing ownership of the corporation than they could accept giving up their arms or legs.

Others who start businesses may prefer to share ownership with a few "partners," rather than with hundreds or thousands of strangers.

However the decision is reached, it is a very personal one. While a corporation is still owned by its founders, it is often an extension of their needs and desires. Later, the corporation will take on a character and value system of its own, derived from its shareowners, managers, workers, community, and customers.

Many corporations remain private because the entrepreneur is personally not suited to sharing ownership. A few of these have been willing to go against their nature and have a public offering anyway. This choice may work if the entrepreneur accepts that it is time for a change in role.

For instance, the inventor/founder may turn over management to others, while finding bliss running a research laboratory. Financial security will have come from owning publicly traded shares and from signing an employment contract. Some entrepreneurs welcome exchanging the power and prestige of being boss for the freedom from pressures and anxieties that go with it.

One colorful entrepreneur had the lifetime goal of being the sole shareowner of a company listed on the New York Stock Exchange. Since broad public shareownership is a requirement for listing, this was obviously impossible. But many entrepreneurs never reconcile themselves to the clear conflict between sharing ownership with outsiders and running the corporation as if it were their own household.

Entrepreneurs need to be honest with themselves before they embark on the voyage of public ownership. And careful investors will detect the clues to future conflicts between an autocratic "owner" and the investors who are supposed to share that ownership.

A Steward for Shareowners

Commitment to public shareownership is the first issue. Competence for that step is the second.

It is hard enough to run a small private business. You have to deal with taxes and licenses, bookkeepers and creditors, employees and customers. Then there are all the minor crises that could never have been anticipated. Public shareownership will add new dimensions to these complications. An entrepreneur needs to achieve a sense of comfort and control over the elements of a private business before moving on.

Having a public company means much more than just the same issues in larger sizes. There is the nature of stewardship—taking care of someone else's interests. Every challenge is no longer "what's best for me" but becomes "what's best for the corporation and its shareowners." It is a different mindset, one that is alien territory to some of us. Beyond honesty, public ownership means public disclosure.

Candor takes on a new meaning in corporate stewardship. It becomes more than complying with the laws and meeting a personal code. There are disclosure obligations beyond those that might come naturally. One of the reasons some corporations stay private is to avoid the "fishbowl effect," where actions are looked at by shareowners, analysts, regulators and lawyers. Corporate managers need to be sensitive to what will look right, as well as what feels right and is within the law.

Imagining What Public Shareownership Would Be Like

Securities lawyers and investor relations consultants can give you an understanding of the impact of public shareownership. Another sensible step is to talk with fellow entrepreneurs who have gone through the transition to public shareownership. Imagine being in their shoes for a month or so.

Imagining through the experience of others is probably the best preparation for testing your own commitment and competence for public shareownership. Some entrepreneurs can get on the board of directors of a public corporation. Others may belong to an association that includes public corporations and fosters assistance at an open, intimate level. Sometimes the entrepreneur can spend a few days tagging along with a counterpart in a public corporation.

Other windows on public shareownership include continuing education programs sponsored by organizations for lawyers, accountants, and executives; attending trade shows and talking with officers of public companies; reading copies of company filings with the SEC.

The Right Time to Go Public

The decision about timing can mirror the decision on the amount of an offering. It becomes a major part of your corporate business plan and your personal objectives.

Perhaps it is too soon. When corporate life begins, it is all dreams. Strangers may be excited by your dreams, but not many will pay to share them. Startups are for friends, relatives, and every dollar of your own.

When a beginning has been made, but there is not a steady growth of revenues, it will probably still be too soon for public shareownership. Some of the problems with going public while still in this bumpy, toddler stage:

> You will have to spend too much time and money educating your market about what you expect.

> The percentage ownership you will have to offer may be too much for the cash you get in return.

> Surprises happen more and bigger early on. They can frighten shareowners away.

> Servicing costs of shareowner and SEC reporting are high for a single small sale.

This sprout stage, after operations have begun but before the proof of profits, is what venture capital is all about. But you have heard stories about what you may give up in order to get money from venture capitalists. One choice you may lose is when you go public and how you market the shares. There can be less costly alternatives for getting through this development stage. For instance, your suppliers, key employees, and affluent acquaintances may be willing to invest privately if they see you have a practical plan for going public within two or three years.

Holding on Until the Time is Right

Controlling costs during development, doing everything "on the cheap," is one way entrepreneurs have stayed out of the clutches of venture capitalists. Taking more time with development is often better than giving up the kind of control that venture capitalists have been demanding.

This stage may seem so promising that you are now willing to tap some resources you left alone during the startup phase. Your own borrowing power. Family or friends who would be using their "rainy day" funds. Suppliers, customers, and employees.

A caution on tapping friends, relatives, and business associates: When the time comes for the public offering, you may need some big hitters—individuals who buy in quantity and who are trendsetters for others. If they have been allowed in earlier, for a lot less money, you have lost this leverage.

Financing techniques are available to you in development that can help you keep control and have 100 percent ownership going into a first public offering. Creditors can be given rights to buy shares after the public offering. Customers can get incentives to pay in advance.

Your lawyer will caution you about having a string of negotiated stock sales that may be aggregated into a single, and illegal, public offering. Part of keeping it simple is avoiding any embarrassing delays when you file your public offering with the SEC and state securities administrators.

"Keep it Simple" is a guiding principle in development stage financing. Legal, accounting, and marketing advice comes before any arrangements. Otherwise, you can find yourself trying to renegotiate terms with an investor at a time when you are over the barrel to make a public offering deadline.

Even when it is clear that your corporation will be accepted by public shareowners, timing issues still come up. Some of the dilemmas:

> We really need the money to move ahead now, but we'll be so much more profitable if we can get through next year. I'll have to sell 30% now, while next year we could get twice the money and sell only 20%.

> This is when the corporate story would be most clear and promising to the investor markets we have in mind. But our plan calls for some steps next year that will hurt profits. How can we price an offering fairly now and not have the market price collapse on us later?

> Borrowed money could get us through another 18 months, when the price to public shareowners could be a lot higher. But the balance sheet will look pretty risky, and we'll have to accept a lot of conditions from the lenders.

There are no easy answers to these kinds of questions. You have to make decisions in the way you have found works for you. A difference is that you can begin to appreciate the conflict between what is best for you, personally, and what is best for all the shareowners.

Corporations Without Investor Appeal

Corporations may be ready, and entrepreneurs may be willing, but some shares probably just will not sell. Marketing corporate shares means deciding who might like to invest in them and then communicating effectively with those people. Some businesses are not going to appeal to a sufficiently broad audience.

Your corporate business may be clear to you and yet look confusing to an outsider. It is usually easier to market a single concept than a multiline business. For example, making bicycle frames from a patented process suggests some target markets and a persuasive story. Adding the manufacture and lease of metal scaffolding, or the importing of bicycle parts, makes the market less clear and the story less focused.

It helps if your corporation has an uncluttered financial statement. Complex accounting strategies often reduce your taxes or accommodate some short-term financing. But they can mess up your balance sheet. Lengthy explanations are too much for the attention spans of most public offering prospects.

Investors will also want to see where you plan to take the corporation and who is on board to get it there. Your basic business plan needs to come across in a few short sentences and be met with a nod of the head and a muttered, "Ahh, that makes sense."

What Makes an Attractive Investment Proposition?

Investors in young businesses sometimes say that the three most important things to look for are "management, management, and management." But most of us individual investors want more than good credentials and an honest face. We would rephrase the three most important standards as something like "concept, management, and staying power."

Individuals who buy shares are deciding not to save that money for a future need and not to spend it on a pleasure of the moment. We are expecting to give up the use of that money, for at least a year or so and maybe forever. In return, we must be offered a chance to realize a dream.

There are insured deposits and government securities, where we can get our money back with interest and not take any risk. Or we can buy lottery tickets, for fun and the fantasy of being rich in a week. Sharing ownership of a young corporation is somewhere in between, and we need a way to evaluate the element of risk involved.

Your basic investment proposition will need to (a) make sense and (b) convey real hope that we investors could achieve some of our personal goals through shareownership in your business venture.

Your corporate concept needs to match some of our fantasies, but as an "investment." Shareownership has elements of both gambling and saving, so it has to generate the thrill or risk and, at the same time, sustain a rational analysis of that risk. Dreams of hitting it big have to be coupled with the comfort of not being taken for a fool.

In this spectrum between gambling and saving, it is the concept behind the corporation that will attract most individuals. Perhaps some pop star of the corporate wars can say, "trust me to do something big," but most of us will want to make our own judgment on whether this is a successful plan.

Corporate Concepts

Learning whether you have an attractive business concept begins with the question: "attractive to whom?"

Marketing your shares will require finding the natural constituencies for shareownership and persuading them to come aboard. At the beginning, it is only necessary to project whether the corporation is based on a concept that should have appeal to one or more groups and whether those groups are likely investors in corporate shares.

Elements of the marketable corporate concept are (1) it is exciting to people who share your interest in the subject, (2) that group of fellow enthusiasts represents enough money to buy your share offering and (3) the story can be told simply, with documented facts and assumptions.

People Who Can Make It Happen

You have the elements for a marketable corporate concept. Your corporation looks clean. It has an exciting yet reasonable story. Now you need a picture of management that looks capable to meet the challenge.

Individuals who are invited to be shareowners will ask whether your concept can be carried out by the people in charge. How this is answered becomes part of the share marketing program. But clever marketing is no substitute for the entrepreneur's informed conviction that the right team will be on the job.

People who actually read prospectuses and annual reports often say they go from the first couple of pages back to the section on management, to see who is on the board of directors. If they are not impressed, they won't bother reading anything more.

Investors want to know that someone competent will be keeping the books and seeing that there is enough cash to pay bills on time. They need to feel there is a single boss who can manage this kind and size of business.

Your Own Role in the Corporation

Inventors or other creative leaders are often not the right people to manage a corporation after it brings in public shareowners. Far better to face this issue before you go public than after. It is no good having the founder leave the helm after the offering. Better to move from president to chairman of the board ahead of time, while continuing to work full time on development and promotion.

This is the very stuff of your dreams. No rule says you have to do everything, wear every hat. You have reached the stage where you can finally do what you like and what you do well. Before you begin the going public process is the time to resolve any "Is this all there is?" issues and settle into your role.

The Power to See It Through

Staying power, the third essential, means adequate resources—in people, money, and access to supplies and markets.

Before starting on the road to public shareownership, you and your management team will need to have imagined facing the worst-case scenario. A big one may be management succession. Who is there to step into your shoes—suddenly, if that should become necessary.

The business plan will have some assumptions about sales, production, financing, and other events that are educated guesses. Staying power means the ability to keep the corporation going if those assumptions do not work out—comfort that the corporation can adjust, can hang in there or do something to survive and move on with its program.

Measuring Your "Affinity Group Appeal"

First-time share offerings are not sold by the numbers, by comparative price-earnings, or debt-to-equity ratios. There is too much risk involved to rely on estimates of future earnings and growth. Decisions are highly subjective.

Most investors will have some personal interests that make them willing to take a chance on your shares. Identifying and measuring the buying power of these people is like the affinity group marketing used to sell such other financial products as insurance and credit cards.

"Affinity groups" are segments of the public with interests that overlap with your business. Most obvious are employees, suppliers, distributors, neighbors. Others are people whose work or play can make them believe in the value of your business.

Some corporations may be in businesses that are dull and that barely earn enough to pay good salaries to their owner/managers. Without the hope of either fun or profit, strangers will have no attraction to shareownership.

Other corporations may be in interesting, profitable businesses, but they will have trouble finding affinity groups with enough potential investors to make a successful share offering.

For instance, if a corporation (1) has only a handful of employees, (2) has no brand names, (3) does no retail business, (4) handles a boring product, (5) deals with only a few suppliers, (6) is mostly unknown in its local community and (7) has no celebrity managers or directors, there are not likely to be any affinity groups large enough to make a public offering possible.

As you get into this kind of marketing analysis, you are ready to consider how you will choose to market your shares. Should you use a securities firm to do an underwritten offering? Is that option available to you? What about marketing your shares directly to investors, without an underwriter?

CHAPTER 4

HOW AN UNDERWRITTEN IPO IS DONE

The basic concept of an underwritten IPO is that part of a corporation is sold to an underwriter, who then resells it, in much smaller pieces. A managing underwriter usually divides the sale among other securities firms in an underwriting syndicate.

The corporation's steps are to find an underwriter, negotiate the terms, and go through the preparation process. It is then up to the managing underwriter to put together the syndicate and see that its members do their job.

The chore of shopping for an underwriter may be over before it begins. If there is to be an underwritten IPO, the choice of managing underwriter is often predetermined. An entrepreneur may already be tied in with a securities firm that manages IPOs, one with the required capacity and commitment. This often happens when venture capital financing has been arranged, through a securities firm or its affiliate.

IPO underwriting is not really price competitive. Commissions are almost always seven percent for IPOs over $10 million and thirteen percent for smaller IPOs (including a three percent "nonaccountable expense allowance"). Underwriters usually get warrants to buy shares, and some additional rights. Any difference in terms between underwriting firms becomes insignificant to the larger issues of pricing the shares timing the sale, and the firm's reputation for completing underwritings.

Underwriting commissions (called "the spread") are divided three ways: The managing underwriter keeps 20 percent; another 20 percent is for the underwriting syndicate, although it is used to pay for the underwriters' lawyer and other expenses; the remaining 60 percent is for the firm whose broker gets the customer's order. The split between the firm and its broker is usually 60 percent / 40 percent.

Competition among investment bankers is on the ability to get transactions done. Word of failures gets around. Rivals see to that. To maintain a reputation, it may be necessary for an underwriter to go through with an offering when there are orders for less than all the shares. Although they have no legal obligation under the letter of intent, competitive prestige may lead them to risk owning leftover stock at a price above the after-market.

Whether an underwriter can be attracted to a particular company's IPO depends upon timing. There are cycles in underwritten IPOs, times when nearly any entrepreneur can go public and times when the entire new issues market seems shut down. The number of underwritten IPOs has peaked, for instance, at nearly 1,300 in 1969, only to go below 30 by 1975. Within the cycles are the fads. If a company is part of the favored industry, investment bankers will seek it out and rush its shares to market. A year or two earlier or later, no one will touch it. Entrepreneurs who plan to go public will monitor market activity to sense when a new issues boom is developing and when interest is turning to their industry. They subscribe to magazines and newsletters that follow the new issues market. They develop information channels to securities analysts and watch their industry peers.

When the time looks favorable, an entrepreneur checks to see which securities firms have been managing IPOs for similar corporations. Meetings with as many as a dozen firms are set—through friends, a securities lawyer, or directly. Preparation for the meeting is mostly in understanding how investment bankers react and make decisions. Publications and speeches emphasize that the company should have a thoroughly documented business plan, at least a million dollars in profit, ten million in sales, and a 20 percent growth rate. Experience shows that what really works is being in the right business and making the right impression on investment bankers.

One securities lawyer/underwriting advisor told a group of entrepreneurs in 1988:

> The ability of a company to go public is primarily a function of market climate, not the operational performance of that particular company. The next thing that is most important is the manner of selecting and presenting your situation to an underwriter, or group of underwriters. And only lastly is the operational performance critical.

Shopping for an underwriter becomes a matter of selling the entrepreneur and the corporate image, then selecting among the firms which show an interest. Then it is time for a letter of intent.

Underwriter's Letter of Intent

When the entrepreneur and securities firm have chosen each other, the underwriter furnishes a letter of intent. It says that the underwriter will buy shares to be issued, as soon as the offering is cleared with the Securities and Exchange Commission and any required state securities regulators. A price range and number of shares are spelled out.

Those who have not been through an underwriting usually believe that a handshake and letter equal a firm commitment, that the underwriter has agreed to buy the shares and assume the risk of reselling them. But the letter of intent is just what its name implies. There is nothing at all about it that is legally enforceable, except the corporation's obligation to pay the underwriter's expenses if the entrepreneur calls off the sale. An obligation to buy the shares does not exist until the final price is negotiated between the company and the underwriter and the underwriting agreement is signed. That happens only after the shares have been resold. There is no commitment to buy until the selling is done. For purposes of signing an underwriting agreement, the selling is done when stockbrokers have gathered "indications of interest" from their customers. Legally, there can be no sale until the customer has received a final prospectus, cleared with the SEC. The prospectus is sent along with a confirmation of the sale and the customer has three days to pay for the shares or to back out, to "renege." Underwriters try to have indications of interest for at least 150 percent of the total number of shares, to cover reneges. The underwriting risk, of being left holding unsold shares, is limited to the few days in which customers may renege. Most underwriters will also take on some risk in buying and selling shares after the offering, to stabilize the market price.

A letter of intent is about three pages and covers only a few topics. Among those may be:

Lock-up. Most people buy underwritten new issues in the hope that they can soon resell the shares at a higher price, because demand will have exceeded the supply in public hands. This image requires that the shares held by the founders be kept off the market until the underwriter's customers have had a chance to take their profit. So the private shareowners are expected to "lock up" their shares for three months to a year after the IPO.

Green Shoe. Underwriters may find that fewer buyers renege than expected, so they have to deliver more shares than they have agreed to buy. To cover the shortage, underwriters buy shares in the trading market. This can drive the price above the offering and create losses to the underwriting syndicate. In an IPO by the Green Shoe Manufacturing Company, underwriters began getting an option to buy more new shares, at the same underwriting price, "to cover overallotments." The number of additional shares is usually limited to 15 percent of the underwriting.

Other provisions may give the underwriter the right to do future financings, to arrange a buyout by another company, and appoint a representative to the board of directors.

This is the structure for a "firm commitment" underwriting. A securities firm can also agree to use its "best efforts" to sell shares, usually with a minimum and maximum number. Very few best efforts IPOs are done, and each one is tailor-made, unlike the rigid formula for a firm commitment IPO. Firms who do best efforts offerings are not the ones invited into underwriting syndicates. Entrepreneurs are told that it is a second-rate way to go public and could ruin the corporation's reputation in the capital markets.

The IPO Preparation Process

Management of the IPO preparation process usually falls to the lawyers, either for the corporation or the underwriter, depending upon experience and personality. The first thing they do is schedule an "all hands" meeting, inviting corporate officers, investment bankers, auditors, financial printers, and anyone else who will be important in the proceedings.

There may be four to six of these all hands meetings over the four months or so of preparation. They usually last 8 to 16 hours a day for one to three days. The first one is to go over a schedule of the steps involved, who is responsible for each, and the deadlines. Major issues may come up, such as legal and accounting barriers to a public offering, or whether the corporate name should be changed. More sensitive subjects, like changes in the board of directors, are discussed at a private dinner between the entrepreneur and the investment bankers.

One of the lawyer teams will prepare the first draft of the prospectus, the document that is sent to investors with confirmation of their order for shares. The remaining all hands meetings are mostly prospectus editing sessions. All hands meetings are also part of the "due diligence" process. Underwriters and others involved in the IPO can be liable to investors for misrepresentations and omissions in the prospectus. Securities laws provide a defense for those who use due diligence in reviewing the corporate history and other facts which should be important to investors.

There will be a "night at the printer's" just before the prospectus is filed with the Securities and Exchange Commission and state "blue sky" securities regulators. This last-minute editing ritual will be repeated when an amendment is filed, in response to comments from SEC reviewers.

Tension really begins to build when the amended prospectus is filed. There is usually only three more weeks until the "effective date," when the prospectus is cleared and confirmations of sale can be mailed. The investment bankers will be calling the entrepreneur with the latest news from their syndicate department—what securities firms want to be included, how many shares have been "circled" by a brokerage office, and which mutual fund managers have shown an interest. There will be good news and bad news, always with uncertainty about whether the shares will get sold and what the final price will have to be. Climax comes the night before the effective date, when the entrepreneur and investment bankers meet to agree on the price and sign the underwriting agreement. This is the last movement in the "pricing dance," an elaborate ritual which began with the very first introduction.

Underwritten IPOs generally lack any real process management. Lawyers usually take charge of the schedule, since so much depends upon writing the prospectus and getting regulatory clearance. Accountants go off to do their job and come back to argue with the lawyers. Financial printers, who now usually handle the electronic filings as well, are the servants of the lawyers and usually spare no expense to accommodate them.

An entrepreneur's only control over the price, timing and expenses is the ability to call the whole thing off. Otherwise, the corporation will go public when the underwriter says the market is favorable, the price will be what the underwriter says is necessary to get the deal done and the corporation will pay the expenses that have mysteriously built up since the process began.

How the Underwriters Sell the Shares

During that last three weeks before the effective date, the managing underwriter's syndicate department begins putting together an underwriting syndicate of securities firms. Each member of the syndicate has an allotment of shares, which it is responsible for buying under the Agreement Among Underwriters. There is a Selected Dealer Agreement for local securities firms that are not in the syndicate but are allowed to sell shares for a split of the commission.

The "Red Herring"

A final draft of the legal offering document, the preliminary prospectus, helps firms decide whether they want into the syndicate and how many shares they expect to sell. The bold red letters on the cover explain that the preliminary prospectus is only a "red herring," used to build interest in the real thing to follow. [The slang remains, although the letters no longer have to be in red ink.]

Names gathered from the entrepreneur, directors, and employees are usually turned over to the managing underwriter's own brokers for processing the order. Investment bankers insist that all shares be sold in the underwriting. The managing underwriter prepares an internal memorandum to help the syndicate candidates decide whether they can sell an allotment. This often becomes a four-page flyer for individual brokers to use in their telephone calls to customers and prospects. There is a summary of the business, capsule financial information, key selling points, and how to answer questions investors might ask. Key phrases are in bold face type.

The Road Show

In addition to telephone selling by syndicate brokers, there are "due diligence meetings," for institutional money managers, where corporate officers answer questions and make an impression. This comes just before the underwriting agreement is to be signed and may include a week in Europe and Japan, as well as a week across the U.S. top management (often split into two teams for separate towns) is expected to do two group meetings and several "one-on-ones" with major fund managers every day.

Telemarketing

The road show is for the big institutional money managers. The rest of the selling is done through telephone calls made by brokers (actually, "registered representatives") of the firms included in the underwriting syndicate and more extensive "selling group." Many brokers know which of their customers want to hear about new issues and who might be interested in a particular industry. By concentrating on these pre-qualified customers, they can reach a favorable ratio of shares sold to calls made. Underwritten IPOs are the last holdout from the days of fixed commissions. That means that a selling broker can make five thousand dollars from calling a money manager who buys 10,000 shares, as compared to making fifty dollars from calling an individual who buys only 100 shares. Why bother with individuals if the whole issue can be sold to a relative handful of people who buy for institutions? And why do any underwritings at all unless they can be sold to institutional investors? This leaves the corporation with maybe 500 shareowner names after it has gone public. Since most of those will be institutions, there are probably only 100 decision makers involved. One money manager may put the shares into several different client accounts. The underwriter is the common bond among all these investors, especially if the entire issue has been sold without a syndicate of other brokerage firms. That means they are all likely to react to future news in the same way at the same time, leading to price swings of as much as 50 percent or more in a day or two. This further discourages any individual investors and keeps ownership concentrated.

With most marketing programs, telemarketing can be useful as one component. But all by itself, telephone selling is usually not an effective way to introduce a complicated new product. Yet, for most sales to investors, it is the only marketing tool used in an underwriting, where the prospect is someone who has probably never heard of the corporation being sold.

Brokers have only a minute or two to arouse some interest and then another few minutes to close the sale. There is no market research to help package the offering and target likely investors. There is no strategy about what aspects of the business should appeal to what kind of person. There is no supporting message in print or electronic media. No one trains the brokers about the corporation.

In an underwritten offering, the corporation gives up any say over who buys the shares. These are the people with whom the entrepreneur is going to share ownership. Yet their identity is determined by the underwriter's priorities, not the corporation's. The new shareowners' first impression of the corporation will have come from a broker who probably first learned of the company a day or two before. The entrepreneur will never know what was said to induce a purchase of the shares.

A "hot new issue" is an IPO that becomes effective at the peak of a fad for its industry. They provide brokers with a chance to reward customers and attract prospects by letting them have some of their allotted shares.

A History of Underwriting

The concept of corporate shareownership began when business ventures started needing more capital than the entrepreneur could provide. Sixteenth-century merchant ships became the model for corporate IPOs.

Ships were expensive to build. A crew and supplies had to be financed until the "ship came in." And someone had to bear the risk that all would be lost at sea. Entrepreneurs began selling shares in the ships and voyages. Courts developed precedents for dealing with disputes that arose over the rights of shareowners. When railroads and big manufacturing enterprises came along, legislatures had created the corporation as a separate "person," able to enter contracts, to be defended by the courts and police, to enjoy nearly every right but voting. Rules were made to serve the economic realities. Most important was the concept that a shareowner is not at risk for anything except the amount paid for the shares. No fear of "my partner ruined me." No calls for more money. No contingent liabilities.

Stock exchanges were organized, as places for people to get in and out of shareownership. This brought the magic of liquidity. The corporation could keep forever the money it got from selling shares, but shareowners could sell for cash at any time. With a stock trading market, an entrepreneur could offer investors shareownership in a way which (a) let shareowners cash out at any time, (b) limited their loss to the price they paid, and (c) provided them with clear legal rights. In return, the entrepreneur got money which (a) never had to be paid back, (b) required no interest payments ever and (c) left management free to run the business.

As corporations increased in number and size, making a market for stocks grew into a business of its own. The customer base for the new securities industry was the growing class of investors—people who bought stock for the long haul because they believed in the business concept and its management.

Brokers act as the agent for investors and traders, matching orders to buy and sell. As the market grew, with more choices available, investors needed a source of information and expert opinion about companies and their stocks. Brokers were willing to fill this need, getting paid by commissions from executing the resulting orders to buy and sell.

Traders make a business of buying and selling shares for a speculative, short-term profit. They help give the market a volume of activity that allows prices to be quoted on a regular basis.

Dealers are in the business of buying and selling for their own account, making small price markups as they turn over their inventory,. and smoothing out price fluctuations. They may be a specialist on an exchange or a market maker for shares traded over-the-counter, where their function is to balance the flow of buy and sell orders. Dealers may also buy large blocks of stock and redistribute them among many buyers.

Those came to be the financial intermediary roles in the stock market:

Brokers, who perform the market mechanics and provide a source of information and advice.

Traders, who create an active market through frequent speculative buying and selling.

Dealers, who make markets liquid through continuous buying and selling.

Since the 1800s, these functions have served to keep a trading market going for shares of corporate ownership. Most of the Wall Street securities firms are brokers, traders, and dealers, all at once. They are also the underwriters of IPOs, but that is not the way it began.

Money to build and launch ships was raised by selling shares among the merchant class. As the Industrial Revolution began, English joint-stock companies were financed the same way.

There was always the risk that enough shares would not have been sold by the time the money was needed. So the early entrepreneurs went to people in the business of "underwriting" risks. The original underwriters were insurance companies who would agree to purchase any shares left unsold, in return for an underwriting fee. To spread the risk of large stock issues, the insurance companies joined together in underwriting syndicates. So, the original underwritten IPOs were marketed directly by their entrepreneurs, who paid underwriters to assume the risk of an uncompleted offering.

Corporate shares began to be used as a medium of exchange in commercial transactions. Money, in the sense of government currency, was not that reliable. Commercial banks and large merchants began purchasing new issues of corporate shares as a way of investing extra cash and settling accounts. This investing and trading led to buying new issues of stock from entrepreneurs for resale. For the larger issues, the merchants and banks began forming syndicates to share the marketing with an allotment of shares to each syndicate member. The risk of unsold shares was divided the same way. Eventually, firms began to specialize in financings.

By 1900, after the vast railroad financings, there were a dozen or so major firms that marketed the shares of any public offering. They had become specialists in corporate finance and called themselves investment bankers. These few firms became respected and powerful. When investors and traders bought an IPO, it was based on the reputation of the investment banker. If an entrepreneur could not convince one of these titans to underwrite the new issue, it just did not happen. Owning corporate shares was still limited to the wealthy few, and they relied upon J.P. Morgan's firm and a handful of others to screen the right companies. There had been too many stock market "panics" since the Civil War for them to take a chance on their own. Endorsement was what investment bankers had most to offer. Their contribution was not so much selling as it was placing their stamp of approval on a stock.

Before the 1920s, investment bankers dealt with a few wealthy families in Europe and the United States. Not many people trusted financial assets, values represented only by pieces of paper. Attitudes toward investing were changed by the immense success of Liberty Bonds sold by the U.S. Treasury to finance World War I. They were printed in small denominations and could be bought on the installment plan. Securities firms were used to sell the bonds into a market estimated in 1917 at only 350,000 individuals. Instead, the first series of bonds was subscribed by over 4 million people and, by the fourth bond issue, there were over 22 million investors.

After the war was over, a vast new group of investors had been revealed throughout the land. The public demand for securities, stimulated by advertising and promotional campaigns, was insatiable, and the profits to be made in underwriting and distributing new issues was lucrative. The result was a marked decline in banking judgment and ethics and unscrupulous exploitation of public gullibility and avarice. (*Investment Banking in America: A History*, by Vincent P. Carosso)

According to Professor Carosso, the Crash of 1929 and the Congressional investigations that followed, "completed the transformation of the investment banker's image from the folk hero of the prosperity years to the scapegoat of the depression era." Congress passed laws creating the Securities and Exchange Commission and making crimes of practices that contributed to the Crash. One of the laws would have separated brokers and dealers, so one firm could not act as agent for customers and also be buying and selling securities for its own account. That would have taken underwriting away from brokerage firms. The provision was lobbied out at the last moment.

Another attack on investment bankers came in an antitrust case, U.S. v. Morgan, which charged 17 Wall Street firms with monopolistic practices in underwriting corporate securities. It was dismissed after the government's case and never appealed.

Underwritten IPOs have become an ever tighter bottleneck for the flow of capital from individuals to entrepreneurs. Changes in the securities industry have been the major cause. Investment bankers are not preparing IPOs and underwriting syndicates are not selling them. But the problem is not all in the diminished capacity to prepare and distribute IPOs. Entrepreneurs who can attract an underwriter still have many reasons to look for alternatives to an underwritten IPO.

When an Underwritten IPO Makes Sense

Even with its problems, an underwritten IPO may still work for some corporations today. Those include situations where the corporation is already in the hands of custodial management, where the objective is to cash out private investors, where going public is just a step in a strategy to sell out entirely, and where the entrepreneur is confident that one public offering is all that will ever be needed.

Accommodating Custodial Care

Control of a corporation sometimes passes to managers who have no ownership interest. The entrepreneur may have died or been ousted. Those in charge may be motivated by the first principals of bureaucracy: (l) avoid work, (2) have a clean record and (3) network to a better job.

Work can be avoided by turning over the going public project to an underwriter and the lawyers. Hiring a name securities firm shifts responsibility for the financing off the manager's record. Getting to know corporate finance people in major securities firms, and granting favors to some of them, can be seen as the big chance to move on as a winner.

Cashing Out Investors

Venture capitalists and other private investors need an exit plan when they decide to invest. It is not enough to have the corporation be successful if there is no way for the financial backers to realize their profit. An entrepreneur can avoid being forced to sell the whole business if investors can be cashed out in a public market.

Many recent IPOs have really been extensions of venture capital financing. Buyers at the public offering have been a handful of institutional money managers. But the IPO will have generated some trading among big investors, providing a chance to unload all or part of an early private stake. Several IPO underwriters have close relationships with venture capital firms and have an interest in helping them cash out.

Preparing to Sell It All

Founding investors often start a corporation with the objective of selling out when they can reach a target price. Going public can accelerate that process. Investment bankers who do underwritings also look for follow-on fees from arranging acquisitions, and the letter of intent can specifically provide them with that opportunity. Being public brings a corporation to the attention of prospective buyers and provides readily accessible information.

Doing an IPO not only invites acquisition interest, it can increase the acquisition price. When a company is privately owned, negotiations for its acquisition involve pricing formulas related to earnings, sales, and assets. Public stock trading generally brings much higher valuations. Since management would never sell at less than the market price, going public can establish a floor on any future acquisition price.

Going Only Once to the Well

Most disadvantages of an underwritten IPO have to do with what happens after the sale—the trading market, future stock offerings, relations with shareowners. There may be entrepreneurs who are not concerned about those issues, because they never expect to need shareowner money again. They may plan to wait for the price to drop and then buy the shares back. If the corporation's business coincides with a new issues fad, it can make sense to say "yes" when an investment banker suggests doing an IPO. The stock price may drop when the fad passes. Shareowners may become disillusioned. But if the entrepreneur is convinced that a one-time injection will last forever, it may be worth it.

CHAPTER 5

HOW TO DO A DIRECT PUBLIC OFFERING

Direct Public Offerings are a way to raise capital by selling securities directly from the company to large groups of prospective investors. DPOs are an alternative to the traditional underwritten public offerings, where securities are sold by brokers to their customers. DPOs can also be used instead of private placements of securities through negotiations with venture capital firms, larger corporate strategic partners or private "angel" investors.

Companies that are already public have begun using Direct Public Offerings as a way to bring more individuals into their investor base. They find that having a direct relationship with their security holders, rather than going through mutual funds, brokers, and other intermediaries, leads to more stability in the trading market, along with increased support for their products and services.

All of the securities laws that govern underwritten IPOs also apply to DPOs. When a company completes its direct offering, it still needs to have a market for trading its securities and it has the same obligations to furnish reports to shareowners and to securities regulators. The big differences between a DPO and the underwritten IPO are: (1) who ends up owning the securities, (2) how the securities are priced for sale to the public and (3) how much it costs to do the offering.

What Decisions Need to Be Made to Start a Direct Public Offering?

We have had enough experience by now with DPOs that predictions can be made about what will happen if a particular company starts down that path. We usually recommend something like a Decision Analysis Seminar before a company begins to incur costs and make commitments toward doing a DPO. This can be a gathering of the company's management and its closest advisors, as well as those employees who would be most involved in doing a DPO.

The Decision Analysis group would review the capital formation alternatives that seem reasonable for the company. Members of the group would have gathered information about private financings, traditional underwritten public offerings and such exotic avenues as reverse mergers into shells or Regulation S offshore offerings. Then the discussion would focus on the Direct Public Offering alternative, including such matters as the amount of ownership that might need to be given up for a certain level of capital raised; the limitations upon management's ability to run the business that might follow the transaction; the state and federal securities law requirements for each alternative; how much it would cost in fees and expenses; how long the process could take and how much of management's time would be involved.

An agenda for discussing the DPO process might look something like:

Decision Analysis for a Direct Public Offering

(a)   *Objectives for Amount of the Offering, Timing and Pricing*

Amount: minimum_____ maximum_____
Timing: filing date_____ commence offering_____
         conclude offering_____
Pricing: minimum amount =_____% of company
          maximum amount =_____% of company

(b)   *Choice of Securities Regulation Filing*

Comparison matrix of SEC forms
Availability, cost of audited financials
States in which offering will be made

(c)   *Market and Marketing Methods*

Marketing pyramid for levels of prospective investors
Steps to profile market segments, media to reach them, probabilities

(d)   *Objectives for Aftermarket (company, present shareowners)*

Matrix of numerical requirements for trading markets
Consideration of broker-dealer for order matching service

(e)   *Corporate Preparation*

Choice of corporate structure
Board of Directors
Title of officers
Intellectual property protection
Employee benefit programs (including share ownership)

(f)   *Selection of the DPO Team*

Internal roles
Outside participants
Communication channels

(g)   *Schedule and Budget*

Responsibility schedule
Budget

Our experience with Direct Public Offerings, with underwritten IPOs, and with venture capital private placements tells us that they are each more complex, and take more time, than the owners and managers thought they would be. But that experience also says that the DPO is no more complex than the other routes. And, because it is a direct offering from the company to the investors, it is the most manageable way to go. In other words, you do not have to accommodate a financial intermediary, like an investment banker or venture capital firm staff, and wonder what they are doing. You can manage a Direct Public Offering just like you would manage any other project. Yes, you need outside help from accountants, lawyers, printers, and other service providers, but you are the one who decides who you want to work with and how you want to manage them.

Before you begin committing time and money to a DPO, you will want to fine-tune that first item of the Decision Analysis, particularly the pricing of the company.

When we talk about pricing a DPO, we don't mean the price per share to be set for the offering. That's a marketing decision, with some securities law considerations. Generally, the lower the price the higher the connotation of potential risk and return. Mature corporations usually trade in the market at prices of $40 to $100. Ones that have been public for only a few years may trade in the $20 to $40 range, while underwritten IPOs are usually priced in the mid-teens.

So-called "Penny Stocks" are, by legal definition, those priced at less than $5 per share. There are specific rules that make it difficult for securities broker/dealers to act as market makers in these shares and regulators may view them with particular caution. We almost always advise against a price below $5. Above that, the price is selected to "tell" the prospective investor something about the company's stage of development and prospects for the future.

The real "pricing" decision is this: "How much of our company do we give up to raise the capital we want?" Put the other way, it is: "How much of the company should the new investors get for the capital they are contributing?"

Estimating the Amount and Price

There is a lot of art in the pricing of a corporation, most especially in its initial public offering. Final decisions will be made after you have your whole offering team on board and up to speed. But you will need a pretty clear idea in mind when you decide to go public.

Going public involves a tradeoff between the amount of money raised and the percentage of the corporation you give up to public shareowners. Is $10 million for 25 percent fair? Is 40 percent really only worth $2.5 million, too small to make a public offering worthwhile?

Take a look at a few corporations that are most like yours, except that they already have publicly traded stock. Figure some ratios of their earnings, revenues, and book value (assets minus liabilities) to their stock trading price. Talk it over with your accountant and other confidential advisers.

If your corporation has not yet received any significant revenues from its main business, you probably should continue looking to private money sources. Sometimes, like the birth of the biotechnology industry, public shareownership works to finance long startups. Mostly, the shares will not sell or, if they do, the new shareowners will become discouraged. The danger is then that you have ruined the corporation's image as a public company and have closed off that source of capital.

All you want at this point is some ballpark answer to (1) how much could you raise by giving up a comfortable percentage ownership—no more than 40 percent, and (2) does that amount make a public offering worthwhile—it needs to be at least $2 million and more comfortably over $4 million? In the last five years, we have completed DPOs as small as $468,000. While that was an exceptional marketing opportunity, we now believe that most offerings of at least $750,000 can be cost-effective.

You can estimate that fixed costs, such as legal, printing, and accounting fees, will run between $100,000 and $200,000. Marketing costs are harder to estimate, but the minimum to do the job is likely to be around

10 percent of the total offering price. The $468,000 offering mentioned had total costs of $104,000, or 22 percent. Marketing costs were about half, while fixed costs were kept unusually low.

Then you need to consider the strain on you and your staff. That often translates through to lower earnings and lost opportunities for the business.

Considering the fixed costs, the minimum needed for marketing and the attention needed from management, it is hard to justify a public offering for less than $4 million, but experience has shown that offerings of $1 million, and even less, can be justified.

Going out for too little money is dangerous. Fixed costs will use too much of the proceeds. When the need arises again, the timing may be bad for another offering, either because of the general economy or because of a temporary setback in the corporation's results.

Less obvious is the problem of having too large an initial public offering. If you raise more capital than you need, you will have given up more ownership of your corporation than necessary. As the corporate business advances through each stage of its development, you should be able to raise more and more capital by selling less and less a percentage shareownership.

Compounding the hit you take in an initial public offering is a "new issue discount" that lowers the price by 20 percent or so, just because the shares have no trading history and the corporation is unknown. You only go through that discount once, so it helps not to sell more than you need to in the first round.

As your corporation prospers and grows, the public will pay a higher price for each percent of ownership. You give up less per dollar in every successive round.

After the first time, the other shareowners participate in that dilution of ownership. Each additional offering of new shares reduces the percentage ownership of the existing public shareowners, as well as your percentage.

Here is an example of an offering program:

Amount of the Offering	Percent of Ownership Sold	Founder's Percent	Ownership Market Value
$5 million	25%	75%	$15 million
$10 million	20%	60%	$30 million
$10 million	10%	54%	$54 million
$25 million	10%	49%	$122 million

This kind of program will only work if you accept that marketing share-ownership is a major part of your ongoing business. You cannot wait around for the experts to tell you that the market is right.

Marketing shareownership becomes a priority at the level of new product development, growth in market share and cost control. It is your competitive edge, through access to low-cost, permanent capital.

If you are ready to put selling shares at this level of corporate priority, then public shareownership can be right for you.

How Do We Get Started Doing a DPO?

The two beginning steps are (1) getting the company ready for public shareownership and (2) putting together your team for the DPO. These can both be started immediately after making the "go" decision and they can continue in parallel until you're ready for the next steps.

Getting the company ready includes some "corporate cleanup," image issues, reconsidering your board of directors and management structure, and making some decisions about the mechanics of how the corporation will be governed.

"Corporate Cleanup"

Is a term used to describe the rearranging and tidying up of corporate affairs. Some of those are minor, such as proper minutes for meetings of directors and shareowners. Others can be touchy, such as getting rid of devices you may have used to save taxes, take care of family members, or protect the original investors. In a private company, decisions of corporate structure are likely to have been dictated by tax advisers, bankers, and by chance. The result may not lend itself to public shareownership.

Land, buildings, and related mortgages may belong in or out of the corporation, depending on their importance to the corporate business. If they are not to be property of the corporation, this real estate should be owned by outsiders and under long-term leases. Airplanes, mountain retreats, club memberships, and expensive cars are sometimes accumulated in private corporations, with some fuzziness between business and personal use. You could no doubt defend their value to the corporate purpose. It would be far better to get rid of them. Shares are not sold by good defenses.

Some discoveries may delay the DPO, like finding that shares sold to friends and associates along the way were technically an illegal "public offering." This may even require a "recission offer," giving those investors the choice of getting their money back or retaining their shares. It is not unusual for the offering to be abandoned for a couple of years because audited financial statements cannot be produced to satisfy the securities laws. (This issue is part of the "Screen Test for a Direct Public Offering," described in Chapter 3.)

Image Issues

Your corporation will be making a first impression, giving signals about its true identity. You want to have that image be accurate and persuasive. Here are some of the issues:

Corporate Name. Whatever the history may have been, the corporate name needs to communicate to prospective investors your vision of the future.

Headquarters. Your address tells whether you are a part of daily operations or in a remote control tower, whether you are a hometown business or a financial center operation.

Corporate Structure. Holding companies and multiple subsidiaries may be necessary for some kinds of business. Usually, they reflect holdovers from tax and financing considerations in the private company context. If they can be collapsed into one entity, it will probably help marketing and regulatory clearance. Generally, the simpler the better.

The Business You Are In. The business concept has to be understood at first glance. This may be the time to create your concept's expression through a corporate slogan or a new logo. Going public has caused companies to hire a corporate image consultant to create a clear, consistent expression of what the business really is or is becoming.

Culture. In marketing your shares to thousands of prospective shareowners, you are letting in another group of participants. They need to have some feel for the atmosphere. Is this a "one big happy family" organization or is it formal and serious?

Outside Professionals. You hire your law firm, auditors, and other professionals according to your own standards. Their names will communicate an image by association. If you are thinking about a change, now is the time to do it and to consider what image your choice of outside professionals will convey.

Most important to your corporate image will be the people on your team—management and the board of directors. Image may not influence your choice of executives, but it is certainly appropriate in picking directors.

The Board of Directors

Corporations are structures like parliamentary governments—directors are elected by all the shareowners to make policy decisions and to appoint executives to carry them out. As a private company, the board of directors is hand-picked by its initial backers. Now it needs to present a board that can represent the interests of its new public shareowners as well. Regulators at the state securities review level will often insist that certain transactions by the corporation with its employees be approved by "outside," non-employee, directors.

Selection of directors is among the most neglected of corporate decisions. Entrepreneurs are often casual about it, considering directors to be a technical necessity. Some become obsessed with personal loyalty and load the board with relatives and cronies. When most of us pick up a prospectus, we first get a general impression of the business and then we flip to the parts we feel competent to understand—the people. We make some quick judgments about the officers and directors. We will be more inclined to learn more, and buy shares, if your selection of directors inspires confidence and comfort.

Picking a board of directors can even be a part of the share marketing campaign. Some entrepreneurs have been very blunt about establishing an "entry fee" to be on the board. They require that each director buy at least a certain amount of shares in the public offering. This needs to be disclosed to other prospective investors and, properly handled, it can be a positive quality.

Corporate Governance

Corporate governance is one of those subjects that is periodically all the rage among politicians and academicians. Most people never think about it—until they suddenly feel slighted by the way an issue has been handled. Corporate governance means: "Who is in charge here, and how do I get treated fairly?" Corporations are governed by their charters and bylaws, which describe how groups of interested people are to relate to each other. Most issues of corporate governance have to do with the relationship between shareowners and management. Before a corporation goes public, the shareowners and the management will probably be the same people. But corporate cleanup for public shareownership includes making some choices now with an eye to possible future conflict.

Your corporation was formed by filing papers with a state agency. If it is not the one in which you are headquartered, the selection probably was based on the rights of management, directors, and shareowners. You will have to explain some of those rights in the offering documents. Reincorporating from your home state to Delaware or Nevada, for instance, may suggest that corporate governance is going to tilt in favor of management over shareowners.

Basic to corporate governance is whether the corporation will have more than one class of shares. When some big private corporations finally went public, the founding family ended up with more votes per share than the class of stock sold to investors. Sometimes the dividend rights are different on the insider class than on the outsider class. If your corporation is already well known, there may possibly be plenty of demand for shares that are "second class" to the ones you keep. But in most cases, you will be offering the public the only class of common stock. There may be preferred stock outstanding, from rounds of private financing, and you will need to consider whether that stock is convertible into common or, if not, whether a concession should be negotiated with the holders.

Cumulative voting becomes important with one class of stock. Without it, the owners of just over 50 percent can elect all the directors. Cumulative voting means that directors can be elected in proportion to shares owned. If there are seven directors, for instance, one of them could be elected by people owning only 15 percent of the shares. (Some states, like California, may require cumulative voting as a condition for sale of shares to their residents.)

You will decide whether the entire board is up for election each year or is a staggered board, in which a third of the directors are elected each year for three-year terms. Staggered boards can turn shareowner revolutions into evolutions. Then there are management protections like supermajority voting and "poison pills." In almost every corporation, it will be best to keep it simple, standard, and favorable to investors. Remember that you will be asked to explain anything that is not.

Selecting the Team

If you want to build your company with public capital, selling shares will become a continuous part of your corporate business. Daily activities will be influenced by their possible effect on shareowners. In the continuous marketing of shareownership, everyone within the corporation is on the team. This sounds like a lot of work. It is. But public shareownership needs to be viewed as a profit center. The "income" is what you save in borrowing costs, the freedom from loan agreement restrictions, the ability to grow more rapidly than you could with money from banks or private investors. Viewed this way, you can afford to have a team devoted to servicing shareowner capital.

Your initial direct public offering is a special effort. It will have a beginning, end, and measurable stages. The process is like a political campaign: Lots of strategy planning, dealing with the unexpected, building to a peak—and then it is over until the next offering. This special effort calls for its own team. Some of the members of your DPO team will be independent contractors, on board for the duration of the project. Others will be employees, permanent and temporary, full-time and part-time.

Essential members of the team include your project manager, financial person, lawyer, DPO adviser, and auditors. Each of those roles is described here, as well as several others you are likely to need.

Project Manager. The captain of the DPO team should be a full-time employee of the corporation but *not* the chief executive or chief financial officer. It won't help to have the business miss opportunities and ignore warning signs because a successful DPO became the obsession of top management.

That kind of obsession is just what the project manager *should* have so that the DPO's success is not just top priority, but the only major concern for the six months it will be underway. If the manager is called off on another matter for even a few hours, the message to the rest of the team runs against all they have been told about the importance of their project. Nothing so promotes success as the single-minded dedication of the project manager.

When it comes to running the offering, your project manager needs to have all the authority of the chief executive and be specifically backed by the board of directors. When asking for information from employees not on the team, or talking with the corporate lawyers or accountants about the DPO, the project manager should receive the same treatment as you at the top would expect for yourselves. For that, your project manager will need your unwavering support, whatever private discussions you may later have.

One of the most successful DPO captains was a recently retired top legal officer for the corporation. It was a great advantage to have someone who knew everybody but did not have to work with them after the offering was over.

Another corporation had a successful DPO almost in spite of making a classic management mistake. The president, who expected to retire in a few years, had refused to designate his successor. Then he appointed as co-managers of the DPO project the two executive vice-presidents who were competing for his job. Their rivalry was played out in the scramble to take credit and avoid blame for each project decision. The experience did lasting injury to the corporation.

Most young companies will not have someone they can spare for this six month period. They may be able to hire a project manager who can later move into a permanent position. There will be the risk of an unknown quantity, and the CEO and CFO may have to be more personally involved than is ideal. But someone who comes through as a successful project manager will likely have a lot to contribute to the ongoing business. It may work for you to hire an independent contractor to be project manager. As a result of a series of recent direct public offerings, there are now experienced people who can sign on for the duration.

Financial Person. Financial statements and accounting issues become very important in explaining the corporation and in meeting securities law standards. Gathering financial information and presenting it effectively can chew up huge blocks of time. The role needs someone who is smart, understands accounting, works well under pressure, and gets along with people—those are the qualifications for the chief financial officer in most businesses. If there is also a controller, chief accountant, or other person under the CFO's direction, they can be assigned to help with the DPO. If there is no such person in management, you may want to fill the gap before you proceed with the DPO.

Outside auditors are qualified to do this gathering and presenting. But paying their billing rates is just the beginning of the extra cost. Because they are auditors, they accept some professional responsibility for the work. That means review procedures, meeting the standards of their firm and profession. It also means you have only indirect control over the people doing the job.

Priorities of your auditing firm will often conflict with those of the corporation, as expressed through the project leader. Nothing is so costly, in time and money, as the resolution of conflicts among members of the team. That is especially true when a team member is accountable to another employer, like an employee of your outside accountants. Temporary, contract employees may be the best choice in some cases, particularly if the project manager is able to make the judgment calls in accounting presentation.

The ideal financial person, like the ideal project manager, is someone for whom this assignment is a stepping stone for a career with the corporation. Financial data will come not only from the accounting function, but considerable information needs to be presented about the market, source of supply, competition, employees, and, often, technical matters. Being responsible for this part of the project teaches a lot about the corporation and its operating environment.

You may already have seen the potential for problem, in considering just these two members of the DPO team. The project leader is responsible to the chief executive or chief financial officer and has been delegated top management authority *for this project*. The financial person reports to the project manager *for this project*.

Career ambitions and anxieties can get in the way. That is one reason why the CEO and CFO, and even the directors, must be informed all along the way. Pep talks will be necessary, as well as individual "and I really mean it" sessions. Everyone on the team will need to internalize the belief that their personal goals will best be met through a successful DPO.

Lawyer. Many lawyers have done the legal work to comply with their state's laws for issuing corporate shares to a few inside shareowners. They have processed the paper for transferring shares from one owner to another. These do not a securities lawyer make. Securities lawyers are a rarefied breed. They come in subspecies of litigation, dealmaking (mergers and acquisitions), and financings. Within the subspecies of securities lawyers who specialize in financings, some may be most experienced in municipal bonds and others in private placements or in international transactions.

For the traditional underwritten IPO, a company must have someone who has been through a public offering registered under the federal Securities Act of 1933. They wouldn't need experience with filings at the state level, since underwritten offerings are generally so large that they qualify for exemptions. (More about state regulation in a few pages.) Lawyers for DPOs, at least those using the recently adopted "small business" filings, don't need to be "securities lawyers." With the database and experience of your DPO advisor, the legal work can be handled by your regular corporate lawyer.

In fact, you need to be wary of lawyers who have had lots of experience in underwritten offerings. They are accustomed to a process that is not "managed" by the client company, nor by anyone else, in many cases. You are, in a DPO, doing for yourself a job that has always "belonged" to securities firms. Most securities lawyers get a lot of work from securities firms, directly as clients or from referrals. You may run into "but you can't do it without an underwriter" or a smoother "let me introduce you to a really good investment banker." After all, that is probably the only way they have seen a public share offering done. And they will have friends and clients who are investment bankers.

Your lawyer may get a sharp reminder of these securities firms' connections from another partner in the firm. It is true that no major investment banker may be interested in your offering and that there is no local securities firm capable of doing it. Nevertheless, this is their historic turf. You should raise this issue specifically and be sure you feel satisfied with the assurances you get.

We have seen companies select a law firm for a DPO, only to be told that the firm's "policy committee" had decided they could not take on the assignment. The reason given by one large firm was a "concern about distribution" of the shares.

Most DPOs simply can't afford the legal fees that companies have to pay in underwritten IPOs—generally, over $200,000. You can do a good job with a lawyer whose commitment and willingness you trust. If ego and pride do not get in the way, your lawyer can rely upon the database and experience of your DPO advisor.

DPO Advisor. Until the 1980s, direct public offerings were mere anecdotes in the history of corporate finance. Maybe, once or twice a year, some corporation would decide to market its shares directly to its local community or customers. Whatever was learned in the process would stay with the team who did the work, probably never to be used again.

When government regulations allowed "mutual" financial institutions (technically, membership structures with no owners) to convert to the stock form, it was a requirement that the new shares first be offered to the institutions' depositors and borrowers. Only the leftovers could be sold through securities underwriters. There was suddenly a search for knowledge about how to market shares and how to manage a direct public offering. Experiences from one offering could be carried over to another.

As direct public offerings spread into non-financial businesses, this body of experience was expanded and improved. With 28 DPOs estimated to have been completed in 1994 and about 40 in 1995, there are now a few professionals who are in a position to pass on their knowledge.

You can find a DPO advisor by talking to satisfied customers—management at companies who have successfully completed DPOs. There are, however, many more who claim to be experienced and are not. One individual tells prospective clients that he "did" an early DPO for a company that had never even heard of him. He apparently figured that, like a job resume, prospects wouldn't check to see if what he said was true.

What you contract for with a DPO advisor will depend upon what you need to allow your team to do the best job possible. The DPO advisor may supply the forms and guidance for the federal and/or state regulatory work. They may help you find an individual who would become your project leader, as a temporary employee. By drawing upon their experience, and database, you can save hundreds of hours and many thousands of dollars.

One DPO advisor designs a relationship solely as a resource for the DPO team. It provides forms and sample documents for the decision analysis, planning, marketing program, regulatory compliance, and process management elements of the DPO. It responds to questions as they come up, usually with how similar issues were resolved in other DPOs.

Auditors. Nearly every company that is ready to consider a DPO will have an outside accounting firm, if only for tax advice, preparation of tax returns, and furnishing financial statements required by the bank. The ideal is that the independent accountants have also been issuing annual audit reports with "clean" opinions in accordance with the profession's accounting standards and auditing principles.

That ideal is more often not the case with companies that are still privately owned, particularly if the only shareowners are the founder, top management, and perhaps, a few family members or close associates. Why pay for an audit if everyone trusts each other?

It is technically possible to do a DPO without an audit. Regulators at the federal SEC level permit the use of Regulation A offering circulars with unaudited financial statements for offerings of up to $5 million. Some states will allow unaudited financials, especially for offerings under $500,000, where the accountants have "reviewed" instead of audited.

As a practical matter, attempting to sell shares to the public without an audit should be reserved for only the most extreme cases where an audit is just impossible. You will need to answer the question, "why aren't the financials audited?" If the answer is that your accounting records are so incomplete that there is no audit trail or that you persist in using accounting methods that are not generally accepted, then you aren't really ready to accept money from strangers who may rely on your financial statements.

Perhaps the most frequent reason why a company cannot get an audit, despite having good records, maintained in accordance with generally accepted practices, is that the amount of inventory cannot be confirmed to the auditors' satisfaction. If inventory is a material part of the business, as it usually is for a manufacturing, wholesale, or retail business, then inventory is usually a material part of the financial picture. It is not so much the amount of inventory shown on the balance sheet. More important is the effect of inventory, at the beginning and end of each year, upon that year's income statement.

It is standard procedure for companies with significant inventories to take a physical count of those inventories at least every year-end. The company's auditors send someone from their staff to "observe" the taking of a physical inventory. What if that didn't happen at the end of last year, or the year before, or the year before that? (Two years' audited income statements, involving both beginning and ending inventory amounts for each year, require three years of inventory verifications.)

There are alternative procedures within the accounting literature and practices. Sometimes, an observed physical inventory can be taken after a year end to demonstrate the reliability of the continuous inventory records. An analysis of accounts payable, shipping, and receiving documents may work.

Before an audit firm is selected, issues like the inventory one need to be identified. Then, each firm can suggest how they would deal with them.

The accounting profession has had all the problems of a mature market for a generic service. The total number and size of public corporations has not been growing the way it did before the 1980s. The managements of public companies see the annual audit as a commodity—it has the same use and value from one well-known firm as from another. When there is no perceived difference in quality, competition is based on price, extra benefits, or personal relationships with the decision makers.

Extra benefits might include valuation or management consulting services. Keep it simple. Do not buy anything except an audit and their advice on accounting and tax issues. Those extra benefits will involve people outside the audit team who have objectives that may just confuse things.

Selecting an auditor on the basis of friendship between the accounting firm partner and the corporate CEO or CFO is a bit touchy. Auditors are there to provide shareowners and others with an independent review and an opinion on the fairness of financial presentations. They must be objective. Better that you use your friend as an advisor and go to another firm for the audit. Personality is important, however. The audit partner can be practical and friendly, or stubborn and hostile. When dealing with the SEC and your securities lawyer, you need practical and friendly.

Public corporations have audit committees, usually made up of directors who are not employees. Those committees are supposed to pass on auditor selection and talk directly with the auditors about their work. You might as well have your directors pick an audit committee and let the committee get started by helping you pick the accounting firm for the pubic offering. There may be some accounting issues in your corporation that involve judgment as to how they are reflected in the financial statements. Your interview with audit firms can cover those.

Do not choose an auditor solely on the basis of what he or she says will be allowed regarding issues to be resolved. Chances are, the people making those assurances can be overruled when their work is reviewed by others in their firm. This is likely to happen just when you are in a hurry to start selling shares. It is probably better to find a way of dealing with the issue that is not controversial, an accounting method that will come out the same with any auditor.

Like the securities lawyer and DPO advisor, you want your auditor's references to tell you that they get the job done on time, within their cost quote and without causing a hassle.

Becoming a public company often means you have to change accounting firms, or add another layer to the one you have been using. Many accountants will either not have the capacity to do an audit or they will have an "independence" issue.

Most accounting firms you would find through a telephone directory do not even perform audits. Those who have an audit capability, and a willingness to keep up on the necessary professional knowledge, may not feel comfortable auditing a public company. However, one of the most helpful actions in the "Small Business Initiatives" from the Securities and Exchange Commission in 1993-94 was the requirement that financial statements for "small businesses" need only be in accordance with the accounting professions' standards, not also with the SEC's additional rules in its Regulation S-X.

If your accountants are willing and able to perform an audit, it still needs to be determined that they are "independent." For instance, if they have been actually performing much of your regular accounting work and preparing internal accounting statements, they may not also be able to issue an opinion on their fairness and conformity to accounting standards. If a partner of your accounting firm is on your board of directors, there goes the firm's independence.

One last consideration on choosing an outside accountant: should it be one of the "Big Six" international accounting firms? Actual experience seems to show that neither regulators nor your affinity group investors will be swayed one way or the other by the big firm's name. Marketing might even be enhanced by a "home town" name or one especially known within a particular industry. However, the regulators, at least, will definitely be influenced by the quality of the work, as shown in the financial statements and their notes—and by the response provided to the inevitable regulatory comments on the accounting presentation. You will need to do everything you can to assure a satisfactory level of competence.

Advertising and Direct Marketing Person. If you have an advertising agency for the corporate product and image, they will be accustomed to a certain way of handling the relationship—who originates ideas, who makes decisions, who supervises costs and timing. Some will be able to handle a new way of doing things and some will not. You probably have experience with a general advertising agency, one which prepares and places advertising in any media. Even if you use a general agency, you may need to supplement their work with a specialist.

Advertising gets a message out there, to inform and persuade. But the results are indirect—some other marketing steps are needed before a sale is ready to close. Direct marketing tells the audience precisely how to respond. It gives a telephone number or furnishes a coupon to mail. There are mechanics in place to deal with responses to the specific campaign. Direct marketing (sometimes called "direct response marketing") has four elements in a share offering:

> **Proposition.** The audience members are told that they will receive a prospectus if they respond to the advertisement; instructions are given about how to respond.

> **Response.** There is a procedure for receiving and processing responses; systems are set and people are trained to evaluate and screen.

Fulfillment. A prospectus and related marketing materials are furnished, just as they were promised.

Conversion. Follow-up and closing methods are supervised so that shares are sold in accordance with the securities laws and your own standards.

Direct marketing, particularly direct mail, is the most likely gap in a full-service agency. Many of them subcontract out the direct marketing component. Marketing shareownership relies heavily on direct mail and you may need to be forceful with your agency about getting a direct mail wizard as part of the team.

Market Research Person. Market research can be a key to bringing all of your objectives together, that is, to sell an acceptable percentage of your corporation at a fair price, to bring in shareowners who are likely to support your vision, and to complete the offering within a reasonable time and cost.

The answers you want from market research could include: Who are the people most likely to be interested in sharing ownership of your corporation? Which ones can also afford to buy corporate shares? What else do they have in common—knowledge that will tell you how to reach them. Where do they get their information? Whom do they trust for recommendations and endorsements?

Good market researchers will come up with far more useful questions once they understand your purposes. Practical experience will guide them to identify market segments that can be reached and sold at an efficient cost. Their service will be interactive—you can fine tune your market selection as the program moves along. You are buying a member of the marketing team, not a research report.

Training Director. Your officers, directors, and employees are going to be carrying the corporate message to prospective shareowners. They could probably use some help in learning how to do that most effectively. Much of that training is defensive—you do not want to violate any securities laws, or have a shareowner later complain of having been misled. Everyone in the corporation will be educated to internalize the different "feel" arising from being publicly owned. They will at once become more guarded in what they can say about the corporation and more promotional in the way they express themselves about it.

It is helpful if the public offering training director is either drawn from within the corporation or will be on call after the offering. Public shareownership is a continuing part of corporate life and training directors will be needed to teach new employees about it and to explain how big corporate events should be handled in light of public shareownership. You may already have an employee practiced in training sales or production people. If not, you can see if someone already in the corporation has the interest and aptitude to do training.

Having in-house training directors means bringing someone in from outside to "train the trainers" about public share offerings. This will be a short course in legal precautions and effective communication about selling shares. There will be role-playing sessions with typical prospect questions and responses. And there should be an instruction booklet and written quiz. You will have a tape of the sessions to complete your compliance record.

Shareowner Relations Manager. Once your offering is sold, your corporation will always, ever after, be in the business of marketing its shares. Actual share offerings will occur only as you need to raise money or meet other objectives, but individual shareowners will have personal reasons to sell. That will mean a continuing need for market research and targeting market segments, for developing name recognition and favorable perception and for publishing information. All these mechanics are necessary to keep a constant demand for your shares. Your shareowner relations program helps produce a waiting list of interested people to buy those shares.

Building interest among prospective new shareowners is probably less important than preventing blocks of shares coming on the market because of uninformed selling. Shareowners who do not get current information tend to get nervous and sell. Worse, they rush to sell when there's bad news, creating sudden price drops, which cause other shareowners to panic and sell, and on and on.

Marketing shareownership is like marketing any other product. Your shareowner relations manager will prepare a plan, budget, and progress reports. The job will include market research and interaction with the securities firms that make a market in your shares. There can be coordination with other parts of the corporation for cross-selling or cooperative promotions. Your investor relations manager will be most effective after being a part of the offering team, if not the team captain, than someone who has other marketing responsibilities.

A big part of the shareowner relations manager's job is to comply with the laws about disclosure of information. What requires a public announcement and when should it be made? How should the information be treated so that there is no selective disclosure to people who can trade before others know? When is it appropriate to keep a secret? Because of these concerns, many corporations have their investor relations officer report to the legal department or the chief financial officer. As a result, the investor relations program looks like something run by lawyers or accountants. Better to have the ideas and communications start somewhere else and be screened later for legal and accounting compliance.

If investor relations is to be part of marketing, you will need clear, intelligent mechanics for legal and financial review of the regular communications with shareowners. A system must also be in place and tested for crisis management so shareowners and prospective investors do not abandon the corporation from fear of the unknown in a catastrophe.

Shareowners who bought through your marketing programs will be natural allies in many marketing, political, and other corporate issues. Part of the investor relations job is to marshal those efforts effectively. With some careful supervision, you could let an investor relations person become a kind of advocate or ombudsman for shareowners—their pipeline to management. It may work well to have the investor relations function report directly to you or your top manager. That is, if the boss appreciates the importance of the job and takes a personal interest.

Electronic Communications Person. Chapter 7, "Selling Shares on the Internet" has been added to the second edition of this book. You will need a "webmaster," "web producer," or some similar employee or consultant who can translate the legal and marketing requirements into an operating electronic communications system.

Allies in the Campaign

There is only so much you can do in direct communication with your target groups. Your messages are about your corporation, its past, present, and future. Who will tell your prospects about what it is like to be a shareowner? Shareownership will be a new adventure for many of them. It involves adding to the image of who they are—an addition they need to visualize before giving it a try. Many individuals in your target markets will need to become comfortable with seeing themselves as shareowners before they can consider the merits of your particular corporation.

There is very limited time and money for accomplishing these changes in self-perception and then completing a sale of your shares. You need all the allies you can get. These allies are people who are perceived by your market as independent experts on the subject of investing. They can include the local banker, minister, barber, accountant, and lawyer. Two groups worth special attention are securities brokers and financial planners.

Securities Brokers. Even if you do not pay them commissions, securities brokers may be a big help to you. They want to be known for recommending winners. Suggesting your shares to their friends and customers can create that image and build goodwill for them. Even if brokers do not recommend your shares, it will surely help if they do not discourage anyone who asks about your offering. What could be more natural for someone considering a share offering than to ask the opinion of a stockbroker? Most of us react negatively when asked about an unknown, especially if we are supposed to be experts on the subject. How good could it be if we have not heard about it? Brokers need to be able to respond with, "Sure, I've talked with their president and read the prospectus."

One corporation marketed all of its first offering to people in the communities where it did business. On the eve of the offering, it had a cocktail party at the country club for all securities brokers in the area. Everyone there got a copy of the mailing that was about to go out and the newspaper ads that would soon appear. Reasons for using a direct offering were explained. Brokers were encouraged to ask questions and assured of access to corporate officers in the future. As a result, brokers were at least neutral when asked about the offering. Many actively encouraged their customers to buy a few shares from the corporation.

You will want to identify the brokers most likely to be consulted by your prospective shareowners. Then plan an information program just for them. Your securities lawyer may let you use a preliminary prospectus for this purpose. Even if the brokers are lukewarm, they will appreciate the advance knowledge of your offering.

We have used securities brokers in DPOs in three capacities. One is that there are still a few states that either require participation by a broker-dealer or require that a company employee has passed the most difficult of examinations. In those cases, we have affiliated a broker-dealer registered in those states.

Another role for broker-dealers has been to have an agency agreement for them to sell the company's shares to their own customers and prospects. The third has been to refer names to them for follow-up, usually people who have received the offering materials but not yet sent in a purchase agreement. These uses of broker-dealers call for written agreements and specific disclosure in the offering document.

Financial Planners. The term "financial planner" does not convey any clear picture in today's lineup of finance and investment professionals. Securities firms or life insurance companies use "financial planners" as a title for their brokers. Others who call themselves financial planners may really sell real estate syndications or other single-product investments.

There are "fee-only" financial planners, who are compensated only by their clients. They are far fewer in number than the financial planners who make most of their income from commissions on products they sell to their clients. Accountants and tax return preparers may double as financial planners, whether or not they use the title. Part of your market research and planning will be to come up with a useful list of people who really serve the function of financial planners.

Your list of financial planners will include the ones who might be consulted by individuals in your target markets. Your marketing program can then include a way to reach them and get their participation. This financial-planners component can include a campaign to educate people who are regularly asked for recommendations. They will include accountants, bankers, some lawyers, real estate brokers, and others who are expected to know about investing in corporate shares.

Other advisers will become apparent from your particular investment proposition. If you manufacture a health-care product, you can expect prospective investors to ask opinions from members of the professional group who would use your product. If it is software for managing construction, you will need to distribute shareownership marketing information to architects and contractors, especially those you know have a good opinion of your product.

Your basic goal is to get the shares sold within the brief time available. But you should also plan a continuous program for informing the people who will influence opinions about your corporation. They can generate fresh demand in the trading market for your shares. Keeping them informed will make your next offering much easier to sell.

Direct marketing of shareownership is like an election campaign. You go with what will win this time. But you must immediately start work to keep the interest up and build a base for the next offering.

Managing the Process

You have selected a manager and assembled a team. Now they need to manage the process to success, while causing as little disruption as possible to the ongoing business. Such tools as newsletters, CCs, and meetings, daily progress reports, incentives, and recognition are used in direct stock offerings to smooth the path.

Newsletters, "CCs," and Meetings

Everyone on your team needs to know what is going on with the whole project, as frequently as possible. Other people involved—employees, brokers, the staff at your advertising agency, and so forth—should get reports at least weekly during the thick of the campaign. This can be done with catchy newsletters or whatever is most effective.

Visual communications within the team are mostly read-and-throw-away. Once the offering is over, no one needs to keep anything, except a legal compliance record and a file of prototypes for the next offering. Sending "CCs" (copies of written work product) can keep everyone informed and give them a chance to contribute, without making a ceremony of it. Showing, by the symbol "CC:" at the bottom of the document, who has received copies, can emphasize the team nature of the endeavor.

Meetings are particularly treacherous in a direct share offering. Things move too quickly to keep everyone current on what the rest of the team is doing. And you certainly do not want the diffused responsibility of decision making by consensus. Decisions need to be made by the person responsible for the task, with the knowledge and approval of the project manager.

Daily Progress Reports

Your major contractors are the ad agency, lawyers, accountants, and financial printer. Their work is described in proposals and they operate largely independent of supervision by your project manager. This can mean nasty surprises not only in cost overruns but in conflicts, duplication, and waste. These contractors can keep logs or diaries of what they do each day, who does the work and how much was spent that day in time and money. They need this for their internal purposes, although that is not any guarantee that they always do it. Insist on it. Make it a part of your request for proposal. Your project manager will collect and study these daily progress reports and quickly follow up with questions or directions.

Incentives and Recognition

You cannot pay commissions for selling stock unless you have complied with extensive SEC broker-dealer regulations. This means you should stay away from any compensation arrangements that could be mistaken for commissions.

You will be asking people to make a special effort, work extra time, and take on some difficult assignments. They need some incentives and some recognition for a job well done. In addition to rewarding contribution, there is benefit from simply keeping up a level of awareness and excitement among the team and all the corporate employees.

Some corporations have taken a very conservative approach and kept awards entirely apart from performance. They had prizes for contests, such as guessing the time when the first stock order would be received or the number of shareowners there would be after the offering or the number of prospectus requests a particular ad would generate. Other companies have tied incentives to performance, not to results. The number of follow-up telephone calls made in a day, how many people showed up at an investment seminar—all without regard to whether shares were sold.

Pricing Your Offering

When you were deciding whether to share ownership with the public, you estimated how much money you wanted to bring into the corporation and about what percentage ownership you would be willing to sell. The market research and advice you have received during the preparatory stage may have modified these numbers.

How much you raise in the offering relates directly to the percentage ownership you are willing to sell to the new shareowners. If you want to retain 70 percent after the first offering, the question is whether you can raise the capital you need by selling 30 percent. Valuing your company for an initial public offering is very different from valuing when you want to sell the entire business. It also involves different considerations from those in a private sale of an interest in the business. Shareowners in a public company have no role in management, but they have a liquid market in which they can sell their shares at any time.

You have to be satisfied that your offering price is fair to you and the new shareowners. You also need to know that it is a price prospective investors will be willing to pay for your shares, rather than buying shares of another corporation, or using their money for some other purpose. Be willing to price at an "introductory bargain." If you sell shares now, and they have continuing increases in trading price, it will help you sell shares in the next offering at a "quality premium."

Corporate valuation is the subject of many articles and entire books. Specialists charge large fees for preparing thick valuation reports. Their methodologies have long mathematical formulae and elaborate justifications. But at the bottom of any fair market value is a guess at what price would be reached between a buyer and a seller.

Market Prices for Shares of Comparable Companies

For new corporate share offerings, most valuations are based on a "peer group" of other corporations. The ideal is to find companies that are just like yours in every respect—except that they are already publicly traded. In theory, the price the trading market sets for those stocks predicts what investors would pay for shares in your corporation. Once a peer group is assembled, the process is like reverse engineering a competitor's product. The market prices of their shares are taken apart, to see how they relate to such factors as revenue, earnings, and cash flow (all for the past and projected future). The prices are also compared with various categories of assets, liabilities, and equity.

These results are then given something called a "sensitivity analysis" or similar jargon. That is, attempts are made to compare the quality of customer base, management, market share, supply relationships, and other factors that should make one business more valuable than another.

Price-earnings (P/E) ratios are the most common in comparative valuations. If your corporation and its peer group have all been earning a profit for a few years, and have about the same growth rate, the P/E ratios will do nicely for your decision-making purposes. P/E ratios vary considerably over time. For the S&P 500, the stock price times average earnings has averaged 14.4 since 1926. But the ups and downs of the stock market have pushed P/E ratios to nearly 20 and to only about 7 within a few months. P/E ratios that are based on past earnings only work for companies that have long ago completed their period of rapid growth. Entrepreneurial corporations usually have to project future earnings to come up with a price. For a ratio based on past performance, they have to use a substitute for price earnings, such as price revenue, or even price to projected revenue.

From the investors' point of view, the stock price is based on their expectation of what they will receive back from holding and eventually selling the stock. Then they have to consider the risk that their expectation will not come true. One way to approach that is to estimate the future cash flow into the corporation and then use a discount rate to put a present value on that stream of cash.

Discounted Cash Flow

The theory behind this method of value is that the cash generated by a corporation will benefit the shareowners, one way or another. In the very long run, the return could be in cash dividends. It could all come at once, if the corporation were acquired for cash. More likely, a shareowner will realize a cash return by selling shares into the trading market. The buyer will pay a price based on a current estimate of future cash flow. Discounted cash flow means estimating how much cash the business will generate and then dividing that by a percentage rate of return. It cuts through all the accounting standards that are involved in calculating "income."

"Cash" means the money left over from receipts after paying the bills. Because it measures the entire life of the corporation, a cash-flow analysis treats major capital outlays, such as a new building, the same way as everyday operating expenses, such as paying the utility bill. There is no attempt to spread the amount over some estimated useful life, as with the accounting practices of amortization and depreciation.

On the other side of the equation is the rate of return investors would require for shares in your corporation. That starts with simple rent on the use of their money, forgetting any risks at all. Usually that has been between 2 and 3 percent per year.

To the rental rate, we add the return required to cover the general risks of having money tied up for a long period. These include investors' expectations about the decline in value of the dollar through inflation and international monetary exchange rates. In the United States, most of us do not add a factor for possible revolution, expropriation, or occupation.

The third element of the discount rate covers the particular risk of seeing your corporation achieve the expected cash flow.

Putting these three components together is seldom done in pure analysis. Instead, we use surrogates. The interest yield on 30-year U.S. Treasury bonds becomes the measure of the first two elements—rent plus general economic risk. Rent on money, and the price for risking devaluation, is the rate of return we would require on U.S. Treasury obligations. They are generally considered to have no risk of loss or delayed payment.

For the risk of owning shares of American corporations generally, we look at the average dividend rate plus price appreciation for blue-chip stocks. That has run from 4 to 7 percent over Treasury bond yields.

Your corporation will be considered a higher risk than the blue-chip market. As a consequence, your corporation's price will fluctuate more than blue chips do, both up and down. That relative volatility is its "beta." You can figure your beta by looking at relative price fluctuations of your peer group of publicly traded companies that are most like yours. If those shares are twice as volatile as the market, their beta is two. These elements all come together by multiplying the equity risk premium times your beta, then adding that to the current Treasury bond rate.

For instance, stocks may be returning 6 percent more than Treasury bonds. With a two beta, your shares need a 12-point premium. At an 8 percent yield on Treasury bonds, investors will value your shares to get a 20 percent annual rate of cash return. This seems like a lot of detailed academic theory. But your board of directors will be setting the price on the portion of the corporation you will offer to the public. They need a record of rational analysis to support that value.

Price per Share

When you have decided on the offering amount and the percentage ownership that you are selling, you are ready to set a price per share for the public offering. In an underwriting, you would negotiate this price with the investment banker. Early on, the number of shares would have been fixed so last minute price reductions would usually mean getting less money for giving up the same number of shares. When you market directly, the arithmetic is a little different. You decide on a price per share that you believe is best for the investor prospects you have selected. Then you divide that number into the total dollar amount you expect to raise. After a little rounding, that will tell you the number of shares to be offered.

Price Influences Perception

The art is in coming up with a price per share that creates the most favorable image. Folklore has it that an initial public offering priced at over $20 per share is intended for a sophisticated market of institutions and the wealthy. The price conveys that this is an established business not subject to rapid price movement, up or down. In analysts' terms, it is a "low beta" investment, one that will move closely with the stock market averages.

In the $15 to $20 range, shares represent a higher expected price fluctuation, because the company is young. However, it is probably marketing an established product, so the risk has to do with its ability to gain market share and be profitably managed. Wall Street investment bankers will often push for an initial public offering price of between $10 and $15. Since established corporations usually have trading price ranges of $30 to $60, there is clearly room for seeking that level. A single-digit price has been looked on by Wall Street as a second-class position, a corporation that would not likely make it onto the NYSE listing—perhaps an interesting little stock, but not for proper investment portfolios.

Below $5 a share puts a corporation in the penny stock category. That is the high-risk, double-your-money-in-a-week class. If a price gets into that game, it might as well be set at 10 cents and really catch the speculative fever. Between $5 and $10 may work best for a Direct Public Offering. There is still some sentiment for buying at least 100 shares, and it may still be cheaper to sell a "round lot" (100 share multiples) in the trading market than an "odd lot."

Pricing your shares becomes another challenge for market research and intuition.

Designing Your Marketing Program

Wall Street brokers will often quote that: "Securities are not bought. They are sold." The process may be very different with a DPO, but the adage is still true. Individuals are not going to (1) get the urge to own a company's shares, (2) initiate their own information gathering, (3) make a decision to buy, and (4) complete a purchase—all by themselves. The urge, the information, the decision, and the action will happen because of a marketing program—one with tools for packaging, advertising, servicing, and closing. A share marketing program begins with packaging—the way you are presenting what you have to sell, your investment proposition.

Your Investment Proposition

Somewhere there is a sentence that tells a person why he or she wants to share ownership in your corporation. It is an invitation that makes sense and makes an individual want to know more. In ten words, more or less, your one truthful sentence will tell that person what the corporation is and what is in it for that individual to buy some shares. In the "Screen Test for a Direct Public Offering," we suggested that if your investment proposition does not fit in about ten words, perhaps your business is not ready for public shareownership. You may be better served shopping for capital with people who can listen to the whole story over lunch, and then take home your business plan to study. Venture capitalists. Wealthy acquaintances. People who can invest an amount of money that will justify the time you each will have to spend.

That certainly does not mean your business must be simple. It can be extremely technical and complex. But its money-earning potential must be clearly apparent to your shareowner profile.

Market Research

Every private company that might be a candidate for selling shares will have done some informal "market research." Some will be convinced that their shares will "sell like hotcakes" because so many people have expressed interest without any prompting. Others will see how apparently effortless another company's public offering seemed to be and just know that theirs is a better investment and should go even easier.

That's not really market research. You certainly want to know if enough people will buy enough shares each so that all the shares offered will be bought—the basic "will it work?"

In securities law terms, the market research to find out whether people will buy your shares is called "testing the waters," and regulators have spent a lot of effort on ways to allow you to answer that question before you start spending a lot of money to do an offering. The federal SEC adopted a "testing the waters" rule for certain small offerings. The states, which had been working jointly with the SEC, are still involved in pilot programs. Currently, you can use a written questionnaire in certain states, if it is in the prescribed form, provides only certain specific information about the company, and asks very limited questions. Before trying this kind of "if we offered, would you be interested in buying" research, you will need to catch up on the current state of "testing the waters" regulation. [See Chapter 6, "The Regulatory Framework."]

There are other reasons for doing market research, involving methods that won't bring into play the securities law issues about whether you are really making an "offer" or "conditioning the market" for your offering.

Who is most likely to buy our shares?
What medium will reach them cost-effectively?
Which messages will work best with each group?

Tools of market research include matching published demographic information with the facts about your corporation, conducting telephone interviews, and running focus groups. It can all be very academic, with results expressed in statistical probabilities. But when it is conducted and interpreted by skilled practitioners, market research can save you far more money than it costs.

Through market research, you can begin living with your new shareowners before you ever start marketing to them. Who are the people who should want to own shares in your corporation? What are their interests, motivations, and dreams? How have they spent their extra dollars so far—expensive cars, lottery tickets, getaway trips? What do you share with these people, other than an interest in your corporation? Can you be comfortable in their heads and hearts for a few minutes?

Share Marketing Pyramid

Marketing DPOs follows the four steps of direct marketing: (1) offering to send information to prospective investors, (2) their response in asking for those materials, (3) your fulfilling your offer by sending the offering package and (4) the conversion of those active prospects into shareowners. From your market research, and your own intuition, you will need to select the groups of prospective investors to whom you will offer a chance to buy shares and then estimate how many will ask for them, how many of those will buy shares, and how much they will invest.

There are three variables that can be compared to the growing body of experience with other DPOs:

> *How many persons are there in your various "affinity groups?"*
> *What percentage of each affinity group will buy shares?*
> *How much will the average investment be in each group?*

The term, "affinity groups," was used in tests five and six of the Screen Test for a Direct Public Offering. You wouldn't be designing a marketing program if you hadn't already concluded that you could communicate with enough people who would be sufficiently interested in owning shares in your company. Now, you need to be more specific about who and how many they are. These steps, and the accompanying "Share Marketing Pyramid," can help you quantify your affinity groups' likely investment:

1. From your experience, and talking with others, describe the markets you think exist for the shares.
2. Put those markets into groups, based on the average amount each investor would likely invest.
3. Estimate the number of individuals in each group you would be try ing to reach with your marketing program.
4. Apply your best-informed guess as to the percentage of each group that would buy shares.
5. Multiply the numbers in 2, 3, and 4, and add the resulting amounts.

If you figure you could probably be successful with a $10 million sale of shares, the formula could look like this:

Marketing Pyramid for a $10 Million Offering of Shares

Average Investment	Number in Group	Percentage Who Would Buy	Amount for the Group
$100,000	100	30%	$ 3,000,000
$40,000	2,000	3%	$ 2,400,000
$10,000	12,000	2%	$ 2,400,000
$2,500	100,000	1%	$ 2,500,000
		Total Investment	$10,300,000

Announcing the Offering

There is a firm regulatory overlay to all your marketing steps. This is particularly so when you are trying to let people know that you are offering shares and they can get the offering materials. These regulations are described in Chapter 6, "The Regulatory Framework."

Direct Public Offerings actually get sold the way Congress seemed to have envisioned—people first learn only that an offering is being made and how they can get detailed information, then they request and receive a prospectus (or similar offering document), then they read it and make their decision.

Getting the attention of prospective investors, so they'll request a prospectus, is a big challenge. A few companies have simply sent the prospectus to their entire affinity groups after some screening to reach the most likely to invest. Most DPOs, however, need to send (by mail or electronic delivery) an announcement to their affinity groups or publish an announcement in selected print or broadcast media. There is very little room for creativity in the wording of that announcement, except for the permitted brief (10 words, or so) description of the company.

The permitted news release allows essentially the same few items of information as the announcement. The room for creativity is in the presentation, the targeting of the groups who will receive it, and the selection of media. Your marketing and legal team members will become a sub-group to get the most effect from the announcements, at the lowest cost, while staying within federal and state interpretations.

Receiving Requests for the Offering Materials

With all the work getting requests for your offering package, it is essential that you fulfill their requests quickly and in a manner that leaves a good impression about your company.

Electronic delivery of the announcement and the offering materials has been successfully accomplished. The SEC and the states have taken action to make it easier for companies to use electronic media—e-mail and web sites—for direct public offerings.

Installing and having trained staff on 800 or 888 numbers will probably continue for a while as the primary media for receiving requests. A software program needs to be used to help your telephone service people record the information (including how the caller learned of the offering, for marketing feedback) and your staff needs to be trained so that (1) they don't say anything that would violate securities regulations and (2) the callers gain the right impression from their experience with your staff. Also of top importance is having the persons handling calls know how not to say anything that would cause legal or relationship problems.

Fulfilling Those Requests

Speed and accuracy are essential. Once someone has expressed an interest, you want them to be able to act as quickly as possible. Electronic fulfillment is ideal for speed and accuracy. It is also a big cost-saver, over the approximately $3.00 cost of printing and postage for the printed version of the prospectus and related materials.

Your system will have the materials on their way within 24 hours, with a notation of that in the database for the individual prospect. The database is kept current to initiate follow-up steps for each prospect and to generate reports, at least weekly, of the requests (and which media created them), fulfillments, and conversions to completed sales.

Converting to Sales

Your marketing pyramid estimates a percentage of each affinity group that will ultimately invest, as well as the average investment amount for each group. There are two steps in the percentage of the group that will become investors: first the number who will respond to the announcement by requesting offering materials and then the percentage of those respondents who will be converted into sales.

In the brief period for which we have been keeping records for DPO marketing efforts, there is not much of a basis for predicting the initial response rate—it varies so much on whether the medium is mail, print or broadcast and how close the relationship is between the company and each affinity group. We do see a pattern in the rate at which responses are converted to sales.

Generally, the conversion rate has been between 12 percent and 25 percent for successful DPOs. That is, about one person ultimately buys shares for each four to eight who receive the offering materials. Conversion rates depend upon several factors but a major one is the quality of the follow-up effort.

Follow-up has been accomplished mostly by mailed letters (or, more recently, e-mail) to those who have had the offering materials for a while and not yet sent in their investment. Those letters must be filed with some of the regulators (a matrix of filing requirements—which states, on what time schedule—will have been prepared). While there is room for considerable marketing creativity, the basic rule is that the prospectus must still be the source of all information for making an investment decision. Comments from regulators on past letters have suggested where the lines are on "selling" through the follow-up letters.

The other major follow-up media is telemarketing. The basic decision, if the telephone is to be used at all, is whether you are going to restrict calls to a very limited inquiry about whether the offering materials were received and whether they intend to invest, or whether the caller will try to help the prospect make an investment decision. This choice involves both regulatory issues (agents must be licensed in many of the states and there are "safe harbor" rules about what a company's employees may do, without being licensed) and marketing/cost issues. For instance, if the follow-up is going to involve "selling," you may need to use a securities broker-dealer, licensed in each of the states into which calls will be made. That means paying a substantial commission. It also means changing the tone of the offering by introducing a third party to the company/affinity group relationship. Most DPOs have been completed without broker assistance. It is a very involved, major decision and each company will need to look at all aspects of the choice.

Geography may play an important part in your DPO. We have found that people prefer to invest in businesses near their home. Even national companies, with customers all over the country, have found that half of their DPO is purchased by people who live within 100 miles of their headquarters.

When a company's affinity groups are largely from its own part of the world, or when the local allegiance seems like a marketing theme, the use of seminars or other gatherings can be very effective. However, they are major consumers of time, both in the planning and execution. Top management of the company needs to be there. Some training may be necessary, as well as careful orchestration and choreography. Without that attention to detail, one negative person in the audience can change the whole tone of the meeting and turn it into a disaster for sales and for morale.

Planning a Trading Market

Every thoughtful investor wants to know how the shares may be converted back into cash. For some, it is an "exit plan," because each investment involves both a buy and a sell decision. Less sophisticated people simply want to know how they can get their money out if they need it or when they have something else they would rather buy.

Planning a trading market for your shares must become part of the work at the very beginning because your prospective investors will want an answer before they part with their money. There are several levels of trading market and several paths to consider.

"Trading" or "Order-Matching"

A trading market exists when prospective buyers and sellers can get information about offers to buy and sell, and recent transactions in the shares, and when there is a mechanism for them to execute a purchase or sale of securities. For a trading market to exist, there needs to be an intermediary (limited by regulation to a registered broker-dealer) who offers to buy or sell shares for its own account, as a way of assuring "liquidity." That is, the ability to make a sale of shares on very short notice.

Trading Markets

The traditional trading markets are stock exchanges and over-the-counter market makers. Stock exchanges include the New York, American, Boston, Chicago, Cincinnati, Pacific, and Philadelphia. (The Cincinnati is more specialized and not really available to new share listings.) Each exchange has certain numerical standards for its listing of shares for trading, including a company's assets, net worth, and income, as well as the number of shares in the public's hands and the number of shareowners.

The Pacific, Philadelphia, and Chicago Exchanges have created two tiers of numerical listing requirements, one for smaller companies. The Pacific has also launched a "SCOR Market," for companies that have had offerings under the SEC's Rule 504 or Regulation A.

The over-the-counter market is a less formal way for particular broker-dealer firms to "make a market" in a company's shares, by offering to buy and sell at quoted prices. Other broker-dealers can then communicate with the market maker to effect a trade. Information about the quotes and trades in the over-the-counter market are available in four levels of reporting systems, all now owned by the National Association of Securities Dealers:

NASDAQ National Market System
NASDAQ Small Cap Market
Electronic Bulletin Board
"Pink Sheets" printed daily

Any NASD member firm may decide it will be a market maker in a company's stock, whether or not the company even knows about it, if it follows NASD rules about how market makers perform their function.

We generally recommend that companies try to arrange for listing their shares on an exchange, for trading after the DPO is completed. Considering the types of investors a DPO attracts and the objectives of management for its shareowners, the carefully-watched and regulated exchange specialist market has seemed the better choice.

Order-Matching Services

Some offerings will not meet the numerical standards for an exchange listing. They may or may not attract a broker-dealer to become a market maker. Since the real objective is to provide a way out for the people buying in the DPO, and a way for new people to become shareowners, we often help a company arrange for a broker-dealer (usually one registered representative at a brokerage firm) to act as an order-matching service.

The order matching service works like this: Persons who express an interest in buying or selling shares are referred to the responsible registered representative at the broker-dealer firm. Their interest, in number of shares and desired price, is noted by that representative. Whenever there appears to be a match of buyer and seller interest, the representative notifies both sides. They both open an account with the broker-dealer and are charged a transaction fee. (At least one broker-dealer is offering credit card transactions as a substitute for opening an account.) The representative provides assistance in having the certificates canceled and issued and the money transferred. This practice has considerable precedent among several broker-dealer firms. The service is different from the work performed by a market maker in that (1) no bid or asked prices are quoted by the broker-dealer representative, (2) no purchases or sales are made by the order matching broker-dealer for its own account and (3) there is no public reporting of bid, asked or last transaction information.

The brokerage firm providing the order-matching service maintains a "book" of persons who have expressed an interest in buying or selling shares, including the number of shares and price objective. These persons will have been referred to the broker, usually by someone at the issuer who has been instructed to respond to inquiries. One national firm, for instance, handles these services through its trading department, which quotes bid, asked and last transaction information in the "Pink Sheets." Another national firm has a designated registered representative in a local office to do all transaction processing and record maintenance and that person provides bid and asked quotations to the local newspaper. Another issuer's order matching service was a local broker who provided price information upon request but did not issue quotations for publication. That was an offering of only $1,000,000.

In all of these cases, investors have been able to sell their shares. Investors have not been required to sell at a price representing a significant discount from the initial offering price and/or then-present value of the shares.

Participating brokers generally charge fees similar to those of discount or full-service brokers. For instance, a trade of less than 100 shares has been at a minimum of $37.50 and up to about $65. Other small trades are likely to be around 3 to 5 percent of the transaction amount. A recent example from one of these order matching brokers was a sale of 166 shares, at a total price of $1,400, for which the commission was to be $52.50, plus a $2.50 service charge. Each side of the transaction is expected to pay a fee. These amounts and practices are similar to those of brokerage firms for individual customers buying and selling shares listed on an exchange or quoted in the NASDAQ National Market System or Small Cap Market.

These order-matching service practices are illustrated in three of the case histories in Chapter 8: California Financial Holding Company, Summit Savings Bank, and Real Goods Trading Company. In all three cases, sales through the order-matching service were always at prices above the public offering price. In the first case mentioned, the price was volatile in that it continued to go up during the first year, between the direct and the underwritten offerings. There were no significant price declines in that year. In the other two cases, transaction prices were within a narrow range, relative to what is customary for listed or actively traded over the counter stocks. There appears to have been no case in which any investor in any of these three companies has been unable to sell shares or been required to sell at a price representing a significant discount from the initial offering price and/or the then-present value of the shares.

Electronic Matching Services

There are currently experiments being made in providing information electronically (Internet web sites) for persons to make their own purchases and sales, without going through a securities broker at all. Over 50 proposals have been submitted for review by the SEC, and a few have already been launched, including SCOR-NE, for companies that have completed offerings under the SEC's Rule 504 or Regulation A. Some issues remain to be resolved, such as the most effective mechanics for someone to act as "stakeholder," to see that the buyer's check is in the right amount, and clears, and that the seller has properly endorsed stock certificates for the right number of shares.

In the Real Goods Trading Corporation case history in Chapter 8, you will see described the first matching service which the SEC has allowed a company to operate for its own shareowners.

Closing and Beyond

Part of that initial planning will have included what to do when the offering is over. There are forms to be filed with the SEC and state regulators. A result of the offering may be that your company is now filing reports and having proxy statements reviewed at the SEC. This compliance can be very expensive and cumbersome, particularly if it is farmed out to your law firm and independent accountants. It can also be done by your staff, with carefully controlled professional review.

Once a company has brought in public shareowners, it is forever in the business of marketing its shares and the concept of shareownership. Having shareowners among your customers, employees, neighbors, and others can be a powerful competitive advantage. Ready access to equity capital is surely a big help to any business. Having a share price that steadily increases with your business growth will bring benefits to everyone. Public shareownership can be a profit center, providing money and support whenever it is useful.

CHAPTER 6

THE REGULATORY FRAMEWORK

Orson Welles once said that "The enemy of art is the absence of limitations." If that is so, then the art of marketing shareownership has been blessed with many, many limitations. Doing a Direct Public Offering of shares in your business means dealing with all of the laws regulating the sale of securities. The federal government and each of the states have built an extensive set of rules about how securities can be offered to the public and who can be involved in selling those securities.

The reason that so many rules exist around selling securities is because so much money has been lost by investors through dishonest or negligent behavior. And the reason for the bad behavior is the same as the one given by Willie Sutton, when asked why he kept robbing banks: "Because that's where the money is."

Few business activities are so heavily regulated as the sale of securities. This is not the place for a treatise on securities law and practice. You will have acquired access to that knowledge in selecting your lawyer, auditor, and DPO advisor. There will be decisions to be made, however, that require management to weigh marketing, financial, and legal consequences. This chapter is intended to provide a regulatory overview that will help you make those decisions.

The relationship between many of the securities rules and the way people have been cheated will not be apparent. In fact, it often seems that the regulations apply to the law-abiding majority, while the criminal minority is left alone. For instance, the major source of foul play in public offerings is telephone selling by persons licensed as broker/dealer representatives. But the regulations principally deal with what is in the written offering materials and whether people need licenses to work on the offering.

It is necessary to keep a sense of acceptance that the securities rules are simply part of the price of access to capital from the public, like payroll taxes come with having employees. Your ability to raise permanent capital by marketing shares to your affinity groups is a great competitive advantage, putting you well ahead of those companies in your industry who must rely only upon traditional sources of capital. Once you have been through the regulatory thicket, you will have a new set of abilities that will allow you to raise capital again and again, when it will help your company grow or become more profitable.

We have to begin with a basic rule of securities regulation: "Every sale of a security must be registered, both with the federal Securities and Exchange Commission and with the buyer's state securities regulator, unless an exemption applies." A related rule is: "Every person engaged in selling a security must be licensed, unless an exemption applies."

Securities and Exchange Commission

Congress and the Franklin Roosevelt administration set about to restore faith in America's securities markets after the Great Crash of 1929 and the securities frauds that had been exposed. First came the Securities Act of 1933 to govern the offer and sale of securities by a business. Then they enacted the Securities Exchange Act of 1934 for regulating the trading in securities. The '33 Act applies principally to the "primary market," in which a company is selling securities to investors (whether directly or through broker-dealers). In contrast, the '34 Act is intended to regulate trading in securities, after a company has issued and sold them to investors. The '34 Act covers stock exchanges, broker-dealers, and others who are involved when securities are being bought and sold (the "secondary market").

The '33 Act is structured around the concept that securities may only be offered by use of a "prospectus," a document that has been reviewed by the SEC staff and complies with detailed regulations. The logic then follows these steps:

A. *Any communication, in print, radio, or television media (which includes the Internet, but does not include telephone or in person communications), will be a "prospectus" if it "offers" a security.*

B. *A communication "offers" a security, even if it just "conditions the market" for an offering to be made.*

C. *The only exceptions are a "tombstone" announcement complying with Rule 134 under the '33 Act, or a news release, complying with Rule 135. (Most states have a similar requirement for offerings made to their residents.)*

As a practical matter, we all know that securities have been sold almost entirely by telephone calls from brokers and occasional in-person meetings. Those communications aren't subject to the limitations imposed on written (including electronically delivered writings) or broadcast media. When the telephone or in-person communications are used to generate interest in buying securities, the prospectus is usually first seen by the typical investor when it arrives in the mail with the "confirmation," which is the invoice to be paid within three days of the purchase. Nearly all of the abusive sales practices we read about occur in what was said on the telephone or in person. Nevertheless, those are exempt from the same limits a DPO must face when announcing the offering by letter or other print media, or by radio or TV.

Once you understand and accept the regulatory framework for your Direct Public Offering, you will select a path with the federal regulator, the SEC. Your proposed offering must either be exempt from registration or you must select a mechanism for filing with the SEC.

Exemptions

Offerings of Not More Than $1 Million. Congress gave the SEC the authority, in section 3(b), to exempt securities from the '33 Act "by reason of the small amount involved or the limited character of the public offering." A limit was placed on the size of offering that could be exempted, and Congress periodically raises the amount, now at $5,000,000. One of the 3(b) exemptions is Rule 504 for offerings which have not totaled more than $1 million within 12 months. (These are often referred to as "SCOR" offerings, because of the state regulatory process, described later.)

There is also the Regulation A exemption under this section 3(b) authority, for offerings of up to $5,000,000, but it requires a filing and SEC review that is nearly the same as a registration. It is mentioned below under "SEC filing choices."

Intrastate Offerings. In deference to state's rights, Congress added Section 3(a)(11) to the 33 Act for securities sold by a company only to residents of its own state. Because this "intrastate" offering exemption deprives the SEC of any review authority, it has been interpreted very narrowly. A few years ago, the SEC issued its Rule 147 as a "safe harbor" for companies trying to stay within the intrastate exemption. This means that if the company does all the things required by this Rule, it will not have to worry about the SEC later claiming the exemption did not apply. Among the elements of Rule 147 is one that all resales by persons buying in the offering may only be made to other residents of the same state, through a period ending nine months after the offering was over.

Most securities lawyers have been wary about trying to guide a client through an intrastate exemption. The "safe harbor" rule has not encouraged any apparent expansion in the number of intrastate offerings. No more than the rare public offering avoids SEC registration through this exemption.

Foreign Offerings. It is *theoretically* possible to do a direct public offering that is exempt from SEC registration because all the shares are sold to residents of countries other than the United States. The SEC adopted Regulation S to guide companies through this process. However, the practice has been abused, particularly in the restriction on resales back into the United States.

DPOs are complicated enough without imagining how to comply with this exemption. That will probably change so that, once a company is comfortable with doing DPOs, it would make sense to do direct offerings to specific affinity groups in other countries.

Private Placements. There are many different kinds of securities sales that can be included in the term "private placement." For instance, when an entrepreneur first incorporates and issues stock for the start-up money — or for the transfer of a proprietorship business — that is a "private placement." At a much later stage, when a few venture capitalists put several million dollars into the company, that, too, is most likely a "private placement."

The '33 Act doesn't use the term "private placement." The exemption it provides, in section 4(2), is for "transactions by an issuer [the company] not involving any public offering." There is also an exemption under section 4(6) for "transactions involving offers or sales by an issuer solely to one or more accredited investors."

Rule 506 under the '33 Act was adopted by the SEC to provide another "safe harbor" for relying on these "private placement" exemptions. Its companion, Rule 505, relies on the Section 3(b) authority, to exempt offerings of not more than $5 million. These two rules are part of the SEC's Regulation D, along with Rule 504 for offerings of not more than $1 million in any 12-month period. When people refer to a "Regulation D offering" or a "Reg D private placement," they mean offers and sales of securities that meet the requirements of Rule 505 or Rule 506. (The rest of Regulation D, Rules 501, 502 and 503, provides definitions and requirements that apply to offerings made under Rules 504, 505, or 506.)

There are important differences between Rule 505 and Rule 506 and all sorts of cautions to be observed in trying to use these exemptions. For many businesses, however, they are definitely the right way to go. In Chapter 3, we suggested a "Screen Test for a Direct Public Offering." Many companies who are missing some of the elements in that test may be able to use the "private placement" exemptions. For instance, your business may be at a very early stage, when the risk of complete loss is the highest. And yet, you may need a considerable amount of capital to get going. The concept of "accredited investors" is arguably made just for this situation.

Rule 501(a) defines "accredited investor" as including certain institutional investors, trusts, and the company's own officers and directors. It then goes on to include any individual with either (1) a net worth (personal assets, minus personal liabilities, with or without the individual's spouse) of more than $1 million or (b) individual income in excess of $200,000 in each of the two most recent years (or $300,000 jointly with a spouse) and "reasonable expectation of reaching the same income level in the current year."

Among the ways to use these exemptions is to follow the same preparation and marketing process for a DPO, as described in Chapter 5, but to limit the prospective investor group to persons who will fit within the limits of Rule 505 or Rule 506. (If the offering is for not more than $1 million, the Rule 504 exemption may apply, but the concept of a limited number of informed, risk-appropriate investors is the same.) We refer to these as "direct private placements," and they are clearly the right way to go for many companies who do not have the capital needs, the affinity groups, or the operating history to do a DPO.

These "direct private placements" differ from venture capital or "angel investor" financings in that they are not negotiated. Instead, a document is prepared, much like a public offering prospectus, and furnished to prospective investors, who then decide whether they want to participate or not. While they have access to the company's management to ask questions, the terms are set and negotiations are not part of the process. Careful guidance is necessary in preparing the private share offering memorandum and complying with federal and state securities laws, although the expenses are generally about a fourth or less of what they might be in a Direct Public Offering.

"Integration." You are always taking a risk by selling securities without regulatory filings and review of the documents to be furnished investors. (There are still risks if you do have securities law filings, of course, but at least you will have exposed the offering to prior regulatory review.) Among the risks is that you will turn out to have been wrong when you thought an exemption applied to your "private placement," or "under $1 million" or "intrastate" or "foreign" offering.

The trickiest of these risks is the doctrine of "integration." That term means aggregating together what were intended to be separate capital formation transactions, then applying the aggregate to test the exemption requirements. For instance, two transactions together are over the $1 million/12 months limit for Rule 504, or the $5 million/12 months limit for

Rule 505. Or they bring the total non-accredited investors to over the 35 maximum in Rule 505 or 506. As one commentator called it: "Integration is the tender trap unfortunately frequently overlooked."

There are reasons to just go ahead and file with the SEC, even if you believe an exemption may apply. If your company is likely to be doing repeated offerings, the additional cost of regulatory review may not be so important when amortized over the whole financing program. It may also be that your particular marketing methods may be enhanced by having an SEC-cleared offering. Some companies figure they need a trading market to make investment in their shares sufficiently attractive, and that points toward an SEC filing.

Once you decide that you must—or choose—to file with the SEC, you need to decide which filing path will fit your company and its offering.

Filing Choices

Regulation A Filings. Regulation A is nominally an exemption under the Congressional authority of section 3(b) of the '33 Act. However, it is really the same process as filing a registration statement. Some of the nomenclature changes: The filing is a "qualification," rather than a "registration," and the prospective investors are furnished an "offering circular," rather than a "prospectus."

There are some differences in the requirements between Regulation A filings and "full" registrations. Nearly any operating company of any size can use Regulation A so long as it is not already a public '34 Act "reporting company." The maximum amount of each offering is $5 million within any 12-month period (with some "integration" issues like those mentioned for private placements).

Regulation A gives the company three choices for the format of its "offering circular." Two of them are those used in registered offerings, while the third is the question-and-answer format adopted by the states as Form U-7 for the "SCOR" offerings mentioned later. Regulation A filings can still be made on paper, while all registrations are now required to be filed electronically, using the SEC's Electronic Data Gathering Analysis and Retrieval System (EDGAR).

Reading Regulation A makes it seem that a company could avoid having audited financials, which would often mean a big cost savings. However, it almost certainly follows that any of the state securities regulators would require audited financials, at least for any offering of over $500,000.

There are some other interplays between choosing Regulation A and filings with the states, as well as the availability of certain trading markets for after the offering is over. You will need to get an analysis of pros and cons from your advisors, if Regulation A is an available path.

Registration. Most DPOs will require SEC registration. Several registration forms have been developed over the years by the SEC, some of which apply to special kinds of businesses or special types of transactions. Fortunately, simplified forms were created by Regulation S-B in 1993 for "small business issuers" (generally, companies with annual revenues of not more than $25 million). The major difference is that all accounting presentations are in accordance with generally accepted accounting principles (GAAP), rather than the SEC's Regulation S-X.

(Until October 15, 1996, these small business registrations could be filed with the SEC's regional offices. Now they must all be filed in Washington. At least during a transition, they have been assigned for review to the Office of Small Business Review.)

Securities lawyers have been referred to as "interpreters," meaning that they function as translators of dense legalese from securities regulations into plain language that business people can understand. Given the hourly rates for these specialists, it was a real service for the SEC to devise some forms that can be understood by most entrepreneurs. Regulation S-B also allows filings which omit some of the more esoteric financial charts that appeal to professional securities analysts who make decisions for institutional investors. As a result, the S-B prospectus can be made quite readable by individuals who are not full-time investors.

Forms SB-1 and SB-2. These were the two forms adopted by the SEC for use by businesses with annual revenues of not more than $25 million. Form SB-1 is very much like Regulation A in allowing a choice of format. However, nearly all the SEC-registered small business public offerings, including DPOs, have used Form SB-2. That registration alternative had been around for many years, as the old Form S-18.

Under any of the SEC filings, you can take advantage of the SEC's Rule 415 under the '33 Act that allows "an offering to be made on a continuous or delayed basis in the future." Without this rule, direct public offerings would have been blocked by the marketing methods used in underwritten offerings, where the "selling" goes on before the SEC registration statement is declared effective, and the offering is all over on the day it clears regulatory review.

Rule 415 describes ten situations in which continuous or delayed offerings are permitted. The ninth one is an offering "which will be commenced promptly, will be made on a continuous basis and may continue for a period in excess of 30 days from the date of initial effectiveness." Those words describe the DPO process very clearly.

There are some particular problems that come up, however, when the offering is marketed over a period of several weeks or months. For instance, when does the prospectus need to be updated with new information; what do you do when some important event happens during the course of the offering, good or bad; do you have to file reports with the SEC under the '34 Act requirements? Answers to these and other questions need to be already in the mind of your securities lawyer, so you can act quickly when the time comes.

State Regulation

Every state has its own set of laws (called"Blue Sky Laws"), regulations, and forms for securities and for the people acting as agents in the sale of securities. Not only are the laws different in each state, but they are administered by a civil service staff (usually, under a politically appointed head) that may have its own unique attitude about corporations and investors.

The different approaches include New York's relatively quick and simple practice of gathering information about the corporation and its officers and directors (for use in case there is any fraud committed). Many states are concerned with what's in the prospectus and have the same "full and fair disclosure" approach as the SEC. There are other, so-called "merit review" states, which decide whether the proposed offering of shares is good enough for the residents under their care. The securities regulators in those states are charged by their legislature with, for instance, determining whether the proposed offering is "fair, just, and equitable."

In practice, some of the "merit review" states act more like New York's "prepare for fraud enforcement proceedings" or one of the "full and fair disclosure states," while a few states that are nominally concerned just with disclosure will have some "merit" issues they always raise, like the number of stock options held by management or the price paid by the founders for their shares.

How each state handles the company and its shares is only half the subject. Then there is the requirement for licensing a "broker-dealer" and an individual as "agent" or "representative." For both the registration of securities and the licensing of firms and individuals, there are patchworks of exemptions.

Exemptions

"Limited Offerings." For your corporation to market shares, about the only exemptions from state registration that may be available will result from the limited number (usually, from as few as five to as many as 50) of persons to whom you offer shares in a state. Every state has a different set of standards and a different way of counting the number it takes to have

a "limited" offering, rather than one that requires registration. For instance, some states limit the number of persons to whom you can "offer" the shares, while others base the count on the number who can actually invest. Some states count only the number of their own residents participating in the offering, while others include everyone, wherever they live. Some states will not apply the "limited offering" exemption to SEC-registered or Regulation A offerings. A filing may be required before the exemption may work in some states, although others are "self-executing," with no filing requirement. These factors become part of your decision matrix.

There are generally at least two sets of "limited offerings" exemption rules in each state. One (often called the "Uniform Limited Offering Exemption" or "ULOE") was created to fit with the "private placement safe harbors" of SEC Regulation D, Rules 505 and 506. The other set was generally around before the SEC rules and is based simply upon the very minimum size of the offering, in terms of the people involved in investing.

There are a couple of themes that are common with nearly every state's limited offering exemptions. One is that there can be no "advertising or general solicitation" in the offering process. The other is that no commissions may be paid for selling shares (in the original "limited offering" exemptions. They can usually be paid in ULOE offerings.)

In the last few years, California and Texas, with some cooperation from the SEC, have created exemptions for limited offerings to people who have certain minimum levels of income and net worth. They have allowed those offerings to be advertised. Use of the Internet is creating some tension around what is "advertising or general solicitation," as well as how some of the other structures for limited offerings are to be adapted.

Broker-Dealer, Agent, and Issuer. All but about ten states will allow a company to sell its shares directly, without hiring a registered broker-dealer firm or having the company register itself in the state as a broker-dealer. It may still be necessary for your company to have an agency agreement with a broker-dealer if you need to sell shares in some of these states. Most states, however, specifically exempt the company issuing the shares.

A wide variety of rules apply to licensing of your company's employees who will be involved in "selling" the shares. Some states exempt officers and directors (with various definitions and limitations). Other states require a license application, on Form U-4, and several also require that the employees to be licensed must pass the Series 63 examination administered by the National Association of Securities Dealers. A few states require passage of a second, much more difficult examination, such as NASD Series 7, although waivers may be applied for.

Some securities lawyers have raised the question whether any broker-dealer or agent needs to be licensed, or exempted, when all communications are in writing between the company and prospective investors. For instance, if the offering is announced only by "tombstones" that reach the prospective investors by mail, print media advertising, or company website; if the prospectus request is then received and fulfilled by regular mail, e-mail or the website; and the purchase agreement and payment are sent by regular mail to the company — who is the person who has been involved with "selling" the shares? There have been no telephone conversations and no in-person conversations. No personal letters have been composed for any individual prospect.

Someone may have a reliable answer that would encourage a company not to follow a state's licensing provisions. However, the general concept is that the states would like to have a jurisdictional "handle" over some real individual who is involved in the process. Many states make the decision relatively easy — someone needs to be licensed before they will allow registration of the securities.

Filing Choices

SCOR — For Offerings Under $1 Million. A long political pilgrimage is finally leading to some real help in matching entrepreneurs and individual investors. Public offerings for up to $1 million can now be made without a registration statement filed with the SEC. Cost savings of as much as $100,000 have been estimated by entrepreneurs who have used the process.

Congress enacted the Small Business Investment Incentive Act of 1980, calling for federal and state cooperation to diminish the burden for small businesses trying to raise capital. Two years later, the SEC adopted its Rule 504, exempting small public offerings from federal registration if they follow state requirements, including a disclosure document for investors.

Then a subcommittee of the American Bar Association spent three years coming up with a uniform filing and disclosure form that the states could use. In April 1989, the proposed form was approved by the North American Securities Administrators Association (NASAA), which named it the Small Corporate Offering Registration (SCOR). NASAA added SCOR as Form U-7 to its uniform state securities filings. A very short and simple filing has to be made with the SEC, after an offering is sold. Frequent progress reports are filed with the states during a selling period that can take up to a year.

Several state legislatures quickly adopted the necessary securities laws, which have included relaxation of some of their own requirements. The SCOR process can now be used in 43 states.

The features and savings available under SCOR are described in each state's instructions. They follow the Small Corporate Offering Registration Form, as adopted by NASAA on April 29, 1989, from which the following summary has been drawn:

Marketing. A "firm commitment" underwriting is not permitted (that is, one where securities firms commit to buy and instantly resell the shares). Sales are made through direct marketing or by using commissioned securities agents. Telephone and in-person marketing is permitted (participants may have to be registered under state law). No limit is placed on the number or status of the persons to whom the offering is made.

Documents. There has been a real effort to make the "disclosure document" (the term used instead of "prospectus" or "offering circular") serve as the marketing tool. Both the series of required questions and the company's answers are included in the document. (Some people still find the format more difficult than the SEC prospectus style.) Any ads or other written materials must be cleared by the state regulators and limited to brief announcements and instructions for getting a disclosure document.

Lawyers. Legal compliance can be accomplished by most small business attorneys without hiring a special securities lawyer. The only legal opinion required is one that states that the shares have been duly authorized and will be legally and validly issued, fully paid, and nonassessable and binding on the company. Offerings have been done with legal fees as low as $10,000.

Auditors. Audited financial statements are not required (in many SCOR states) for the first $500,000 of securities offered by a company. The accounting profession has announced it will follow this procedure and permit "reviewed" financials, in accordance with accounting standards. Even when an audit is made, there is no "comfort letter" requirement (unless a securities broker-dealer is used), and very little extra cost for auditors should be necessary. Auditors fees for SCOR offerings have often been in the $10,000 to $15,000 range.

Printing. Because there is no firm commitment underwriting, special financial printers need not be used. The disclosure document can be a desktop composition or a camera-ready form on a word processor. It should be many pages shorter than an SEC prospectus.

Filings. Since SCOR is a uniform filing, the same documents can be used in any state that has passed appropriate legislation (with some additional items required by a few SCOR states). "Regional review" has been created in the West and Northeast United States, so that one state regulator reviews the filing for the others in its region. The instructions are short and in plain English. Completing the form is a process of answering questions (which some states will provide on computer disk). The resulting disclosure document will include a business plan and a listing of the principal risks to investors. Filing fees in most states are under $500.

In addition to making small public offerings easier, some states are actively promoting the offerings. Washington state created publications and seminars to teach entrepreneurs about the new small public offering opportunity. The state economic development staff even compiled its own mailing list of prospective investors by sending questionnaires to a list it developed of people who would probably have the requisite ability and interest for buying the shares. Companies could have an announcement sent by the state to those on this list, telling people where they can request that firm's disclosure document. Washington published a booklet for the investor side called "A Consumers Guide to Making Venture Investments in Small Business." This was later adopted by NASAA and required by some states to be delivered with the disclosure document.

After Arizona's legislature unanimously adopted SCOR in May 1990, a special assistant to the securities division director was hired to help the program become active. Several states later adopted the program and have been even more active in encouraging its use. Others, like California, have made the process very difficult and expensive. (California's $2,500 filing fee can end up being $3,500 if the review staff spends additional time on a company's application.)

More information about SCOR may be available from any state's securities regulator.

Registration by Coordination or Qualification. Using limited offering exemptions, or a SCOR filing, have their obvious limitations of size. The number of prospective investors or the dollar amount you seek to raise may be over the maximums and eliminate these alternatives. There may also be good reasons why you need to register your shares rather than structure some other way of marketing them. Most states have at least two types of registration, that are usually referred to as registration "by coordination" or registration "by qualification."

There are always surprise nuances in a state's statutes or regulations, or in their forms or practice. Generally speaking, however, registration "by coordination" means a filing with the state that leaves review of the prospectus and related documents up to the SEC. Registration "by qualification" means that the state regulators must review the details of the offering, including the prospectus or other offering document.

When you are just dealing with one or two states for your prospective investors, the choice is one of the considerations you will mix with deciding your SEC filing method. For instance, some states allow "by coordination" for SEC Regulation A filings, while others permit it only for registered offerings. For offerings to be made into several states, the decision process is more complex.

Multi-state Offerings. If the great majority of your affinity group members are in your home state, rejoice! Your DPO is going to be much simpler than it would be if you were contending with the securities laws of many states at once.

For companies doing business within one state, it may be possible to rely solely on that state's securities regulation, with no SEC filing. Great care is required, however. As soon as there is even one investor outside the company's own state, there is no chance of using the "intrastate" exemption from SEC registration. (See "Exemptions — intrastate offerings," earlier in this Chapter.) There is a proposal pending to extend the "intrastate" exemption to certain defined geographic regions. The same caution would be required for compliance, however.

Every state has a different set of laws, and people administering them. Part of your planning process will be to review a matrix of those laws and administrative approach, compared to your own data base of affinity groups by residence. You will do a cost/benefit analysis, comparing the prospective sales to be made in a state with the cost and difficulty of complying with its rules for exemption or registration. Right selection at this stage can save you a lot of time, money, and disappointment later on.

A first step is to prepare a schedule of prospective investors by state. Because many DPOs are directed toward the company's customers, this often means listing states in descending order, by the number of customers in each. Before doing this, you may want to apply selected screens to those customers, to zero in on the ones who are really prospects for investing in your securities. One company, for instance, sorted out customers who had not made a purchase within the last year or who had bought less than some minimum amount. The idea is to include those in each state who really represent future investors in your company.

If the offering is above the $1,000,000 Rule 504 "SCOR" exemption amount, you will need to file for a multi-state offering with the SEC under Regulation A or by registration on the SEC form that applies to your size and situation. If you qualify for a SCOR offering, then you will need to check the laws of each state in your proposed DPO market, to be sure they provide for SCOR offerings and to see what special rules they may have. By the end of 1996, regional review of multi-state SCOR offerings (filings on Form U-7) were provided in the western states and the northeastern states.

Your choice of filing form with the SEC may depend upon the number of states in which you will market and which states those are. Nearly all states allow registration "by coordination" for offerings registered with the SEC. This means a much more limited state review of your offering document language, and the ability to become registered in the states at the same time your SEC registration becoming effective. Regulation A filings receive the "by coordination" treatment only in a minority of states. (This choice between Regulation A or registration involves other considerations, as well. For instance, by using Regulation A, you will avoid having to file reports under the Securities Exchange Act of 1934 for the year in which a registration becomes effective under the Securities Act of 1933. Among the aftermarket options, your shares may be tradable through the Pacific Stock Exchange or SCOR-NET only if you have used Regulation A.)

That listing of potential investors for your cost/benefit analysis shows you the benefit side for each state. For the cost side, you want to know what your chances are of being able to legally sell securities in each state and how expensive it will be to comply with that state's regulations. Preparing a matrix of registration and licensing fees and forms is time-consuming and complex. The more subtle issues to be considered are what kind of effort will need to be made by the people you've asked to do your state securities compliance work, and what "sacrifices" may be required by the company, its founders, present owners, and managers.

A state-by-state difficulty analysis requires some experience in processing DPOs or the ability to learn from someone else's experience. Each state has its own set of requirements—both at the policy level and in the detailed forms to be completed. States can be generally classified in such categories as "not difficult," "difficult," and "very difficult." But the important analysis is one that takes into consideration the issues that your particular offering may raise when being reviewed in each state.

Every state is different. This cannot be overemphasized. However, state regulators do try for some uniformity and the North American Securities Administrators Association (NASAA) has issued "Statements of Policy" which may be followed, if a state chooses. They deal with issues like "cheap stock" and the fairness of the public offering price.

Some of the issues raised by states can be met by creating impounds for a minimum amount of sales. (If the minimum is not sold, the bank acting as impound agent sends the money back to the investors.) A state may also suggest that you can sell to its residents if the present owners will place their shares in escrow with a bank, for over six years or until certain performance levels are met. You may need to elect outside directors, who will vote on certain transactions involving managers or major shareowners.

Your cost/benefit analysis will need to weigh how reluctant you are to go along with conditions like impound of minimum proceeds, escrow of present shareownership and restrictions on certain transactions, on management stock options, and other conditions likely to come from particular states.

Multi-state offerings can have great benefits, especially for companies expanding nationally. Shareowners have proven to be better customers and to become ambassadors of goodwill for "their" company. You may need to spread your direct public offering across state lines to reach enough prospective investors. A careful cost/benefit analysis at the outset can save you surprises and costs later on.

State securities law issues are only part of the cost/benefit analysis for a multi-state offering. Businesses with national or regional markets also have some special challenges in marketing securities directly to their affinity groups. A few of the issues for multi-state offerings have to do with how the securities are marketed. For instance, the most effective tool for selling DPOs has often been the personal meetings, or seminars, to which customers, neighbors, and other interested potential investors may be invited. If those people are spread over thousands of miles, it may not be feasible to use that tool. Marketing plans for multi-state offerings may need to involve more personalized telephone and mail follow-up.

Other marketing approaches, such as product demonstrations and tours, may be left out of the multi-state offering. This will mean that electronic communication, through e-mail and websites, can become all the more necessary. Use of a national 800 or 888 telephone number, with well-trained and supervised operators, becomes essential for some offerings. Multi-state offerings may also call for the use of national print publications for announcing the offering. These will require careful planning, since they have long lead times before publication. Marketing issues like these, important as they are, usually take a back seat to the regulatory difficulties of a multi-state offering.

In Chapter 7, "Selling Shares on the Internet," there is a description of the process by which the offering is announced and the offering documents delivered, and the rules most of the states have now adopted about Internet offerings.

SELLING SHARES ON THE INTERNET

This chapter is entirely new with this second edition. In fact, the first edition, published in the Summer of 1991, did not contain the words "Internet," or "world wide web," or any of the phrases that have become a part of nearly all our conversational language, like "on-line" or "website" or "hyperlink."

The Glossary to this book is largely unchanged from the first edition, where the closest word to Internet technology was "videotex," a term that disappeared shortly after. It was to have been the use of cable TV to deliver textual material through television sets. When the Internet suddenly came into everyone's consciousness, e-mail, websites, diskettes, and CD-ROMs eclipsed all the other ways of electronic delivery of text and graphics. In another five years, it is possible that something else will have replaced the Internet. What seems more likely, in today's perspective, is that incorporating voice and motion pictures on the Internet will make it an inclusive medium for all the messages that we will use in marketing shares through Direct Public Offerings.

Marketing a DPO on the Internet follows the same four-step process described in Chapter 5 for the use of news print media or the conventional mail. First, the prospective investors are made aware of the offering and the availability of the prospectus. Then, they respond by requesting the prospectus (and providing the company with information about them). The third step is when the company delivers the prospectus (together with the share purchase form and any further marketing materials). Fourth, and final, is receipt of the share purchase form and payment for the shares purchased.

Our challenge is to adapt the computer/modem tools we have to this four-phase marketing program. Fortunately, the federal Securities and

Exchange Commission and the state securities administrators have taken the lead in explaining just how this can be done. They could have been an obstacle, or they could have done nothing and waited for the mistakes and abuses. Instead, they acted early, they acted decisively, and they acted very favorably toward using these new electronic tools for marketing securities and communicating with investors.

In February 1995, the SEC specifically allowed (by a private "no-action" letter, now publicly available) the electronic delivery of a prospectus. When we started the Annie's Homegrown, Inc. electronic delivery process, in August 1995 (one of the case studies described in Chapter 8), we relied upon the February letter. Then, in October 1995, the SEC published an extensive "interpretive guidance" release called "Use of Electronic Media for Delivery Purposes."

Later in this chapter, we will go through those four steps, using some of the 52 examples furnished by the SEC in its electronic media release. (We've edited some of them slightly by deleting parts that would not relate to a DPO.) The SEC's examples will illustrate some of the opportunities and limits on the use of computer/modem technology for (1) announcing the offering and availability of the prospectus, (2) delivering the prospectus, (3) delivering and receiving back the share purchase agreement and (4) follow-up communications.

You may find that some of this chapter goes into quite a bit of detail, describing the various rules we're dealing with and what others have done. The reason is that we are on the edge of adjusting securities regulation to new technology. To be as effective as we can, without crossing the line, all of us doing DPOs need to have an understanding of the legal rationale for the rules and the attitude of those responsible for enforcing the rules.

Announcing the Offering

Telling people that you have a share offering needs to be accomplished in one of the same two ways that were used for regular mail, print or broadcast media, that is, either the "tombstone" announcement, described by Rule 134 under the federal Securities Act of 1933, or the news release allowed by Rule 135. Either announcement can be made by e-mail delivery or posting on a website, just as by regular mail or a newspaper advertisement.

To rephrase some of the explanation in Chapter 6, "The Regulatory Framework," the structure of the '33 Act and the states laws is that: (A) anything in writing, radio, or television that "offers" a security (construed very broadly, including "conditioning the market") is a prospectus; and (B) securities may only be offered by means of a prospectus that has been filed and cleared with the SEC and the necessary state regulators.

The logical consequence of these two rules is that no writing can be used to "offer" the Company's shares, except the prospectus that is cleared with the SEC and the states. Treating the Internet (as well as delivery by diskettes or CD-ROMs) as a "writing" has been accepted as an unchallenged fact of life. As a practical matter of politics, no government is going to regulate securities marketing and leave out electronic media. Telephone calls and "road show" personal meetings were left out when the laws were first adopted. That's not going to happen to computer technology.

Only two exceptions are carved out by the SEC to the law that only a prospectus can communicate any information about a company's share offering. They are described in Rules 134 and 135, both of which are also generally followed at the state level. Rule 134 is a "Notice, circular, advertisement, letter, or other communication published or transmitted to any person after a registration statement has been filed if it contains only the statements required or permitted," which are (1) the company's name, (2) the title and amount and price of the security being offered, (3) "a brief indication of the general type of business" of the company and (4) who will furnish a prospectus and execute purchase orders. This is the model for the so-called "tombstone" announcements, used by underwriting syndicates to announce completed offerings.

Rule 135 is the "notice given by an issuer that it proposes to make a public offering of securities to be registered." It has traditionally been a written news release sent by mail, hand delivery, or wire services to print, radio, and television media. It is limited to similar information as Rule 134, specifically (1) the company's name, (2) the title and amount and price of the security being offered, (3) "the anticipated time of the offering," (4) a "brief statement of the manner and purpose of the offering" and (5) any statement required by state or foreign regulation.

A Rule 135 notice may appear on the company's home page (what comes on the screen when someone first gains access to anything posted by the Company). There may be bulletin boards, user groups or other places where the Rule 135 notice can also be posted. This would be a sample Rule 135 notice:

> Only-an-Example: *Company will offer shares of its common stock directly to its customers and others, for $_ per share, to fund expansion of the Company's manufacturing and for working capital. The offering will be made only by a prospectus, to residents of selected states.*

The last sentence, or the word "prospectus" can be highlighted for clicking, which would then take a person to the next step on the path. There are a number of choices for delivery of this next page, governed by marketing experience, as well as legal compliance. For instance, the next page could be the Rule 134 "tombstone" or it could go directly to the prospectus cover.

Several DPOs have shortened what Rule 135 permits. For instance, they have said something like: "For information about our direct public offering." An alternative would be to place the Rule 134 "tombstone" announcement directly on the page. But design considerations may dictate something that takes up less space.

One of the early attempts to do a DPO using the Internet ran into regulatory problems. The principal difficulty was the apparent ability of anyone to download the prospectus and other materials about the offering, regardless of their state of residence.

By late-1996, more than 20 states had adopted a rule about Internet announcements, and the North American Securities Administrators Association adopted it as policy for all the states. The rule is that, even if the announcement would be considered an "offer" (SEC Rule 134 announcements are generally not "offers" in the states), it is still not in violation of a particular state's laws requiring registration if:

(a) the offer indicates, directly or indirectly, that the securities are not being offered to residents of that state,

(b) the company does not specifically direct the offer to any person in that state, and

(c) no sales are made in that state as a result of the Internet offering until there has been registration in that state.

This is basically the same rule that applied to announcements made in the print media, such as national newspapers. Some companies have listed the states in their announcements in which they had not registered the offering. Others have listed the states in which they have registered, with some "available only in the states of" language. Borrowing from the announcements used by underwriting syndicates, it would seem that the traditional " available only in any state in which" language should be sufficient.

Once the wording is chosen, you will be deciding which media you can use to announce the offering. The simplest step, posting on the company website, is specifically permitted by the SEC's electronic media release:

"(18) Company XYZ places a tombstone advertisement complying with Securities Act Rule 134 on its Internet Web site.

"This would be permissible, provided that the advertisement otherwise complies with Rule 134."

Of course, announcing your offering on your own website is only going to communicate with people who have visited your website, probably for reasons unrelated to your share offering. We have used mixed media to get the word out about DPOs, by sending "tombstone" announcements in regular mail letters, postcards and fold-outs, giving the website as one way to get the prospectus. The release also permits this practice:

> "(19) Company XYZ files a registration statement with the Commission. The Company then places a "tombstone" advertisement in accordance with Securities Act Rule 134 in the Wall Street Journal. In the advertisement the Company includes the location of its Internet Web site where an electronic prospectus can be obtained.

> "This inclusion of an electronic address for obtaining the materials in the "tombstone" advertisement would be permissible under Rule 134."

Requesting the Prospectus

It would seem to be permissible to let a prospective investor go directly from the announcement (even the abbreviated "for information about our offering of shares") to the prospectus. The Annie's Homegrown system was programmed so that clicking on the announcement took the viewer to a page with an invitation to put in their name, address, and telephone number. If they lived in a nonregistered state (where no filing to register the offering was made), they got a regret notice, explaining why they could not buy shares in the offering. Because the regulators in two of the registered states had required extra messages, their residents got one of three passwords. When they entered their password, they got the materials cleared for their state.

Under the state rules described earlier, it may be permissible to allow anyone access to the prospectus and to put a block on acceptance of the share purchase agreement. That does not seem like good marketing or efficient process management. Since most companies will want to capture names, addresses, and telephone numbers (for this and future offerings), the intermediary questionnaire page provides these additional tools.

There are, however, other ways to capture some information about who has requested the prospectus. One of the SEC's examples, dealing with mutual funds, describes an acceptable process:

> "(36) A prospectus is made available through an on-line system that allows users to access, download or print the entire prospectus and has the capacity to track which users accessed, printed or downloaded which documents.

> "A fund may rely upon a user's having accessed, printed or downloaded a prospectus for the fund in order to deliver supplemental sales literature or an order form for the fund or to establish delivery of the prospectus in connection with a sale of fund shares."

Delivering the Prospectus

Most Stringent Rules

The SEC's October 1995 release tells us that we may, if we choose, rely on its February 1995 no-action letter. That would rarely happen, since the later release gives considerably more latitude and covers more situations. However, at least for interpretation, it is useful to know that the February letter says the prospectus may be delivered electronically if these rules are followed:

a. The electronic prospectus must be the same as the paper one, except that graphic and image material that cannot be disseminated electronically is to be replaced with narrative description or tabular representation. This can be considered in the final design of the paper prospectus and any replacement designed for the electronic prospectus.

b. The prospective investor must have voluntarily furnished a written (paper or electronic) revocable election to receive delivery of an elec tronic prospectus. (For state securities law purposes, a company would also need to have the prospect give their residence address. For mar keting follow-up, you would also probably want their voice, fax, and electronic numbers and addresses.)

c. Immediately after the electronic prospectus is available, a paper or elec tronic notification must be provided to everyone who has elected to receive electronic delivery. No share purchase agreement may be accepted until after this notice has been sent.

d. The electronic prospectus must be continuously accessible through the designated electronic system, without charge, until the offering is over.

e. The electronic prospectus can be downloaded or printed, without charge (other than any system subscription or on-line time charge).

f. Whenever requested, a paper copy will be furnished promptly without charge. (A promise to do this will be in the prospectus and any supple mental sales materials.)

October Release Guidelines

The release is unusually readable, speaking mostly through examples. The basic foundation is:

"[I]nformation that can be delivered in paper under the federal securities laws may be delivered in electronic format."

"The Commission believes that the question of whether delivery through electronic media has been achieved is most easily examined by analogy to paper delivery procedures."

"The Commission would view information distributed through electronic means as satisfying the delivery or transmission requirements of the federal securities laws if such distribution results in the delivery to the intended recipients of substantially equivalent information as these recipients would have had if the information were delivered to them in paper form."

This policy language confirms that the easiest way to comply with the securities laws when using electronic media is to imagine that you are using a national newspaper or magazine, or that you are broadcasting on network television or a syndicated radio show.

The release has several pages of text before it begins the examples. From the text and the examples, some general rules seem to emerge. Our reading suggests that these are the elements of what it takes to comply:

Element 1: An "opportunity to retain a permanent record of the information" [downloading or printing, without extra software or expense] "or have ongoing access equivalent to personal retention."

Element 2: Presentation of information "in substantially the same order" as required for paper. (For instance, in example 15, "The sales literature and final prospectus should appear in close proximity to each other on the menu.")

Element 3: "[R]ecord-keeping or other procedures to evidence satisfaction of applicable requirements through electronic means."

Element 4: "[R]easonable precautions to ensure the integrity and security of" the information, "so as to ensure that it is the information intended to be delivered."

Element 5: Provide "timely and adequate notice to investors that information for them is available."

Element 6: "[S]hould not be so burdensome that intended recipients cannot effectively access the information provided."

Element 7: "[A]ccessible for as long as the delivery requirement applies."

Element 8: The company "must be able to make available paper versions of documents delivered in an electronic medium."

Element 9: The company should "have reason to believe that any electronic means ... will result in the satisfaction of the delivery requirements," such as "(1) obtaining an informed consent from an investor to receive the information through a particular electronic medium coupled with assuring appropriate notice and access . . . ; (2) obtaining evidence that an investor actually received the information, for example, by electronic mail return-receipt or confirmation of accessing, downloading, or printing . . . ; (3) dissemination by facsimile; (4) an investor's accessing a document with hyperlinking to a required document . . . ; and (5) using forms or other material available only by accessing the information . . . ."

One of the examples for mutual funds is useful for companies that may be doing offerings over long periods of time, or frequent offerings to the same affinity groups:

> *"(42) A fund transmits prospectuses over an electronic bulletin board. Investors provide specific consent to receipt of the prospectus through that system. The consent states that the current version of the prospectus will be made continuously available and notice of material amendments will be given by mail, e-mail, or some other manner specifically directed to investors.*

> *"The prospectus delivery requirements will be satisfied with respect to subsequent additional purchases by those investors."*

Delivering the Share Purchase (or Subscription) Agreement

The "order form" for buying shares is usually delivered with the prospectus, although it can come after delivery of the prospectus. Particular care must be taken to assure that no one receives the share purchase agreement before they have the prospectus. Since a check must usually be transmitted, you can expect that the only medium for return of the share purchase agreement would be by mail or delivery service. (The use of credit cards, debit cards, or "e-cash" is in such an early stage that we have not attempted to provide any guidance for payment methods other than sending a check in the mail.)

One of the SEC's examples deals with the problem of the prospective investor who has the purchase agreement before the prospectus:

> *"(38) A server available through the Internet contains a fund's prospectus and application form in separate files. Users can download or print the application form without first accessing, downloading or printing the prospectus; the form includes a statement that by signing the form, the investor certifies that he or she has received the prospectus. Logistically it is significantly more burdensome to access the prospectus than the application form (e.g., the investor needs to download special software before accessing the prospectus).*

> *"The statement in the form about receipt of the prospectus would not by itself constitute electronic delivery of the prospectus, and the application form is not evidence of delivery of the prospectus, given the need to download special software before the prospectus can be viewed."*

The next two examples in the SEC's release show permissible ways of delivering the order form and the prospectus:

> *"(39) A server available through the Internet contains a fund's prospectus. Users must download the prospectus to view or print it. When a user downloads the prospectus, the user receives the prospectus and an application form in separate files. It is not significantly more burdensome to access the prospectus than the application form (e.g., no additional software is necessary to read either document, although the documents may be in different formats).*

> *"If the fund can identify the application form as coming from the electronic system, electronic delivery of the prospectus can be inferred. The application form is evidence of delivery of the prospectus."*

> *"(40) A fund's prospectus and application form are available through an electronic system like that described in the preceding example, except that the investor needs to download special software before the prospectus and application form can be downloaded.*

> *"If the fund can identify the application form as coming form the electronic system, electronic delivery of the prospectus can be inferred. The application form is evidence of access to the prospectus."*

There is an important need to be sure that no one is buying shares who is a resident of a state in which your offering has not been registered. Whether you are using electronic delivery or regular mail, it is certainly possible that someone in a nonregistered state may get a copy of the prospectus and share purchase agreement.

You are not required to become a detective and use heroic measures to catch any subterfuge. A "reasonable" procedure is sufficient. Compliance with state laws may actually be easier with electronic delivery than it is with regular mail. It is apparently not difficult to program the share purchase agreement so that, if someone inserts an address in a non-registered state, it will not accept the address and will display an explanatory message.

Other Marketing Communications

It is only the prospectus, cleared by the SEC and state regulators, that may be used to offer your shares. However, it is neither unlawful nor unusual to also use other materials. For DPOs conducted primarily by regular mail, these may be follow-up letters, or they may be company brochures that give more of a "flavor" of the company. These communications, whether they accompany or follow the prospectus, need to be filed with the SEC and the states before they are used.

Regulators may refer to these other marketing communications as "supplemental selling materials" or similar terms. They cannot be used to add information to the prospectus, and they cannot be delivered without being preceded or accompanied by the prospectus. An example from the SEC release highlights this:

> *"(37) A fund's prospectus is available through an on-line service that does not have the capacity for downloading or printing or to track retrieval by a user. Investors do not provide any consent. The fund mails or e-mails supplemental sales literature, or an application to all of the service's subscribers, without including a prospectus.*

> *"Absent other factors that would indicate delivery of the prospectus, the fund may not send the supplemental sales literature or an application in this fashion, because it is not preceded or accompanied by the prospectus for purposes of Section 2(10)(a) of the Securities Act. -[This is analogous to printing a fund prospectus in a magazine of general circulation and subsequently mailing supplemental sales literature to the magazine's subscribers, which would not comply with Sections 2(10) and 5(b) of the Securities Act. See William C. Lloyd (State of Wisconsin), June 7, 1990.]- This would be true even if the general subscription agreement for the service contained a provision consenting to receipt of documents, because such consent would not be sufficient to give the fund reason to believe that delivery requirements relating to the prospectus will actually be satisfied."*

Other examples from the release show how the timing must work in using other marketing materials:

> *"(14) Company XYZ places a copy of its final prospectus on its Internet Web site. The electronic final prospectus will remain there throughout the period for which delivery is required. Company XYZ also places supplemental sales literature on its Internet Web site. Both the sales literature and the prospectus can be accessed from the same menu, are clearly identified on, and appear in close proximity to each other; -[In this example, the prospectus is accessible on the same menu as the supplemental sales literature; consequently, the existence of the prospectus and its location are readily ascertainable by the investor viewing the sales literature.]- the supplemental sales literature may be accessed before viewing or downloading the prospectus.*

> *"Sales literature, whether in paper or electronic form, is required to be preceded or accompanied by a final prospectus. -[Section 5(b) of the Securities Act.]- In this example, the prospectus would accompany the sales literature since investors can access both the prospectus and sales literature from the same menu. The sales literature and final prospectus should appear in close proximity to each other on the menu. For example, the sales literature should not be presented on the first page of a menu while the final prospectus is buried within the menu.*

> *"(15) Company XYZ places its sales literature in a discussion forum located on the Internet World Wide Web. The sales literature contains a hyperlink*

to the Company's final prospectus. While viewing the literature the individual can click on a box marked "final prospectus," and almost instantly the person will be linked directly to the Company's Web site and the final prospectus will appear on the person's computer screen.

"Sales literature, whether in paper or electronic form, is required to be preceded or accompanied by a final prospectus. The hyperlink function enables the final prospectus to be viewed directly as if it were packaged in the same envelope as the sales literature. Therefore, the final prospectus would be considered to have accompanied the sales literature. Consequently, the placing of sales literature in a discussion forum on a Web site would satisfy delivery obligations provided that a hyperlink that provides direct access to the final prospectus is included."

"(35) A fund posts its supplemental sales literature and prospectus on a file server for open access over the Internet. The supplemental sales literature contains hyperlinks to the fund's electronic prospectus and includes a caption referring the investor to the prospectus. The investor would not need any additional software or need to take burdensome steps to access the prospectus and thus has reasonably comparable access to both documents. This system also provides for the downloading or printing of prospectuses and sales literature. An investor would not be required to retrieve, download, or print a prospectus before viewing the sales literature. The system does not require any consent by its users.

"When a user accesses the supplemental sales literature, electronic delivery of the prospectus can be inferred. This scenario is analogous to an investor's selecting an envelope containing a paper prospectus and supplemental sales literature from a display at an office of a broker-dealer. This electronic delivery of the prospectus would be sufficient for other purposes if the fund could reasonably establish that the investor has actually accessed the sales literature or the prospectus."

Mixed media also rates an "OK" from the SEC release, as in this example of combining electronic delivery of the prospectus and print follow-up materials by regular mail:

"(17) Company XYZ places its final prospectus on its Internet Web site. The Company then mails sales literature to individuals for whom delivery through the Internet Web site was effective (regardless of whether the individuals consented to delivery). In the forepart of Company XYZ's sales literature is notice of the availability and Internet Web site location of its final prospectus.

"The mailing of sales literature to these individuals is permissible, provided that notice of the availability of the final prospectus and its Internet Web site location accompanies or precedes the sales literature. When notice is included within sales literature, it should be in the forepart of the literature and

clearly highlighted to make investors aware of the availability and location of the final prospectus."

The very good news is that, if (1) the other marketing materials come with or after the prospectus and (2) they do not get rejected when filed with the regulators, then these other marketing materials can be delivered in effective ways. This is where the SEC's examples are particularly helpful in showing what might be done:

"(13) Company XYZ wants to deliver to investors a CD-ROM version of its prospectus. The CD-ROM version includes within the prospectus a movie illustrating the Company's operations. Investors viewing the CD-ROM prospectus would not have to exit the prospectus in order to view the movie, as the movie is actually a part of the prospectus.

"While Company XYZ may include the movie as part of the prospectus, it would need to file with the Commission as an appendix to the prospectus the script of the movie and a fair and accurate narrative description of the graphic or image material just as it would have to supplementally provide to the Commission scripts and descriptions of such material in sales material."

In addition to being helpful in suggesting effective marketing techniques, it is quite to be expected that the SEC would think of some potential for the kinds of scams that have been around long before computers. One of them is the "independent" buy recommendation that turns out not to be so independent:

"(22) Company XYZ pays John Doe $10,000 to write a report about the Company and post the report on the Internet. John Doe writes the report and places it on the Growth Companies Investment Bulletin Board located on the Internet. The report does not disclose the $10,000 that the Company paid John Doe.

"The Securities Act requires that the $10,000 compensation paid by Company XYZ to John Doe be disclosed in the report, regardless of whether it is in electronic or paper form."

Back in Chapter 6, we mentioned the exemptions from registration, including "private placements." One of the requirements for the "safe harbor" for "transactions not involving any public offering" is that there cannot be any advertising or general solicitation used in the offering. These examples illustrate how that condition fits around the Internet:

"(20) Company XYZ wants to raise $5 million by selling its common stock in a private placement pursuant to Securities Act Rule 506 of Regulation D. The Company places its offering materials on its Internet Web site, which requires various information from a person attempting to access the materials to be provided to the Company prior to displaying the offering materials.

"The placing of the offering materials on the Internet would not be consistent with the prohibition against general solicitation or advertising in Rule 502(c) of Regulation D. -[In Release 33-7185 (June 27, 1995), the Commission solicited comment on the question of whether the prohibition against general solicitation in Regulation D offerings should be reconsidered.]- Where prospective purchasers have been otherwise located without a general solicitation, a proprietary computer service could be used to deliver required disclosure documents.

"(21) Company XYZ wants to raise $5 million by selling its common stock in a private placement pursuant to Rule 506 of Regulation D to certain individuals who have been located without a general solicitation. The Company transmits the offering materials via electronic mail addresses provided by these persons.

"This would not be inconsistent with the offering restrictions in the rule."

These examples and summaries represent the first steps in placing the limitations of securities laws around the art of electronic direct share marketing. We have certainly not heard the last from securities regulators about how a company can sell shares on the Internet. Entrepreneurial ingenuity has just begun to focus on how to make capital formation more effective by using electronic communication tools. Securities lawyers are just beginning to be challenged with how they can help their clients reach objectives without violating the letter or spirit of the law. We are seeing an area in its infancy. Who knows where it all will lead?

Two individuals who should have some pretty strong clues about where electronic communication tools will lead are the founder/leaders of the major computer hardware and software companies. They both authored articles for the December 2, 1996 issue of *Forbes*.

Andrew Grove, CEO of Intel, wrote:

"I have a rule, one that was honed by more than thirty years in high tech. It is simple. 'What can be done, will be done.' Like a natural force, technology is impossible to hold back. It finds its way no matter what obstacles people put in its place.

"The beauty of this rule is that it can be used to look into the future. All we need to do is remember what already can be done:

All information can be expressed digitally.
All information can be transported in digital form.
All information can be stored in digital form.

"If all this can be done, the rule says, it will be. What this means is that digital creation and display of information will predominate over other forms of communication — telephony, broadcasting — at the workplace as well as in our personal lives."

There, we have the leader in computer hardware predicting this digital dominance in all communications. More specific vision for the effect on the marketing of shares can come from the article by William H. Gates III, CEO and chairman of Microsoft:

> "The key mechanism of capitalism is matching buyers and sellers. . . . More and more, information about goods and services, buyers and sellers, will migrate to the network. Once that happens, then the people who have been profiting as middleman passing that information along — well, their world becomes very different. Buyers and sellers will go direct. It doesn't take a genius to figure out that the percentage of middlemen will go down quite a bit."

This short chapter on "Selling Shares on the Internet" will very soon be updated by new DPOs which extend use of the technology. There is something about the philosophy of the Internet — information available to everyone, right now, at an affordable cost — that fits with direct public offerings.

CHAPTER 8

CASE STUDIES OF DIRECT PUBLIC OFFERINGS

Each Direct Public Offering adds to the knowledge base upon which future share offerings may be built. The knowledge base presented in this book is largely drawn from our direct experiences with more than 20 DPOs since 1976. We have also learned from the experiences of others, as they have experimented with different approaches to direct share marketing.

There have been Direct Public Offerings since long before there were securities broker-dealers, investment bankers, or underwriting syndicates. When shares in enterprises were first sold by entrepreneurs, three hundred years ago, the affinity group direct marketing methods were basically the same as those being used in today's DPOs.

Before this book's first printing, however, there had been no published effort to accumulate and organize the lessons that had been learned in the direct marketing of shareownership. This chapter has been added to the original book to provide a sense of the companies that have been through the DPO process and a context for some of the particular issues they faced. Included are very brief descriptions of some of the DPOs for which we were advisors. There are also "interviews" with the principals in others that were successfully completed.

New Mexico Financial Corporation

When Thomas Edison was asked how he had "discovered" the right material for his light bulb filament, he answered that he knew it was the one, because he had first tried everything else. That's how New Mexico Financial came to try a Direct Public Offering.

In early 1973, the legal work necessary to help what was then "Sandia Financial Corporation" prepare for an underwritten initial public offering began. A letter of intent had been signed with the proposed managing underwriter, G.H. Walker & Co., which was one of those smaller but national underwriters that had done several public offerings in the 1950s and 1960s.

Sandia Financial Corporation was a holding company for four separate savings banks, all named "Sandia Savings." By adding "North," "South," and "West" to three of the banks' names, the company had been able to have the only state-wide banking system in New Mexico, despite a law limiting branches to within 100 miles of a bank's headquarters. If you have ever been to New Mexico, you will probably recognize "Sandia" as the mountains which dominate the horizon in the central state. At one of the early "all hands" meetings, the underwriters said the company name would have to be changed because no one in New York would have ever heard of "Sandia." Changing the corporation's name to "New Mexico Financial" later became the major marketing hurdle when its shares were offered directly to customers of the Sandia Savings offices.

Near the end of 1973, all of the work had been done (and the company had paid $144,452 in offering costs) to be ready for the underwriting. A few days before it was to have been completed, the underwriter postponed the offering. The "continuing uncertainty of the stock market" was cited as the cause for delay. As weeks turned into months, the underwriter merged into another firm to be G.H. Walker, Laird & Co. Another few months and that firm was acquired by White, Weld & Co., a much larger brokerage firm. Not much later, White, Weld was absorbed into Merrill Lynch, the largest securities broker-dealer in the country. The company and its capital needs were far below the Merrill Lynch interest level.

Business for the company, meanwhile, was very profitable and growing rapidly. The ability to grow, however, was being limited by the need for more equity capital. The company began meeting with other underwriting firms, primarily those in the Southwest with some experience in IPOs. After furnishing reams of data and conducting several meetings and tours, the time never seemed to be right.

Finally, in May 1976, management decided to try marketing its shares directly to its depositors, borrowers, and others in New Mexico and West Texas. In what was to become an early "Screen Test for a Direct Public Offering," as described in Chapter 5, management saw that it had (1) exciting prospects for sharing in the Southwest's rapid growth, (2) several years of profitable operations under present management, (3) honest, socially responsible and competent management, (4) an easily understood business of accepting deposits and making loans, (5) customers who had already trusted it with their money, (6) customers who would certainly recognize and pay attention to its communications (once we dealt with the underwriter-induced name change problem), (7) those customers' names, addresses, telephone numbers, and account information were all in the company's database, (8) the president's assistant could be available to be the project manager and (9) audited financial statements had been required by banking regulators.

A full registration on Form S-1 was required with the Securities and Exchange Commission, although the offering was only for $1.5 million, since this was long before the SEC's Small Business Initiatives brought simpler forms. There were many issues raised by the SEC staff about why the company was using direct marketing and whether it had to be a broker-dealer (which, as a bank holding company, it could not have legally become). Similar questions came from the banking regulators who reviewed the proposed offering.

The offering was filed with state securities regulators in New Mexico, Texas, Colorado, Arizona, and California. They each had questions, about how we had arrived at the offering price and how the offering price had been arrived at and how shares were going to be sold without using brokers. The offering cleared in each of those states except Arizona, where the Director of Securities himself (long since gone) telephoned personally to say that he did not want "a single piece of paper" relating to the offering "crossing into my state." He did not believe that securities should be sold by anyone except a registered broker-dealer.

Clearing a regulatory path was one major victory, but now the shares had to be marketed, without breaking any of the rules we had just helped to write. The search for someone with experience in the direct marketing of something like corporate shares led to a direct marketing consultant, Joseph Kreuger, who had helped American Express in the direct marketing of insurance products and Wells Fargo Bank with the direct marketing of credit cards. A series of three letters was created (to transfer the relationships with "Sandia Savings" onto the parent "New Mexico Financial") and everyone from the tellers to the board members were trained in how to talk with prospective investors and stay within the rules.

All 150,000 shares offered were sold, at $10 per share, by April 1977. In 1978, a second DPO was registered and completed for 160,000 shares at $11 per share. The company was acquired in 1982, at a substantial gain to the shareowners.

California Financial Holding Company

Stockton Savings Bank had been a small, local savings and loan from the 1930s until its management chose to become a publicly traded institution in 1983. It was one of the early "conversions" from the mutual to stock form of ownership. These "mutual" banks are technically owned by their borrowers and depositors. As a practical matter, there is no real economic ownership. The legal structure is more like a nonprofit social club than the typical business corporation. Born in Depression legislation, these mutuals were a populist concept of families putting in their savings so that their neighbors could take out loans to buy homes.

Federal and state regulators began allowing these mutuals to issue stock in 1982, primarily as a way to get more capital into the industry. In the complex process for conversion, one rule required that the existing "owners," the borrower and depositor members, would get the first chance to buy the new shares, by way of a mandated "direct community marketing." Elaborate formulas would proportion oversold shares among the members in accordance with the amount and timing of their deposits. People who opened accounts or increased their balances after the offering plans were announced would only get shares left over after the first allocation.

More than the total $6 million in shares were subscribed by the depositors and borrowers, nearly all of whom were in the bank's Northern California Central Valley neighborhood. Some "outsiders" from San Francisco, who opened accounts after learning about the offering, were largely shut out, as local customers subscribed for the entire offering.

All shares were marketed directly by the bank, following the same program as New Mexico Financial. A special element was added to try making friends with all the securities brokers in the area, who would be receiving no commissions in the offering. They were invited for cocktails and snacks at the Country Club, where officers explained the offering — why it was being done and how the regulations called for direct marketing. Questions were encouraged. The purpose was to help the brokers avoid the discomfort of learning about the offering from their customers and to have them be able to respond favorably when asked their opinion.

Most of the company's investors had never owned corporate shares before and much of the education process was to explain the risk and potential reward. One farmer, who became one of the larger shareowners, had said he only invested "where I can kick the dirt." The bank's president, David Rea, invited him to come kick his desk anytime he felt like it. Today, the company is ten times the size, at over a billion dollars in assets, and has become the dominant financial institution in its market.

After the offering, two local offices of national brokerage firms began making a trading market in the shares. One of them became lead underwriter in the bank's second public offering. California Financial Holding Company was created to exchange its shares for those of the bank and, at the end of 1996, some 13 years after the DPO, an acquisition was announced. The original shareowners stood to receive about ten times their original investment, in addition to their stream of dividends over the years. Both David Rea, who has been CEO of the company since 1955, and Robert Kavanaugh, who was the bank's CFO from 1960 until his present COO position, have been able to build significant ownership of the bank's shares as well. It was announced in December 1996 that the company would be acquired at a price equal to more than ten times the original DPO offering price.

California Federal Bank

Conversion of this mutual savings bank in 1983 became the largest initial public offering in history, with the sole exception of Ford Motor Company. The total offering was $375 million. Through a direct offering to the bank's customers $45 million in 45 days was sold. The balance was then sold by an underwriting syndicate managed by four large Wall Street brokerage firms.

The bank started out to use direct marketing media to announce the offering in the Los Angeles area, where 80 percent of the their customers lived. Print, radio, and television ads were all prepared, with marketing experts and lawyers teaming up to make them as effective as possible. Two days before the campaign was to begin, management was warned that any advertising could trigger an "investigation" by the SEC, causing a delay in the underwritten portion of the offering. The consequences of that, management was told, could be to miss "the window of opportunity" presented by the institutional investors "appetite" for savings bank shares. The announcement phase of the Direct Public Offering was canceled. (The project manager, Lloyd Dunn, formerly the bank's general counsel, later wrote his belief that the direct offering could have sold half the total offering if the announcement program had been used.)

All other efforts were concentrated on helping the customers who expressed interest to their share subscriptions in before the deadline. Several dinner training meetings were held, to which all the employees were invited. Everyone participated in small-group training sessions. A telephone room was staffed with constant training and supervision. Television monitors and VCRs were placed in every branch, with a continuous message playing about the offering. Tellers were trained to mention the offering to customers and direct them to where they could get more information. Cookie-and-coffee and wine-and-cheese gatherings were held for customers to come with their questions.

California Federal Bank was one of the survivors of the industry shakeout that was to follow. As of the end of 1996, it was to be merged with another large institution.

Farm and Home Savings

The experience with California Federal prompted many calls, including one from Farm and Home Savings, which was a large mutual savings bank with offices in Missouri and Texas. They had a letter of intent to do an underwritten initial public offering with Salomon Brothers as the managing underwriter. Their idea in calling us was to save underwriting commissions on the shares that could be marketed directly in their service area.

Farm and Home followed several other large mutual banks in the new conversion IPO market and that "window of opportunity" nearly slammed shut before they were ready to offer shares. Institutions had gotten their fill, at least temporarily, of savings bank shares. Investment bankers at Salomon Brothers began to encourage sales of as many shares as possible in the direct portion of the offering.

This added incentive for the DPO led to some experiments. For instance, large announcements of the offering were made in the daily and weekly newspapers, shopping news, and organizational newsletters wherever the bank did business. Radio announcements were played on all the local stations. Cable television was used to get the word out and cause people to telephone for a prospectus package. Even billboards carried the news.

One of the innovations was to employ local securities brokers to sell shares in the direct offering. (Regulations did not permit an "underwriting," but the bank could pay commissions for "best efforts" selling.) We met in nearly every brokerage office in their area, both independent and branches of large firms. Some brokerage management officials would not let any of their salespeople participate at all, while others were allowed to participate. The bank paid a commission that was meant to equal what a selling brokerage firm would receive in an underwriting syndicate (60 percent of a 7 percent commission, which we rounded up to 4.5 percent).

When the brief DPO period was over, the bank furnished each participating firm with a printout of the firm's sales, by broker and by customer, and a check for the commission. The broker program had produced about $7 million of the $45 million sold in the DPO. Sales by the underwriters, almost entirely to institutions, were another $27 million. Ironically, the amount sold by underwriters included exercise of their "Green Shoe" option, which allowed them to sell another 15 percent of the entire offering. In other words, the offering was originally to have been for about $63 million. With $45 million sold directly, the underwriters were able to get orders for the balance, plus another $9 million in new shares. On the other side, the bank received $9 million in additional capital for the same costs and effort.

Real Goods Trading Corporation

John Schaeffer started this catalog direct marketing business with a $3,000 investment in 1986 and still owned it five years later when its first DPO was started. Half of its $6 million annual sales at that time were in alternative energy generation (photovoltaic, wind, and hydro) systems and energy conservation. The rest were in a broad range of environmental, "green" products.

A brief description of Real Goods in the *Wall Street Journal*'s Enterprise column suggested that it might fit the elements in the "Screen Test for a Direct Public Offering." The first edition of this book was about to be published and the next step was to carry what had been developed in the savings bank DPOs over to other industries. John was willing to test the concept and to use the new SCOR filing process for offerings of not more than $1 million.

Real Goods selected a target market of customers who had purchased more than a certain amount, or more than three times, in the most recent 15 months. These were sorted by residence and 13 states were picked for the offering, based upon the number of qualified customers and the cost of compliance with state securities laws. A "tombstone" announcement went to 15,000 customers in October 1991. Within three months, there had been 6,200 requests for the offering documents and sales to 674 new shareowners. Another $300,000 had to be returned to 175 customers who subscribed after the maximum had been reached.

A second DPO was completed in 1993, using the SEC's Regulation A filing and simply updating the offering document from the earlier SCOR offering. This time, the $3,600,000 maximum amount was sold and several hundred thousand dollars had to be returned as coming in too late. After the two offerings, John Schaeffer still owned 75 percent of the Company. Shares began trading on the Pacific Stock Exchange in 1994 and over-the-counter trading is reported on the NASDAQ Small Cap Market. In 1996, Real Goods became the first company to begin an SEC-cleared bulletin board for "off-the-grid" buying and selling its shares without a broker.

Three securities brokerage firms were enlisted on a "best efforts" agency basis for the second offering. However, their total sales were less than 10 percent of the offering. Ways to identify and communicate with affinity groups beyond Real Goods customers were also experimented. Most of those were not cost-effective.

Real Goods had learned after its first offering that customers who had become shareowners purchased twice the dollar amount of Real Goods products than non-shareowner customers. The extra contribution to gross profit was well worth the cost of servicing shareowners with reports and certificates. As a result, the minimum required purchase was reduced from 100 shares to 15 shares in the second offering. The states in which the offering was registered was increased to 44. Nearly 5,000 Real Goods customers had become shareowners in the two DPOs, with an average investment of about $900. Total costs of the two offerings, including marketing expenses, had been about 10 percent of the funds raised.

Mendocino Brewing Company

This 1994 DPO presented a new marketing challenge to the DPO process. Unlike the banks and catalog retailers, this 11-year-old brewer of ale, stout, and porter did not have a database of the people who were its customers, except for those who had signed the brewpub guest book. In other words, Mendocino Brewing did not pass one element of the "Screen Test for a Direct Public Offering," the one that calls for a database of the affinity groups to whom the shares are to be offered. The company's products are marketed primarily through distributors and then retailers. There was no way to get the names, addresses, or any other information about the ultimate customers. (Actually, there are ways, but they take years to be effective. See the story about Annie's Homegrown.)

The lack of a database did not change the assumption that only those who bought the product would buy the shares. The marketing was entirely directed to people who drank the company's Red Tail Ale and other ales, ways to let them know they could become shareowners in their favorite brewery were needed.

We projected (conservatively, as it turned out) that 20 percent of those who received a prospectus would buy shares. We also projected (also conservatively) that the average purchase would be $1,000. That meant we needed 3,600 investors to sell out the offering and five times as many (18,000) people requesting the prospectus. An answer to the question, "what media did you use to announce the offering?" would be, "every one we could think of, if it looked to be cost-effective. "

To keep tabs on how well each medium was drawing, callers requesting prospectuses were asked how they had learned of the offering. Responses from half fit the "word of mouth" category. Second highest responses were from a "tombstone" announcement card placed in six-pack containers of ale. Several other media were used, and the combination helped to get the "word of mouth" started. Total costs of the offering were $260,000, or about eight percent of the $3.6 million raised. The shares have been trading ever since on the Pacific Stock Exchange.

Bridge City Tool Works

John Economaki, formerly a high school shop teacher, began Bridge City Tool Works on the basis of his talent for designing "work-of-art" hand tools for serious woodworking hobbyists. He sold the tools through woodworking shows and developed a catalog direct marketing business. After building a team of employees and growing rapidly, the business was hit by some of those unexpected events that can force undercapitalized businesses into liquidation.

To show its ability to survive, Bridge City needed to get some short-term capital, and some patience from creditors. To get beyond that, and back on the growth track, some permanent capital would be necessary.

Short-term capital, by way of investment in preferred stock was available, on the condition that there would be long-term capital to back it up or replace it. A two-step financing was put in place during 1994 and 1995. Two private investors purchased preferred stock, which was to be redeemed from the proceeds of a public offering. Then common stock was registered for a direct public offering. Shares were marketed to vendors, customers, and local investors. Bridge City is now back on a solid footing, able to continue its growth and service its loyal customers, many of whom now share ownership.

Hahneman Laboratories, Inc.

This offering was another significant extension of the DPO experience. For one, it was a test of how small a truly "public" offering could be and still be cost-effective. Secondly, it recognized that the company's customer base was not going to be large enough to support the necessary investment—other affinity groups would need to be defined and reached.

Michael Quinn, a registered pharmacist, had a lifetime belief in homeopathy. He had started a pharmacy, connected to the well-known Hahnemann Clinic in Berkeley, California. (Many hospitals and clinics had been named after Dr. Hahnemann, who founded homeopathy 200 years ago.) The pharmacy made its own remedies, and Michael wanted to begin a pharmaceutical laboratory, in compliance with FDA standards, in order to have nationwide distribution.

The marketing challenge was to find and communicate with people who were true believers in homeopathy. We operated on the assumption that the only investors would be those who had personal experience with homeopathic remedies and believed homeopathy would be a growing part of the health care industry. Michael mailed announcements to the customers of a homeopathic bookseller and a homeopathic software company. Professional organizations' members were told of the offering in newsletters, magazines, and more mailed announcements.

Regulation A Offering Circulars were mailed as requests came in from these announcements. A total of $467,000 in shares was purchased by 242 investors. Hahnemann Laboratories held its first shareowners' meeting a few months after the offering was over. The main event was a tour of the new manufacturing laboratory.

Blue Fish Clothing, Inc.

Jennifer Barclay made block-printed T-shirts in her parents' garage when she was 19, selling them at a festival. Nine years later, she had built a profitable business with $8 million in annual sales, 160 employees, and a goal "to encourage people to believe in themselves and to inspire creativity and self-expression."

Blue Fish Clothing operated three of its own stores and a catalog/telephone sales division at the time it began its Direct Public Offering. Over 75 percent of its sales, however, were through 600 wholesale accounts, ranging from small boutiques to Nordstrom and Neiman Marcus. Blue Fish customers were loyal, enthusiastic, and dedicated to both the clothing and the corporate goal. The problem was how to let them know they could share ownership in Blue Fish with Jennifer.

Announcements of the offering followed the letter of SEC Rule 134 (described in Chapter 6, "The Regulatory Framework"). While the wording was totally traditional, the design and graphics were definitely not. Hangtags went out on all clothing after the offering prospectus was declared effective. Shaped like a fish and in pastel shades of Blue Fish colors, the announcements did not at all have the look that brought notices the "tombstones" nickname to begin with.

Creativity was the theme of the Blue Fish business, and much of that creativity went into spreading the word about the share offering, without going outside the lines of securities regulation. There had been a minimum offering amount of $2,500,000 and a maximum of $4,000,000, with May 13, 1996 as the deadline for reaching the minimum. By early April, prospectus packages had gone out to enough people to have the offering sold out. Still, the subscription agreements had hit a bottleneck. We recommended that the Blue Fish board decide to end the entire offering on the May 13 date for reaching the minimum. That way, a message could go out that action was necessary right away, or they'd miss the opportunity to buy shares directly from the company at a fixed price and no commission.

All $4,000,000 was subscribed by the May 13 date, with half the amount coming in the last few days, and trading began on the Chicago Stock Exchange.

Annie's Homegrown, Inc.

First of the nine items in the "Screen Test for a Direct Public Offering," described in Chapter 5, is that "the company's business would excite prospective investors, making them want to share in its future." Annie's Homegrown, Inc. is in the business of marketing macaroni and cheese dinners, the kind that come in a box and are cooked in hot water. Not very exciting?

The excitement is that Annie's macaroni and cheese is "totally natural," compared with the Kraft product, which dominates the market. Bernie the Rabbit is portrayed on the box. Environmental messages are on the back, and "Be Green" bumper stickers are available for customers who write in for them. Shares in the company's profits are donated in product and cash to charitable organizations in its "Community Enrichment Program." A company magazine, *Be Green*, features articles about helping the environment and society. Founder and "Inspirational President" of the company is Ann Withey, who lives on an organic farm and personally answers customer letters.

Money was certainly an important motivation for the offering. Expanding sales of grocery products these days means buying shelf space in supermarkets. Nearly all the proceeds were earmarked for paying "slotting fees" that have become necessary for the introduction of new products. Another critical objective of the Direct Public Offering for Annie's Homegrown was to bring its customers into shareownership. They would certainly be good future customers, and they could be expected to bring in their relatives, friends, and neighbors. As it turned out, the average investment, excluding one or two larger ones, was under $600. This fits with the customer demographics, people in their 20s and young parents.

Annie's placed a "tombstone" announcement like a "cents-off" coupon in the box. (It tended to go into the boiling water with the macaroni.) A few other media were used for announcing the offering as well. The major innovation in the Annie's offering began once a customer or other prospect responded by requesting a prospectus. Response could be either by telephone to an 800 number, mail to a post office address, e-mail, or by viewing Annie's website.

Only the SEC's February 1995 "no-action" letter was available to guide us in designing the website. (As described in Chapter 7, "Selling Shares on the Internet," the SEC gave much more extensive guidance in an October 1995 release on electronic delivery of offering materials.) Most of us were surprised to find that about 30 percent of the initial responses came electronically. There were four different ways that requests needed to be handled, depending upon the prospect's residence, and the programming mechanics worked smoothly throughout the offering.

Thanksgiving Coffee Company, Inc.

Paul and Joan Katzeff came out from New York City to the relative wilderness of Mendocino County, California. Since 1972, they have operated Thanksgiving Coffee Company in the coastal town of Ft. Bragg. Starting out by buying and roasting arabica coffee beans for local restaurants and inns, they gradually expanded into sales through markets and a catalog mail-order business.

Thanksgiving Coffee added coffee-making and coffee-related products and started a Royal Gardens Tea Company division. Over the years, greater awareness was created for the way coffee beans are grown and marketed. Adopting the motto, "Not Just a Cup . . . But a Just Cup," Paul and Joan have developed "green" coffee buying programs to benefit the independent growers and pickers in Central America and to buy coffee grown organically.

Three overlapping affinity groups were the prospects for the company's shares: customers, neighbors, and believers in Thanksgiving Coffee's socially responsible business practices. Announcements of the offering were placed on customers' coffee bags and in-store bean dispensers. They were mailed to mail-order customers and vendors. Printed announcements were carried in targeted magazines, newspapers, and the company's catalog. Thanksgiving Coffee's website had a "tombstone."

Even with all its affinity groups, initially there simply weren't enough people to allow the offering to just sell on the numbers. The total number of prospects was small enough that it was still necessary to get the interested ones to take action. As Thanksgiving's General Manager, Rick Moon, told *Inc. Magazine*, "you have to put the offering in front of potential investors' faces seven times to get them to take action." Taking the extra effort did the job, and Thanksgiving finally completed its offering.

The Three That Failed

They say that "success is a poor teacher." If that is true, then less may learned from these successful Direct Public Offerings than from the three that failed. Without mentioning their names, following is a brief description of some fatal flaws.

One of the savings banks had to terminate its offering, and remain in the mutual form, because it could not get enough people to pay enough money to sell all its shares. The bank's service area was entirely farm communities in the Northern part of midwestern state. A volume of savings and of loans was sufficient to allow the bank to operate profitably. However, the savings were principally "rainy day" monies, accumulated and put away for the year in which the crop failed, a new tractor was needed, or someone became too sick to work. These were not people who wanted to add another risk investment to lives that were already subject to the big risks of weather and commodity prices. This experience found its way into the "Screen Test for a Direct Public Offering," that the company has affinity groups "with discretionary cash to risk for long-term gain."

A catalog retailer had built a very large base of loyal customers, many of whom wrote personal "thank-you" notes about how much they appreciated the products and service. If only a third of 1 percent of the customers would buy $1,000, the offering would be successful! Prices for the company's products were in the premium range, so surely many of these customers could afford the risk. What we missed was that these customers would have the same issues as any full-time investment professional—what is the risk versus the reward. Interviews showed that they were concerned about the company's three consecutive years of losses going into the offering and that most of the offering proceeds were to pay off bank debt. On the reward side, they did not see how the rapid growth of the past could be maintained in the future. As it turned out, management did turn the company around. The limiting factor in DPOs is that the only place to tell the whole story is in the prospectus. It is hard to convey a sense of what management can do, except by the record of what it has done. This particular lesson, that it must be an attractive investment proposition, is not in the "Screen Test for a Direct Public Offering," because every entrepreneur would answer "of course it is!" Nevertheless, someone needs to look at what is to be offered, through the eyes of the prospective investors. The merit may be there, but it may not come across in the written word and financial statements.

A small chain of home furnishing stores had established a particular style and "feel" in its stores that was drawing rapid growth in sales and frequent inquiries about buying shares in the business. The owner expressed what is often heard from entrepreneurs, something like: "Don't worry about the shares getting sold. As soon as word gets out, they'll be beating down the doors to buy in." It rarely happens that way and getting 10 percent of those people to actually invest is a good record. What happened was that (according to post-offering interviews) customers read the offering document and did not like management's plans for the future, how they were going to spend the shareowners' money. It included going into the mail order business, something beyond management's experience. A few weeks into the share marketing program, the owner became very dejected at the response and called the whole process off. Whether it would ultimately have sold or not, the second unwritten rule was learned: Principals of the business must be complete believers in doing a Direct Public Offering. It won't work if there's an attitude of "Let's give it a try and see if it works."

Those are capsules of our own experience in doing Direct Public Offerings, those that worked and those that did not. We have also tried to learn from the experience of others. Following are interviews with people who have been through DPOs.

The Price REIT (Real Estate Investors Trust)

During the fall of 1991, members of the Price Club invested $73 million in four Price Club warehouses and related shopping centers. Instead of the usual underwriting through Wall Street investment bankers, shares were offered directly to Price Club members.

Before its merger with Costco, Price Club was one of the great success stories in retailing, with 72 merchandising warehouses in nine states and Canada. By the middle of 1991, the company owned nearly $600 million in real estate—largely its warehouses and adjacent shopping centers.

Sol Price, a founder of the company, figured that the seven million dues-paying members would recognize value in an investment, just as they did with goods in the warehouses. Why not offer ownership shares in the real estate to Price Club members? Not only would this generate cash for more growth, it would build even greater loyalty among the member/customers.

To manage the project, Price called upon Bill Birdsall, who had spent two years as President of the Company's real estate subsidiary. The 42-year-old Mr. Birdsall had been in the real estate development business since 1978, after serving as a lawyer for a congressional committee and the state of Arizona.

Following are some questions and answers about the Price REIT offering put together from the prospectus and discussions with Bill Birdsall.

Why did price decide to do a direct public offering?
Investment bankers and other financial intermediaries were ready to help in the offering process, but they wanted to be paid 6 percent to 7 percent of the offering in fees—even when Price would be handing them a list of 7 million likely prospects to sell. We decided we could do it ourselves for a much lower cost. As it turned out, the investors were as interested in saving big transaction costs as we were. Offering the shares directly, without any commissions, was a positive selling point.

Did you have some market research to show the shares would sell?
We thought about using focus groups or other market research tools, but we felt that a real test marketing was the only way to know whether or not this was a service Price Club members wanted.

How did you advertise the offering?

SEC rules limit very tightly what can be said about an offering before someone has a copy of the prospectus. We used a very bare-bones legal announcement, with request for prospectuses to be made to an 800 telephone number or an address. The only thing we offered was a copy of the prospectus.

What media did you use to reach members?

We tested several media. There was a special mailing to some members. Others received an announcement and reply card in their membership renewal notices. An announcement appeared in the Price Club journal. A booth in some of the warehouses was used to pass out fliers. We selected small target groups and tested each method. Some reply cards, for instance, had return postage, and some didn't. We varied the message a little from one group to another. In total, we reached about a million of our seven million members.

How did you close sales?

We answered requests by sending a prospectus, the document called for by SEC regulation. It came inside a wraparound flier that answered 10 of the most obvious questions about the offering. A subscription agreement was included, with instructions on how to sign up and pay for shares. We included an 800 number to call, but no one was allowed to do any "selling."

When someone called the number, a recorded message asked the caller to give name and address to receive the prospectus, or to push another button to get a member of my regular office staff. These staff members had a script for handling simple questions, often by referring the caller to the prospectus. About half the calls were referred to me, and I could "stack" up to 10 calls on hold.

We kept track of all responses, with a couple of personal computers and some software, so we could see what methods led to the most closed sales.

How long did it take to sell?

We received SEC clearance and started the announcements on October 11 of 1991. Within about seven weeks, by December 3, we had sold all $73 million. In fact, we sold more, and had to allocate shares in the oversubscription.

How much did it cost?

The total, "all in" cost was $1.88 million, or 2.575 percent of the amount we raised. Of that, we paid $700,000 to a Wall Street investment bank, to do their due diligence investigation and, in effect, say that this was a legitimate investment. We also wanted them to stand by, in case our members did not buy all the shares and we needed them to sell some to institutional investors.

The other costs were $400,000 for lawyers; $200,000 for accountants; $200,000 for printing; and the balance for postage, telephone, computer, and miscellaneous.

What about a trading market for the shares?

We had approval for listing on the NASDAQ (National Association of Securities Dealers Automated Quotations) National Market System, with two brokerage firms committed to be market makers. Since the offering, we have split the shares 40 for 1, so trading may become more active. Other brokerage firms have said they will also be market makers for the shares.

Where did you learn to do a direct public offering?

Nowhere, really. I got copies of the written materials used by the big savings and loan associations, when they first offered shares to their depositors and borrowers. Mostly, it was trial and error.

Portland Brewing Company

"Hometown" identification can be a strong marketing draw, as demonstrated by Portland Brewing Company's series of Direct Public Offerings. It had opened its brewery and brewpub in Portland in 1986. Six years later, its sales had gotten over a million dollar annual rate and one of its brews took a gold medal in the Great American Beer Festival.

Portland Brewing's initial DPO was for $500,000. Only Oregon residents were eligible to invest. The offering started December 14, 1992 and was sold out by January 8, 1993. Perhaps the fastest DPO on record, it took place over the Christmas holidays, traditionally a time when no one tries to do a public offering. A few months later, another $500,000 was offered at the same $5 per share price to residents of Oregon and across the river into Washington.

That million-dollar direct IPO was successful with the people in Portland Brewing's backyard, even though there was no SEC registration. Relying on the "intrastate exemption" (described in Chapter 6, "The Regulatory Framework") meant that the offering circular spelled out that the shares could only be resold to residents of Oregon and Washington, and went on to warn: "Accordingly, purchasers of the Shares in this offering may not be able to liquidate their investment and must be prepared to bear the economic risk of an investment in the Shares for an indefinite period."

Later direct public offerings included residents of California.

There are now some 5,500 shareowners in Portland Brewing, still without any exchange listing or other real trading market for the shares. The average investment was $1,100, with fewer than ten people who own $10,000 or more of the Company's shares. These were the comments of Tony Adams, its President, about their DPO experience.

Why did you decide to do a DPO?

It was the only way we could get financing. I'd seen DPOs done in other industries and thought it would be right for microbreweries. We have now completed several rounds. When we were getting started, in 1985, we did a private placement with fewer than 25 people. Then, in 1993 we did a two-part, $1 million offering ($500,000 in Oregon and $500,000 in Oregon and Washington.) We followed that with a Regulation A offering and, most recently, an SB-1.

Did you do some market research to show the shares would sell?

We just intuitively knew both microbreweries and DPOs (at least, in Oregon) were hot!

How did you advertise the offering?

For the first one, in 1993, the only ad was a "tombstone" in the local paper, with a Christmas wreath around the copy. It turned out to be an effective way to communicate the idea of giving shares as gifts, particularly to children. An article broke about Bernau's offering (Willamette, mentioned later in this chapter), which was happening at the same time. The article also mentioned our offering and that really helped. In the later offerings, we used print ads and they were very effective in local publications. Wall Street Journal ads were a waste of money. Radio ads were particularly effective in motivating people who had already requested prospectuses to buy shares.

How did you close sales?

Most sales closed themselves. It became more difficult the further we got from Portland (the issue of liquidity for the shares got more important). We followed up after sending prospectuses an average of twice—some phone calls, some "last chance" letters. It was most effective when I called, introducing myself as president of the company. Calling on weekends, I batted 1,000. When we did our SB-1 offering, the mailing of prospectuses was outsourced to a mail house. They waited three weeks to send anything out and the huge delay made closing more difficult.

How long did it take to sell the offering?

Our first offering sold out in three days. Each of the others took progressively longer. We found that sending announcements to names on our mailing list was more effective than advertising. We now have a mailing list of 50,000 people.

How much did it cost?

Each offering we did has gotten progressively more expensive. Costs of the last offering were the equivalent of 15 cents on the dollar.

What About a trading market for the shares?

There is none. We try to have a very loose matching process among the shareowners themselves, but nothing very formal.

Where did you learn to do a DPO?
We taught ourselves, with the help of a good investment banker and a securities attorney who had previously worked for the State of Oregon writing most of their Blue Sky laws.

What was your biggest problem doing a DPO?
During the offering it takes management out of the business you're in for a long time. The DPO is a protracted distraction.

Tully's Coffee Corporation

Seattle seems to have started the gourmet coffee trend that continues to spread coffee shops across the country. Tully's Coffee opened its first store in September 1992 and, by the time of its initial Direct Public Offering. In June 1995, there were ten Tully's retail locations in the Seattle metropolitan area.

Tully's first DPO was a Regulation A offering for a minimum of $1,050,000 and a maximum of $4,200,000. The actual amount raised was $2,400,000. Tom O'Keefe, President and CEO of Tully's told us this about their experience.

Why did you decide to do a DPO?
We'd done a Reg D (an exempt "private placement," as described in Chapter 6, "The Regulatory Framework") for $1.5 million and a Reg A offering was mentioned as an alternative to a second Reg D. In November 1994, I went on vacation and read the book about Ben & Jerry's (the ice cream company, which had done a $750,000, Vermont residents only, DPO in 1975). That convinced me that a "self-managed" offering was right for us. Particularly since we have the same community involvement and visibility as they do. My managers were all ready for the idea, as they said that customers had been asking all along if they would "do what Starbucks did" (that is, go public).

Did you do some market research to show the shares would sell?
We went totally on gut instinct. We figured our customer counts, by store, as a basis for sort of an informal market understanding.

How did you advertise the offering?
We used a combination of radio (all local, AM, various formats) and pretty basic tombstone ads placed in local newspapers. Radio worked well—we got lots of calls from car phones. The tombstone ads were conservative, but so is our management. We didn't push the edge.

How did you close sales?
We didn't. We made no follow-up calls. We only responded to incoming calls (about 40 to 50 in total). The only follow-up mailing was to keep people posted on the status of the offering.

How long did it take to sell the offering?
When we started the offering in June 1995, we intended to go through December. Then we realized that would take too much of our time and December would be an off month anyway. So, we changed to September 30. When we sent a letter to that effect, lots of money came in.

How much did it cost?
We raised $2.4 million (the limit was $4.2 million and our goal was $2 million). Costs were less than expected — $100,000 to $120,000.

What about a trading market for the shares?
There is none. Now we keep a rudimentary list of folks to match buyers and sellers. There are usually about 100 to 125 buyers and 5 to 10 sellers.

Where did you learn to do a DPO?
We were largely self-taught. We did tons of reading and research. We hired a former Washington State securities attorney.

Jim Bernau and His Companies

Jim Bernau is the entrepreneur with the record for doing the largest number of Direct Public Offerings. While holding down a full-time job as Director of the Oregon Chapter of the National Federation of Independent Businesses, he has been doing DPOs since 1989. After his first three DPOs for Willamette Valley Vineyards, he did more for Willamette Valley Brewing and microbreweries in other parts of the country. "When I started the [first] public offering, I had no winery, I had no winemaker, I had no crop. I had a dream that people could share in." Shareowners in his companies have helped pick the grapes, bottle the wine, sell, and deliver the product. Jim Bernau talks about his vision of "consumer-ownership." "I believe very strongly that the public is best served when the consumer owns the business."

Jim Bernau believes that an offering needs to be for at least $1 million to be cost-effective. His offering expenses have averaged about 12 percent of the amount raised. One of his lessons: "You raise 90 percent of your capital within 50 miles of your business."

GLOSSARY OF TERMS USED IN SECURITIES MARKETING

This glossary is offered as a reference for looking up the meaning of terms relating to corporate shares, public offerings, and direct marketing. Reading it is also another way to understand the book's basic message:

1. Companies are not selling shares to the public because the underwriting syndicate no longer works for most businesses.

2. There is plenty of money and motivation among individuals to invest as shareowners.

3. Here is how you can do a Direct Public Offering.

Like any specialty, corporate finance has its own special terms, seemingly designed to intimidate the outsider. Many everyday words take on new connotations when applied to public stock offerings. Then there are the terms created by lawyers, regulators, and practitioners of the relatively new direct marketing specialty. The meanings and commentary in this glossary are the author's own interpretations.

Note: Terms in italics are defined in their alphabetical order.

Acceleration - Securities cannot be sold unless a *registration statement* has become effective with the SEC, or a specific exemption applies. That *effective date* occurs automatically 20 days after it is filed, unless an SEC stop order or refusal order is in effect. The way it really works is that each filing includes a *delaying amendment* so that it cannot become effective automatically. Then the lawyers file a request for acceleration of the effective date to a selected day and time.

Aftermarket – The *trading market* that develops for *shares* after the *public offering* is over. Orders to buy or sell shares are matched in the *over-the-counter market* by a *securities firm* acting as a *market maker*. For *listed shares*, a *specialist* on the *stock exchange* will match orders. The quality of the after-market is measured by its ability to absorb *bid price* or *asked price* orders without major disruptions in the price. That ability is a function of the market's *liquidity*—the number of shares owned by the public, rather than by company *insiders* (called the *float*), and the extent to which the public is active in trading the shares, rather than holding them for the long term.

Agreement among underwriters – In the last few weeks before the *effective date* of an *underwritten public offering*, the *managing underwriter* will be putting together an *underwriting syndicate* of other *securities firms*. When the *underwriting agreement* is signed, the firms who have joined will sign an agreement among underwriters, assigning them an *allotment* of *shares* they are technically required to buy from the company as an *underwriter*.

All hands meeting – Part of the ritual for an *underwritten public offering* is the all hands meeting. These gatherings include an initial planning meeting (the "kickoff meeting") and at least two sessions for reviewing drafts of the *registration statement*. They include two or more representatives each from the company, the company's general counsel and its securities lawyers, the *managing underwriter*, the law firm representing the *underwriters*, and the *auditors*. The kickoff meeting may have people from the *financial printer*, *transfer agent*, and *registrar*. The meetings go on for at least a full day, often for two or three. The kickoff meeting is often consumed with a power struggle among representatives of the *investment bankers*, the company, and their respective counsel to settle who will be the "quarterback" for the preparation process. Some drafting sessions will last through the night to meet a deadline set by the *time and responsibility schedule*.

All-or-none offering – Each *public offering* will have a total number of *shares* to be sold. Sometimes, in a *direct public offering* or a *best efforts underwriting*, a condition of the offering will be that all shares offered must be sold or the offering is cancelled and none of the shares will be sold.

Allotment – In an *underwritten public offering*, each *securities firm* in the *underwriting syndicate* is allocated an allotment of *shares* to sell. As a practical matter there is very little relationship between the allotment and actual sales. Technically, the *agreement among underwriters* could force each member of the *underwriting syndicate* to take its allotment.

Amex shares – *Exchange traded* shares that are listed on the American Stock Exchange.

Angel investors – Also known as *informal investors*, these are people who invest money in the business at its start-up, or "seed capital" stage, before other sources of *capital* would be available. They are usually relatives or friends of the entrepreneur, or individuals with the wealth and experience to take significant risks for possible long-term rewards. Angel investors and entrepreneurs often get together through acquaintances or *finders*. The transaction is usually negotiated as a *private placement*. According to a survey made for the Small Business Administration, angel investors were the largest source of external *equity* capital for small businesses in the United States, at about $30 billion a year.

Annual report – Financial statements and a *management's discussion and analysis* of the company's operations and condition. For companies with *registered shares* under the federal *Securities Exchange Act of 1934*, an annual report must be filed with the *SEC*, following Form 10-K. Most states require corporations to send annual reports to their *shareowners*. These usually require audited financial statements, but their form and content is left to management's preference.

Arbitrage – Strictly speaking, arbitrage is the simultaneous buying and selling of the same thing in different markets without risk, in order to make a profit from the difference in price quotations between the markets. Recent practice has included "risk arbitrage," where the buying and selling are not simultaneous and there is some risk that the price difference will turn unprofitable. (A recent example has been buying *shares* in the *stock market*, expecting a *takeover* offer at a higher price.) When an *underwritten public offering* is expected for a company that already has shares in the *trading market*, the arbitrageurs will sometimes sell the shares short, that is, place sell orders for shares they do not yet own. This drives the market price down. As the *effective date* approaches, the lower market price causes the *underwriters* to negotiate for a reduced *offering price*. The arbitrageurs then buy shares in the *underwriting* to cover their short sales. Where there is no existing market, these short sales may occur in a *when-as-and-if-issued-market*. In a *direct public offering*, the offering price will have been set before any public filing or announcement. As a result, the effect of selling pressure in the trading market would be to cause a postponement of the offering. The company can also remove the incentive for arbitrage by setting a maximum on the number of shares anyone may purchase in the offering.

Asked price – *Shares* traded in the *over-the-counter* market will have prices quoted by their *market makers*, either on *NASDAQ* or in the *Pink Sheets*. The quotations are for the *bid price* (what the market maker will pay to buy at least 100 shares), or the asked price (what it will take to sell shares). For *listed shares*, bid and asked quotations are channeled through a *specialist*, a *dealer* who does business at a post on the *stock exchange* trading floor.

Auditors – A firm of certified public accountants, independent of the company, that reviews the company's financial statements for the purpose of issuing an opinion on their fairness. Most *public offerings* of *securities* require audited financials.

Backdooring – In some *underwritten initial public offerings*, speculators will commit to buy *shares* at the *offering price*, then immediately sell the same shares back through another *broker*. If it is a *hot new issue*, the price will have jumped up in the *aftermarket*, so the speculator makes a fast profit as a *flipper* of the shares. If the market reception has been cool, the speculator's shares will likely be sold "through the back door" to the *underwriting syndicate*, which has committed to buy shares for stabilization of the aftermarket price.

Backing away – When a *market maker* refuses to honor its *asked price* or *bid price* on an *over-the-counter share*. This is in violation of *NASD* and *SEC* rules.

Bad boys – Past offenders under securities fraud laws. When the *SEC* has authorized exemptions from full *registration statements*, such as *Regulation A* and *SCOR*, it prevents their use by a corporation affiliated with persons who have, within the previous five years, been convicted of *securities fraud* or who are subject to any enforcement order by a securities regulator. Filings under the securities laws require disclosure of bad boy affiliations.

Bedbug letter – A major part of any *public offering* of *securities* is compliance with federal and state securities laws. Usually, this requires filing a *registration statement* with the *SEC* and receiving a letter of comment (*deficiency letter*). When the regulatory reviewers consider the company or its registration statement to have problems that cannot be fixed by recommended changes, they suggest that the registration statement be withdrawn. This bad news is called a bedbug letter.

Best efforts underwriting – When a *securities firm* agrees to use its "best efforts" to sell *shares* as an agent for the company. It is not technically an *underwriting* since that term means buying all the shares offered and reselling them to investors (see *firm commitment underwriting*). As a practical matter, most *underwritten initial public offerings* have become like best efforts. They are called *all-or-none offerings*, since the *underwriter* is not legally bound to buy the shares until it has collected *indications of interest* for the entire offering (as well as an additional margin of shares to cover sales to investors who *renege* after they receive their *confirmation*). Most best efforts agency agreements will have a *minimum* as well as a *maximum* number of shares that must be sold within the offering period. If the minimum is not met, the offering is cancelled and all money collected from investors is returned.

Beta – A measure of a company's share price volatility—how wide the ups and downs of its trading price will be compared to the market generally. *Stock market averages*, like the Standard & Poor's 500, will be assigned the number 1.00 to reflect how much it would move on news about earnings, *dividends*, new products, etc. *Shares* of a very stable, mature company might move even less on that news, have a beta of, for instance, 0.74. On the other hand, an *emerging growth company*, especially in a competitive new technology or market, could have a beta of 2.00 or more.

Bid price – The price at which the bidder will buy a specified number of shares (see *asked price*).

Big Board Stocks – *Exchange traded shares* which are listed on the *New York Stock Exchange*.

Big Six – The largest international independent public accounting and consulting firms. Recent consolidations have reduced the "Big Eight" to these six: Arthur Andersen, Coopers & Lybrand, Deloitte & Touche, Ernst & Young, KMPG Peat Marwick, and Price Waterhouse.

Blind pool – Also known as "blank check" *public offerings*. These offerings are made without any specific business described for use of the offering *proceeds*.

Blue Sky laws – Nearly every state has its own securities regulators with whom a filing must be made for any *public offering* of *securities* to its residents. The governing laws were enacted to stop offerings that had no more substance behind them than "the blue sky." There are great differences among the states in their blue sky requirements—both in the standards they impose and the detail work necessary to *qualify* an offering. Many are so-called *merit states*, where the regulatory staff actually judges the quality of the company and the terms of its share offering. The standard for most merit states is that the proposed investment be *fair, just and equitable* to the local citizens. Only limited coordination exists among the states (through *NASAA*) and the *SEC*, so that companies will have to consider blue sky costs and delays when designing their marketing program. The SEC has allowed offerings up to $1 million to occur without registration; several states now permit them to have simplified blue sky qualification under the *SCOR* or *ULOR* program.

Board of directors – The governing body of a corporation, which sets policy and appoints major officers. *Directors* are elected by the *shareowners*.

Bonds – Debt *securities* generally for borrowings due to be repaid several years after they are issued. Bonds are legal instruments to evidence borrowed money. They are generally marketable securities and many are listed on *stock exchanges*. Corporate bonds are often subject to an *indenture*. There is no standardization among bonds; investors need to study the bond terms, as well as the credit and prospects of the corporate *issuer*. Bonds of large corporations are usually rated by Moody's or Standard & Poor's.

Book value – The amount of a corporation's *shareowners' equity*. Also called *net worth*. Literally, the company's value according to its own accounting records. In many businesses, accounting methods and fluctuations in market value make the book value of academic interest only.

Bought deal – When an *investment banker* or other *financial intermediary* has arranged for the purchase of an issue of *securities*, before offering to buy them from the *issuer*. This has become a frequent way for large corporations to sell securities, particularly debt. They can use a *shelf offering*, so that the issue is legally ready for immediate *public offering*, and then wait to be approached with a bought deal.

Bracket underwriters – *Securities firms* with the ability to be *managing underwriters* are arranged by tacit understanding into brackets. This explains the pyramid of alphabetical listings in the *tombstone ad* announcing a *public offering*. The rankings are based upon the number and stature of their corporate clients, their ability to originate new financial products, their coverage of *institutional investor* customers, and the number of their *registered representatives*. From four to seven firms at any one time seem to be at the top—the "bulge" or "special" bracket. Next is the "major" bracket, composed of most other large Wall Street firms. There was, at a point, a large "submajor" bracket of medium-sized Wall Street brokerages dealing primarily with individuals; these are now gone. A "mezzanine" bracket remains, consisting of Wall Street specialty houses and a few active underwriters in other cities. In the bottom bracket are the "regionals," that is, firms with offices only in one section of the country (with a small presence in New York).

Breaking the syndicate – During a period after the *effective date, underwriters* can conduct stabilization activities. These usually involve placing buy orders at the *offering price* and accepting any offers to sell back *shares* purchased in the *underwriting*. The *agreement among underwriters* provides the authority for these transactions and spreads their cost among *underwriting syndicate* members. That authority terminates 30 days after the effective date unless the *managing underwriter* decides to shorten or extend it, usually by breaking the syndicate before the 30 days is over and letting the shares seek their market price in the *aftermarket*.

Broker – Defined in the securities laws as a person in the business of buying and selling *securities* for the accounts of others. In everyday usage, "broker" or "stockbroker" refers to an individual who talks with investors about their investments and causes their buy or sell orders to be executed. This may be a *registered representative* of a *securities firm*, an independent *broker-dealer*, or a *financial planner*.

Broker-assisted – *Direct public offerings* can be successful without using any commissioned sales people. However, the size of the offering, its timing, or other factors may suggest using licensed *brokers* to sell part of the offering. They can be allocated a portion of the *shares* to sell on a *best efforts* basis to their own customers or by *cold calling* to *prospects* they generate.

Or, the company can deliver the names and telephone numbers of people who have requested a *prospectus* to selected brokers and pay a negotiated commission rate for the *conversion* into sales.

Broker-dealer – Individuals who have passed an examination and have met other standards can be licensed as a broker-dealer principal. This gives them and their corporate employer the right to engage in the business of buying and selling *securities*, both for the accounts of others (a *broker*) and for their own account (a *dealer*).

Brokerage firm – The business organization which operates under a *broker-dealer* license, more often and accurately called a *securities firm*. Before the 1960s they were nearly all partnerships. Now they operate primarily as corporations, either publicly owned or as the subsidiary of a large insurance company or conglomerate.

Bulletin Board Stock – *Over-the-counter shares* for which *bid price* and *asked price* information is available on-line through the *OTC Bulletin Board*, operated by the *NASD*.

Caller ID service – Using a telephone company central office switch and an inexpensive computer system, a customer's file can be automatically displayed on a monitor as the customer is calling in (or as an outbound call is being placed). Where available, this service can improve *conversions*, particularly from inbound *telemarketing*. The monitor can display the caller's name, address, dates of the *response* and *fulfillment*, caller's priority for the marketing program, and all *demographic* information accumulated.

Capital – Also known as capitalization. The amount of long-term money available to the company. The total of *shareowner* investment, earnings retained in the business, and borrowings which will not come due for more than a year. By the mechanics of double entry bookkeeping, capital is equal to assets minus short-term debt (due within a year). Equity capital or *equity* is that part of the company's capital that comes from shareowner investment and retained earnings. It is more often called *net worth* or *shareowner's equity*.

Capital formation – The process of adding to a company's *capital*. It usually refers to issuing equity or debt *securities*.

Certain transactions – When money or property has passed between the company and one of its *insiders*, it may require explanation in the *prospectus*. The name certain transactions comes from the instructions accompanying the *SEC* forms for registering a *public offering*. For example, when an entrepreneur hopes to take a company public, it is wise to avoid any of the situations that would need description in the certain transactions section. They may make it difficult to *qualify* the offering under the *blue sky laws* of a *merit state*. Descriptions of certain transactions tend to be lengthy and complicated, causing *prospects* to reject the offering based on their "smell test."

Cheap stock – When *insiders* have invested in the company within three years before the *public offering*, the amount they paid will be compared with the *offering price* to the public. A big difference raises the cheap shares issue, which must be dealt with satisfactorily for the public offering to be cleared through *SEC* and state *blue sky laws*. A *NASAA* Statement of Policy defines "cheap stock" and provides for their escrow as a condition to *qualify* the public offering in some states. While in escrow the shares cannot be traded. Release from escrow is typically conditioned upon meeting a three-year earnings-per-share test equal to 5 percent of the public offering price, a three-month period of trading at 175 percent of the offering price or six to nine years after the offering (see *promotional shares*).

Closing – In an *underwriting*, the company delivers share certificates and the *underwriters* pay for the *shares* they have sold, less their commissions and expenses. The closing date is generally a week after the *effective date* of the *underwriting*. In a *direct public offering*, there will be a date when the offering closes and no more orders are accepted. An allocation is then made when more shares have been ordered than were offered, and certificates are mailed to the new *shareowners*.

Cold calling – When a *broker* or agent makes telephone solicitations to strangers, usually from a list of *prospects*. Securities laws require a prospectus to be delivered before *shares* can be sold, so cold calling can only be for gathering *indications of interest* in the shares.

Cold comfort – Sometimes called "negative comfort." A representation made by someone independent of the company, to the effect that although they have not checked everything, what they did check revealed nothing wrong. The company's *auditors* are required to give the *underwriters* a "cold comfort letter" just before the *underwriting agreement* is signed. It lists several pages of "special procedures" the auditors have performed. The letter explains that this was not an audit and, finally, gives the cold comfort that "nothing came to our attention that caused us to believe that" there are any misleading errors or omissions in the material reviewed. Getting this letter is part of the underwriters' *due diligence* defense against claims by investors who lose money on their investment.

Common shares – Also known as common *stock*. These are the basic units of ownership in a corporation. Their voting rights elect the *board of directors*, which sets policy and hires and fires management. When a corporation is sold or liquidated, whatever is left, after paying off creditors and any senior *securities*, belongs to the owners of common shares. Some corporations have more than one class of common shares, usually as a way to keep voting control in the founders' family.

Confirmation – *Shares* are sold in an *underwriting* when brokers telephone their customers and *prospects*. Since this takes place a week or so before the *effective date*, there is no final prospectus available. Securities laws require delivery of a prospectus before a "sale." That means when an investor agrees to buy, it is called an *indication of interest* or "circling a number of shares." Then, on the effective date, the prospectus is mailed to the investor along with a confirmation showing the company's name, number of shares, and amount due in payment. The investor either pays on the *settlement date* or *reneges* on the sale.

Control person – Securities laws place potential liability for investor losses onto persons who "control" the company. They include executive officers, *directors*, and the owners of more than five percent of the company's *shares*. Control persons are *insiders* subject to special rules about trading in the company's shares and passing on information about the company that would be important to a decision about buying or selling its shares.

Conversion – A *direct public offering* follows the steps of *direct marketing*: (1) the *proposition* (offer to provide a *prospectus*), (2) the *prospects'* response in requesting the prospectus, (3) *fulfillment* through delivery of the prospectus, and then (4) conversion of the prospects into *shareowners*.

Corporate cleanup – When a company is owned by an entrepreneur, it may be used to minimize taxes. Its structure may reflect negotiations with *angel investors* or *venture capitalists*. There can be a certain casualness about corporate proceedings. When presented to the public and the securities regulators, the business should be simple, tidy, and as independent as practicable. This transformation is called corporate cleanup and calls for some balance among the securities lawyer, marketing advisor, and management.

Corporate governance – Corporations are much like the British form of government with each *share* similar to one registered voter. Shares elect *directors*. The *board of directors* makes policy, appoints officers, and monitors their performance. The rights and responsibilities of *shareowners*, directors, and officers are determined by laws of the state from which the corporation has its charter.

CUSIP number – All certificates for *publicly traded shares* require an identification known as a CUSIP number. They are issued by the New York office of Standard & Poor's Corporation, (212)208-8331.

Customer Information File (CIF) – Nearly every business maintains some sort of information about its customers. With such computer peripherals as bar code scanning, information can be gathered about buying patterns. Through access to databanks (available from *list brokers*, credit card companies, credit bureaus, and government registrations), a CIF can provide extensive statistics and *demographics* about customers.

Because of their preexisting relationship, customers are usually *prospects* for a company's *shares* in a *direct public offering*.

Database enhancement – Adding externally compiled information to the company's *customer information file*. There are suppliers who compile and sell statistics and *demographics* on nearly every adult American. Their data can be added for each name in the customer information file.

Database management – Information management is a major part of any *direct public offering*. Information must be gathered, checked, and communicated in order for people to make an investment decision. In addition, information about the people to whom the *shares* will be offered must also be acquired and used. Database management includes names, addresses, telephone numbers, and other useful facts about selected individuals and markets. Some of this data may be purchased, some developed from responses to advertising, and some built from the company's own records as well as the knowledge of its employees and advisors. Database management handles the arranging of that data into categories reflecting the probabilities of investment in certain amounts. It enables the sorting and displaying of data in the most useful form for selecting *media*, preparing messages, doing *telemarketing*, and tracking results.

Dealer – Securities laws define a dealer as one who buys and sells *securities* for the dealer's own account. This contrasts with a *broker* who buys and sells as the agent for others. In the 1930s, Congress had almost decreed that each *securities firm* could be either a broker or a dealer, but not both. The reason was to separate giving advice to customers from also being an investor. Instead, the standard license in the business is a "registered *broker-dealer*." *Underwriters* are dealers, since they technically buy the *shares* from the company and resell them to investors.

Deficiency letter – Often called a "letter of comment." When a *registration statement* has been filed with the SEC or a state securities administrator, it will generate a list of comments from the staff assigned to its review. There are usually separate ones for the text and the financial statements. The process generally involves comparing the filing with the most recent ones the agency has cleared for similar businesses. Since the law does not call upon the SEC to pass upon the adequacy of a registration statement, the comments are only "suggestions." Failure to make changes or otherwise explain each matter may mean that the registration statement never becomes effective and the offering is cancelled. Sometimes the staff will send a *bedbug letter*, telling the company that its registration statement is considered so deficient that it cannot be fixed with an amendment.

Delaying amendment – When a *registration statement* is on file with the *SEC*, it would automatically reach an *effective date* and be usable to sell *securities*. To prevent this, securities lawyers routinely include a delaying amendment in the filing. They then request *acceleration* of the effective date to a selected time.

Demographics – The use of population statistics to classify *prospects* by particular characteristics. *Customer information files* often have little information beyond name, address, and telephone number. When lists are purchased, they are often subscribers to particular magazines, purchasers from designated catalogs, or contributors to selected fundraisers. At its most basic level, demographics is the selection of *target markets* by the ZIP code of their residence, which is some indication of household wealth. Much more demographic information can be added to these files and lists through *database enhancement*. Census data now encourages "geo-demographics," the correlation of location with the propensity to invest. So much information is available from credit bureaus and customer information files that the science has moved on to "psychographics," where a mix of data bits will suggest spending patterns and other characteristics useful in planning and executing a marketing program.

Dilution – Whenever new *shares* are issued, there is some financial effect upon the company's existing *shareowners*. This is usually measured by the increase or decrease in the amount of *shareowners' equity*, or *book value* per share. A decrease in book value per share occurs when the *proceeds* from each new share sold are less than the company's shareowners' equity, which is then divided by the number of shares existing before the sale. (For instance, proceeds from a sale of new shares at $8.00 each would mean dilution for the owners of 10,000 existing shares of a company with a shareowners' equity of $100,000). When the proceeds of new shares exceed the book value of existing shares, the offering is considered "antidilutive." Dilution may also refer to the expected earnings or cash flow to come from the use of money received in the offering of new shares. If those earnings are not at least equal to current earnings per share before the sale, then there is dilution of earnings to the existing shareowners.

Direct mail – One of the *media* used in *direct marketing*. A marketing *proposition* is sent by mail to a list of *prospects* who may communicate their *response* by mail, telephone, facsimile, or other media.

Direct marketing – Some of its practitioners prefer "direct response marketing," and all of them abhor the label *direct mail* or worse, "junk mail." The concept is the same as *disintermediation* in the financial services industry—eliminating the businesses in the middle, dealing directly with the customer. In the language of direct marketing, the process for a *direct public offering* involves:

> The *proposition*: "We'll give you a *prospectus*."
> The *response*: "OK, I'd like to see it."
> The *fulfillment*: "Here is the *prospectus*."
> The *conversion*: "This is my order for *shares*."

Direct marketing has developed several generations beyond the first solicitations by mail to everyone in selected neighborhoods. Now it incorporates *demographics, database management, list brokers*, fulfillment houses, and telemarketing specialists. *Media* used still includes direct mail, but the proposition may also come through radio or television with responses communicated to an 800 telemarketing system. Fulfillment may be effected with a videotape or floppy disk containing the prospectus and *selling materials*. The conversion could be handled by facsimile transmission of an order form, with telephone or computer transfer of funds. Beginning in 1995, Direct Public Offerings have been done on the Internet. The proposition, response and fulfillment have all been accomplished through the Company's website. The conversions have thus far still been completed through the mail.

Direct public offering or DPO – *Shares* are sold by the company to investors through *direct marketing*. This contrasts with an *underwritten public offering* sold by *registered representatives* who work for *securities firms* in an *underwriting syndicate*.

Directed sales – In an *underwritten public offering*, a *money manager* for *institutional investors* will often ask the *managing underwriter* to take an order for *shares* and give credit for the sale to a particular *securities firm*. The designated firm will then be paid the 60 percent *selling concession* portion of the *underwriting spread*. This is a way for money managers to pay securities firms for research or other services provided "free" under socalled *soft dollar deals*.

Directors – Representatives elected by the *shareowners* to the *board of directors* who set policy and appoint executives.

Disintermediation – When money is transferred directly between the user and the provider without passing through a *financial intermediary*. Part of the general trend toward "cutting out the middleman." An example has been the commercial paper market, where large corporations lend and borrow among themselves, rather than through bank deposits and bank loans. A *direct public offering* is a form of disintermediation because there is no *underwriter*.

Disk Marketing – Delivering the *direct marketing fulfillment* on a floppy disk or CD-ROM for computer access by the *prospect*. Providing the *prospectus* and *selling materials* on a disk allows the prospects to use their own programs to compare, project, and analyze the information. The *SEC's* October 1995 release on electronic delivery is a big boost toward this method. However, direct delivery to the *prospect's* computer through the Internet is likely to be the dominant electronic media.

Dividends – Payments of amounts per *share* by a corporation to its *shareowners*. Dividends represent a proportion of the corporation's earnings (except for liquidating dividends and other unusual cases). They are usually paid in cash, but may be newly-issued additional shares. Sometimes, the shares of a subsidiary or other corporate assets are distributed to shareowners as a dividend.

Dog and pony show – The *road show* arranged by *underwriters* for *money managers* who are *prospects* for an *underwritten public offering*.

Due diligence – Securities laws allow disappointed investors to recover their losses in court from persons related to the company or involved in a *public offering* of its *shares*. One of the ways to avoid that liability is known as the due diligence defense. It requires that the defendant make a reasonable investigation into the truth and completeness of the *registration statement*.

EDGAR – The *SEC's* Electronic Data Gathering, Analysis and Retrieval system for companies to file documents by computer *media*. This is part of what had been a very slow progress into the electronic age. By May 1996, the pilot project had become fully operational; individual investors are now able to retrieve data in real time for use in their own analysis.

Effective date – This is the precise moment when the *registration statement* "becomes effective" with the *SEC* and state agencies. Only then can the *prospectus* be used in offering *shares* to the public. In an *underwriting*, timing of the effective date will have been requested by the lawyers to come at the point when the sales efforts are concluded by the *underwriters' brokers*. If those efforts have been successful and the company agrees to the underwriters' final price, the *underwriting agreement* will be signed a few hours before the effective date. Then, *confirmations* of the sale are sent to investors with a copy of the prospectus. In a *direct public offering*, the sales program really begins on the effective date. The final prospectus is sent to those who have requested it by responding to ads or *public relations* efforts. An order form accompanies the prospectus, often as a detachable page.

Emerging growth company – The definition of *growth company* is a business beyond the start-up phase but not yet mature. The term emerging growth company is used to describe a business that is just coming out of start-up and entering the growth company category. Most candidates for an *initial public offering* are emerging growth companies.

Emerging growth stock – A popular term to describe *shares* of companies large enough to have a *trading market*, but still in the early stages of an expected period of growth. They usually have *price/earnings ratios* higher than market averages because investors are paying for the discounted present value of expected future earnings and cash flow. These expectations often change as events unfold, causing the stock price to fluctuate more than market averages (see *Beta*).

Endorsement – A marketing message that uses someone outside the company to express approval of the product or service being sold. A "testimonial" is usually a favorable quotation from an individual who is either famous or someone with whom the *prospects* are expected to identify. Other endorsements are more subtle. Advertising in particular *media* may connote an endorsement, especially if other advertisers are well-known. A powerful endorsement for a *direct public offering* can come from a *sponsor*, especially one making a *standby commitment*—a promise to buy any *shares* not purchased by *prospects*.

Equity – In finance and accounting, this term means the owner's investment in the business. It is used interchangeably with *shareowners' equity* or *net worth*. It includes amounts the owners have invested, plus or minus the earnings or losses that have been accumulated from operating the business.

ERISA – The Employee Retirement Income Security Act of 1974. It cast into stone the "herd instinct" of *money managers* who invest for pension funds by redefining the common-law "prudent investor" rule. Congress changed the fiduciary duty from investing other people's money as the manager would invest its own, to investing the same way as other *institutional investors*. This standard gets tested every quarter when money managers file public reports. One effect has been to turn the *stock market* and *securities firms* into a short-term performance race. This has largely discouraged *individual investors* from buying or holding *shares*. *Direct public offerings* can operate outside the securities markets dominated by ERISA investors.

ESOPs – Employee Stock Ownership Plans are trusts set up to own a company's *shares* for the benefit of its employees. The legal structure was a creation of the Internal Revenue Code sixty years ago and Congress has recently added several tax incentives for companies to form ESOPs. They have also been used to put large blocks of *publicly traded shares* into the hands of a trustee who will protect management from a *takeover*. In most cases employees cannot vote, sell, or receive *dividends* on the shares. Their interest in the trust is cashed out when they leave the company. Most ESOPs have been created with bank borrowings that must be repaid out of the company's cash flow.

Exchange Traded – Shares that have been listed for trading on one of the national securities exchanges registered with the *SEC*. Shares that are traded on an exchange may also be dually listed on another exchange or reported on *NASDAQ*.

Exempt securities – Federal and state securities laws read as if they applied to all *securities*. They then define certain kinds as being exempt securities, to which the registration, disclosure, and some antifraud provisions of the laws do not apply. These include securities of certain types of organizations like banks and government agencies.

Exempt transactions – Securities laws apply to every purchase and sale of *securities*, unless a specific exemption applies. Most *stock market* transactions are exempt, as are *private placements*. The SEC and the courts keep the interpretation of exempt transactions rather narrow. It can be dangerous to sell *shares* without a *no-action letter* or an opinion of counsel that the proposed transaction is within SEC *safe harbor rules* or other defined limits.

Fair, just and equitable – State *blue sky laws* often require their enforcement agency to pass upon the quality of the proposed offering of *shares* to residents. These are the *merit states* and a frequent standard is that the terms of the proposed offering, the investment itself, and the method of sale are all fair, just and equitable to the local residents. Where the offering is limited to *prospects* meeting certain standards (usually wealth and income), the agency may also pass upon the *suitability* of the investment for that class of investors.

Fair price provision – Language in the corporation's charter requiring that all *shareowners* receive the same price in any *takeover* of a controlling interest in the *shares*. This prevents the "two-tier" offer, where the first group of shares tendered in acceptance of the offer receives one price, while the remaining shares get a lower price in a later offer. The fair price provision may not be a particularly effective *shark repellent*, but it does protect shareowners who hold their shares in *street name* or are otherwise slow in responding to a takeover offer.

FASB – Pronounced "fazby," The Financial Accounting Standards Board—an attempt to bring uniformity and understanding to *generally accepted accounting principles (GAAP)*.

Filing date – The day on which a *registration statement* for a *public offering* is filed with the *SEC* (or a filing is made to qualify under state *blue sky laws*). It marks the end of the *prefiling period* and the beginning of the *waiting period*.

Financial intermediary – Someone between the company that wants money to use and the source of that money. Banks get money from depositors and lend it to businesses. *Securities firms* channel money from investors to corporations by selling *securities*. *Disintermediation* occurs when the money flows directly from the source to the company, as in a *direct public offering*.

Financial planner - An advisor to individuals in their financial affairs. Financial planners will review their clients' income, expenses, assets, debts, tax status, and future needs. Then they may recommend a budget and the purchase of financial products, like insurance or investments. There is little special government licensing or regulation of financial planners. Most of them are licensed to sell insurance or *securities* and earn their living from commissions on sales. Some are "fee-only" financial planners who accept no commissions and are compensated solely by an agreed fee or percentage of their client's assets or investment income. Sometimes this includes incentive arrangements for investment results above performance standards. Fee-only financial planners who have a large practice become subject to the federal Investment Advisers Act of 1940 and similar state laws. They are then usually called *investment advisors* or *money managers*.

Financial printers – Printing businesses that specialize in printing documents used in corporate or government finance, such as *prospectuses, annual reports*, and *takeover* offers. What distinguishes them from commercial printers is the intensive level of service—speed, accuracy, and responsiveness to nearly every whim of the company's securities lawyers. There is, of course, an extra price for this service. Word processing, especially computer telecommunications and desktop publishing, make it possible for cooperative lawyers, *auditors*, and other advisors to perform everything but large-scale print runs, eliminating the need for a financial printer. As a consequence of these changes and the general slowdown in corporate finance transactions, there are only three national survivors: Bowne, Donnelley, and Merrill.

Finder – A person who introduces a company to a source of financing—an investor or another *financial intermediary*, like a bank or *securities firm*. Finders typically get paid a fee upon *closing* of the financing.

Firm commitment underwriting – A *public offering* of *securities* by an *underwriting syndicate*, where the underwriting agreement contains a firm commitment by the *underwriters* to buy all of the shares. In practice, the underwriting agreement is not signed until *indications of interest* have been gathered by brokers for sales of more than all the shares. Large, older *securities firms* will usually participate only in firm commitment underwritings and not in *best efforts underwritings*.

First refusal rights – Some *IPO underwriters* will require that they be given the right to be the company's *investment banker* and receive a fee on future corporate finance transactions. They will have no obligation, but will have the first refusal rights to any proposed arrangement with a *securities firm*.

Flipper – There is potential for a "heads-I-win, tails-you-lose" game in *underwritten initial public offerings*. Members of the *underwriting syndicate* will have signed an *agreement among underwriters*, which binds them to buy back *shares* at the *offering price* for stabilization of the *aftermarket*, for a period as long as 60 days after the *effective date* of the *underwriting*. A flipper will buy the shares in the offering, then sell them back within the next few hours or days. On a *hot new issue*, the flipper realizes a quick profit by selling to someone who did not get shares in the underwriting and is willing to pay more for them in the aftermarket. If the price does not go up, the flipper can resell shares back to the underwriting syndicate (often by *backdooring* through another *broker*). The only cost to the flipper is the brokerage fee on the resale, since the *underwriters* have fixed a floor price. Even that can be profitable for the flipper because of a *soft dollar deal*, where part of the *underwriting spread* is credited to the flipper.

Float – This has two very different meanings. As a noun, the float is the number of a company's *shares* that are owned by the public, rather than owned by the company's officers, *directors*, and other *insiders*. A minimum float is required by a *stock exchange* for *listed shares* and by *NASDAQ* for its price quotation system. As a verb, to float shares means to sell a *new issue* through an *underwriting*. The British refer to an *underwritten public offering* as a "flotation."

Focus group – A *market research* tool. A dozen or so individuals, who are thought to be representative of the *target markets* for a *direct public offering*, are invited to meet as a group for two or three hours. Payment is made to them or a designated charity. Trained facilitators ask questions and monitor a discussion of the investment *proposition* and marketing methods. Company officers and advisors watch through a one-way mirror, and the session is usually recorded by audio or videotape.

Founders' shares – Before businesses *go public*, their *shares* are often owned by the entrepreneur and other *private placement* investors. The question will be raised of *dilution* and *promotional shares*. Depending upon the difference between the price paid for founders' shares and the *offering price* to the public, special disclosure in the prospectus may be required under *SEC* rules. If the private placement was made within three years before the proposed *public offering*, the *blue sky laws* in *merit states* may require an escrow of the *cheap shares*, or even prohibit the sale to their residents as unfair.

Free-riding – When shares of a *hot new issue* are purchased by *securities firms* for their own account (or for their employees and their immediate families), rather than for distribution to the public. *NASD* rules prohibit free-riding, but they do not prevent favored customers from getting all the shares available in the *underwriting* or upon exercise of the *green shoe* option.

Free writing period – From the *effective date* to the conclusion of the *public offering*. *Shares* may be offered only by a final *prospectus*, which is available only after the effective date of the *SEC* registration. Any other communication, in writing or on radio or video, may be considered a prospectus in violation of the securities laws. But, during the free writing period, other *selling materials* may be used if accompanied or preceded by the final prospectus. When preparing a *time and responsibility schedule*, the *fulfillment* (delivery of the prospectus to prospects) should come immediately after the effective date. It can then be accompanied with other selling materials and followed with additional marketing tools.

Frontrunning – The practice of some *broker-dealers* in placing an order in the *trading market* for *shares* for themselves, before they place an order for a customer. They allegedly do this when they expect the customer's order to cause a change in the price, so they can then sell their own shares at the resulting higher price (or buy shares at the lower price to cover *selling short*).

Fulfillment – In *direct marketing* terms this occurs when a *prospectus* is sent in fulfillment of a *prospect's response* to the company's *proposition*—that it would furnish a free prospectus.

Fully diluted – Per share earnings or other amounts in a company's financial statements after giving effect to the potential issuance of additional *shares*. This occurs when a company has issued warrants or *options* to purchase shares in the future, often as incentives to employees or investors, or as compensation to an *investment banker* or other *financial intermediary*.

GAAP–Pronounced "gap," an acronym for Generally Accepted Accounting Principles that must be observed in financial statements in order to get a clean opinion from the company's *auditors*—a necessity in virtually every *public offering*. Conforming to GAAP may be painful for an entrepreneur if the company's bookkeeping has principally served to save on taxes.

Glass-Steagall – The Banking Act of 1933, that separated commercial banks from *investment bankers* and prohibited commercial banks or their affiliates from *underwriting securities*. Because an underwriting is technically an investment in securities and a resale, the *underwriter* must have *capital* to cover a prescribed ratio to the amount of the underwriting. Taking banks out of the business severely limited the number of investment bankers which had sufficient capital to do underwritings. The Federal Reserve Board of Governors has been gradually relaxing the Glass-Steagall restrictions, most recently permitting certain banks to form holding company affiliates to act as underwriters of corporate debt and equity securities. In a *direct public offering*, because there is no underwriting, commercial banks are free to act as advisor. Their *broker-dealer* affiliates can also be agents in the *conversion* of *prospects* into *shareowners*.

Go public – When a company owned by no more than a few *shareowners* comes to have *publicly traded shares*. The usual method is through an *initial public offering*.

Go public by the back door – When a business comes to have *publicly traded shares* without an *initial public offering*. This can happen through a series of acquisitions of businesses, paying the former owners in new *shares* of the acquiring corporation. It may result from a string of *private placements* with a gradual widening of shareownership until a *trading market* develops. A third way for a business to go public by the back door is for *promoters* to organize or acquire a *shell corporation* that already has publicly traded shares, or does a *blind pool* offering. Then the shell acquires the operating business.

Golden parachute – An employment contract, requiring a significant amount of severance pay for an officer or director in the event of a hostile *takeover* of the company. Golden parachutes are often justified as assuring the *shareowners* that officers and *directors* will not block an otherwise favorable acquisition in order to save their jobs.

Green Shoe – In a *firm commitment underwriting*, the *underwriting syndicate* agrees to buy a fixed number of *shares* from the company. The selling efforts will have been concluded before the *underwriting agreement* is signed by *registered representatives* gathering telephone *indications of interest* from their customers and *prospects*. Some of these buyers will *renege* by refusing to accept and pay for the shares. Other buyers will be *flippers* who force the underwriting syndicate to buy back shares as part of their *aftermarket* price stabilization. To protect against this, underwriting syndicates take orders for considerably more shares than are included in the *underwriting* (similar to the overbooking of airline reservations in anticipation of cancellations and "no-shows"). But if more shares have to be delivered to buyers than are included in the underwriting agreement, the *underwriters* could be required to cover the shortage through buying shares in the aftermarket. This would likely drive the trading price up, causing losses to the underwriting syndicate. In an underwriting for the Green Shoe Manufacturing Company, underwriters first negotiated an option to cover these *overallotments* by buying more shares from the company (or its major *shareowners*) within 30 days after the *effective date*. The first Green Shoe options were for up to 10 percent of the shares underwritten. The maximum is now commonly 15 percent and the most frequent use of the Green Shoe is to reward the underwriters' favored clients by getting them *hot new issues* at the original *offering price*. (*NASD* rules against *free-riding* prevent underwriters from themselves investing in *hot new issues*.)

Growth company – This term is an attempt to classify businesses that are not yet "mature," but are beyond the "start-up" phase. Mature companies are in markets that are not expected to get much larger (like some public utilities), or have products that nearly everyone owns and will only replace when worn out (for example, refrigerators). They usually have a low risk of failure and a low potential for major growth. Start-ups are very high risk, and if they succeed, can produce rapid growth in size and share value.

Gun-jumping – Rules of the *SEC* and state *blue sky laws* limit the advertising and publicity that can appear before the *effective date* and the delivery of a prospectus to each of the offering's *prospects*. If these rules are violated through gun-jumping, the offering may have to be postponed for a "cooling-off period," or even cancelled. In the words of the SEC, gun-jumping is publicity or other communications that "may in fact contribute to conditioning the public mind or arousing public interest in the *issuer* or in the securities of an issuer in a manner which raises a serious question whether the publicity is not in fact part of the selling effort." SEC Rule 135 permits a very limited prefiling public announcement of a proposed offering.

Hot new issue – An *underwritten initial public offering* that trades in the immediate *aftermarket* at a price higher than the *offering price*. According to rules of the *NASD*, member firms and their employees may not trade in hot new issues.

IPO – An initial public offering, whether an *underwritten public offering* or a *direct public offering*.

Incubators – Start-up businesses are typically financed on a shoestring. They need cheap quarters and they need lots of experienced advice for "free." Incubators are usually sponsored by universities or community development organizations. They provide space for several beginning businesses, pool support services, and provide consultation all at a cost that is usually below market value. Several incubators are also tied in with groups of *informal investors*, from whom tenants may be able to raise capital.

Indenture – The contract among a company, investors, and a trustee, governing the issuance of corporate *bonds*. These are generally very long and must be filed with the SEC under the Trust Indenture Act of 1939.

Indications of interest – When *brokers* write orders for *shares* in an *initial public offering*. No sale of shares can occur until the effective date and delivery of a final *prospectus* to the customer. In practice, the prospectus in an *underwritten IPO* is first sent to the customer when it accompanies the *confirmation* of sale. The customer then has three days to pay for the shares at the *offering price*, or to *renege* and cancel the order.

Individual investors – People who are investing their own money directly. Included are IRAs and trusts for family members. Not included are people who channel their money through mutual funds, pension plans, or other *institutional investors*.

Influentials – People who influence the decisions of others. Members of the community to whom acquaintances turn for advice or a role model because of their position, reputation, or personality. A *direct public offering* program will try to reach these people first.

Infomercial – also known as "infocommercial." A commercial message presented like a feature story. Most advertisements are short and in a rather standardized format, whether the *media* is print or electronic. An infomercial is longer and packaged to resemble news, editorial copy, or programming. There will be some distinguishable mark, like the word "advertisement" in print or a voice-over in television: "This special announcement is brought to you by . . . "

Informal investors – Also known as *angel investors*. There is a period between the start-up of most businesses and their *initial public offering* when *capital* is needed to become established and profitable. These businesses will probably not be attractive to *venture capital firms*, most of which have become institutionalized and unwilling to take risks on little companies. As a result, various networks of informal investors have developed all over the country. They are often coordinated by *incubators*, accounting, firms or management consultants.

Initial Public Offering (IPO) – For a corporation, the initial public offering is like a coming-of-age rite. It signals that a company has joined the ranks of successful businesses. As a matter of practical finance, the first-time sale of *shares* to the public opens the door to large amounts of *capital* with no interest expense, no repayment, and no restrictive covenants on management. For the founders and early investors it places a market value on their investment and provides the *liquidity* for some cash return. In the past nearly every *IPO* was a *firm commitment underwriting* through an *underwriting syndicate*. Today, the developments in direct marketing make possible the *direct public offering (DPO)*.

Insider – A person in a position to control the corporation or to have access to nonpublic information, which, if publicly known, would likely affect the price of the *shares*. The legal definition varies with the particular legal duty involved. Insider trading is periodically the subject of prosecution and publicity.

Institutional investors – Pools of capital under the control of *money managers*. The largest institutional investors are pension funds, insurance companies, mutual funds, and endowments for schools and religious bodies. Nearly half the *shares* of America's largest corporations are owned by institutional investors. Because they buy and sell investments much more frequently than individual investors, over 70 percent of the trading in corporate shares is done for institutional investors. After years of poor performance, money managers of many pension plans have been replaced by index managers who invest in the same shares and proportions as the Standard & Poor's 500 or other market indexes. In recent years, most *underwritten IPOs* have been sold to institutional investors and individual speculators.

Interactive marketing – This occurs when the company and the *prospects* can communicate back and forth immediately, without the delay of going from a *proposition* in one type of *media* (newspaper or TV) to a *response* in another (telephone or mail) and on to a *fulfillment* and *conversion*. The oldest interactive marketing, as well as the most costly and time-consuming, is calling upon prospects in person or by telephone. Electronic means of interactive marketing include facsimile machines, computer modems, and *videotex*.

Internal memoranda – A brief writing, video, or audio tape used to tell *registered representatives* about the offering and give them selling points for their *telemarketing*. It is unlawful to show internal memoranda to *prospects*.

Intrastate exemption – Registration of a public offering with the SEC is not required if the shares are offered and sold only to residents of the same state in which the company is incorporated, has its headquarters, and does nearly all of its business. Most securities lawyers are nervous about recommending use of this exemption since the SEC or the courts may challenge it. If only one offeree or investor is not a resident, or if a buyer resells to a nonresident within the next nine months, the exemption is lost.

Investment advisor – Technically, a person or firm registered under the federal Investment Advisers Act of 1940 or similar state law. (The preferred modern spelling has become "advisor," rather than "adviser.") Under *ERISA*, investment advisors are really *money managers*, having been delegated the absolute decision-making authority to buy and sell investments, within some general guidelines. *Financial planners* may be registered investment advisors. Many are not, because they operate on too small a scale to require registration.

Investment banker – This is not a defined term under the securities laws, like *broker, dealer,* or *investment advisor*. It most often refers to the corporate finance department of a *securities firm* which handles *public offerings* and *private placements* of *securities*, as well as mergers, acquisitions, and other corporate finance transactions. Many securities firms call themselves investment bankers even when the only services they provide are as a broker for trading securities in the *secondary market*.

Investment company – These are generally mutual funds regulated under the federal Investment Company Act of 1940. They are *institutional investors* run by *money managers*. Some of them have a specific investment objective that includes the purchase of *emerging growth stock*, often through an *initial public offering*.

Investment letter – Legal documents used in a *private placement* of *securities* to avoid violating the laws requiring registration of a *public offering*. They state that the buyer is purchasing for investment purposes only and not with a view to the redistribution of the securities. The letter usually has the effect of a contract and may require that the securities be held for a particular period of time, that an opinion of counsel be obtained before any sale, or that the securities can only be transferred to a certain class of investors. *Shares* subject to an investment letter are known as *lettered stock*.

Issuer – *Shares* come from a corporate issuer as fractional ownership interests. Corporations may also be the issuers of debt *securities* and *options* or warrants. For each share or other security, there is an issuer and an investor.

Issuer-directed shares – In an *underwritten initial public offering*, every share must be sold through the *underwriters*. The entrepreneur and company management can request that *shares* be sold by the *underwriting syndicate* to persons who have some special relationship to the company, such as members of the board of *directors*. Some underwriters will not permit the practice and *NASD* rules allow only 10 percent of the shares to be issuer-directed. An *underwriting spread* must be paid on all shares, including any which are issuer-directed.

Junk bonds – Long-term corporate debt *securities* are generally issued as *bonds*. Before the 1970s, nearly all bonds sold in *public offerings* were rated as to their investment quality by Moody's or Standard & Poor's. When the term junk bonds was coined, it referred to bonds of "fallen angels," corporations which had qualified for a rating when the bonds were issued, but had lost their rating when the business fell on hard times. The term carried over to the use of *new issues* of high-yield, unrated bonds for *growth companies* and acquisitions. One reason for the use of new junk bonds was the deduction from corporate income taxes allowed for interest payments on bonds, but not for *dividends* on *shares*. Another was the preference of *institutional investors* for *liquidity*. The *trading market* for shares of growth companies was often too thin to allow sales of large amounts without depressing the price. Junk bonds might be no more marketable, but they substituted an obligation to repay the investment in a few years and a high cash return until repayment. Since most institutional investors are tax-exempt, all of the interest received counted toward the return on investment. Junk bonds allowed *money managers* to show better short-term results than their peers, who invested in stocks or rated bonds. During the 1980s, junk bonds met the *capital* needs for *emerging growth companies* that have traditionally used *equity* to finance rapid growth.

Know-your-customer rule – *Securities firms* and *brokers* are subject to certain standards of conduct under securities laws, *self-regulatory organization rules*, and court decisions. One such standard is they should know about their customers' financial condition and needs before recommending a transaction. The broker can then determine the *suitability* of the proposed transaction for the customer.

Lead underwriter – When there are multiple *managing underwriters*, one of them takes the lead and "runs the books" for the *underwriting syndicate*. The lead underwriter's name will appear on the left side of the first line in the listing of underwriting syndicate members for the *tombstone ad*.

Legal opinion – For an *initial public offering*, securities laws require an opinion of the company's lawyers for the benefit of investors in the *shares*. These are in standardized form and provide the lawyers' opinion that the shares have been legally issued.

Letter of intent – When a corporation and a *managing underwriter* reach an understanding about doing an *initial public offering*, they sign a letter of intent. It describes the proposed *offering price*, number of *shares*, and *effective date*. An *underwriting spread* will be included, as well as an amount of *underwriters' warrants*. However, nothing in the letter of intent is legally binding, except a usual provision for the corporation to pay expenses if it calls off the deal.

Letter stock – *Shares* acquired in a *private placement* where the investor has signed an *investment letter*. Because of the restrictions created on transfer of ownership, letter stock can be sold only to certain persons. As a result, the sales price will often be at a discount of 20 percent to 50 percent of a *trading market* price.

Leverage – The ratio of borrowed money to *equity capital* in a business reflects its leverage. The concept is that a base of equity money can be enhanced in its power by debt capital. The amount of leverage considered prudent varies significantly by industry. Financial institutions, like banks, may be considered very sound if they have $12 of debt for every $1 of equity. Manufacturing businesses often have only $1 of debt for every $2 of equity. In 1983, equity was over 65 percent of the total capital of U.S. corporations. By 1989, the equity portion had dropped to about 52 percent. To get back to the historic average of 57.7 percent equity, American corporations would have to sell over $300 billion in shares. This process is referred to as "deleveraging."

Liquidity – How quickly an asset can be converted into freely available cash. For a company, it is the proportion of its assets consisting of money in the bank, accounts receivable, salable inventory, and the like. For an investor, it means how long it would take to sell and collect cash without a resulting drop in market value.

List broker – Lists of *prospects* are used for *direct mail* and *telemarketing*. They may come from magazine subscription or credit card records. Some are compiled from census data, others from credit reporting agencies or government registration files. A good list broker will help develop a profile of the company's *prospects*, then suggest lists that will *merge and purge* to most closely match that profile.

List maintenance – Companies will develop their own lists of *prospects* for *direct public offerings* from *customer information files*, purchased lists, and other sources. Once these lists have been through a *merge and purge* program, they need to be kept current and secure through list maintenance procedures. Like *database enhancement*, list maintenance is part of a company's *database management*.

Listed shares – *Shares* admitted for trading on a *stock exchange*. One *securities firm* will be appointed by the exchange to be the *specialist* in a company's shares and will process all bid and asked offers. (As the exchanges gradually automate, some orders will be matched electronically.)

Management's Discussion and Analysis (MD&A) – In a *public offering* the securities laws generally require this section in the *prospectus*. *Annual reports* will also have an MD&A. It requires management to comment on changes in financial conditions and results for comparative recent periods, as well as such issues as *liquidity*, and the effect of laws for environmental protection.

Managing underwriter – The *securities firm* that originates the proposed *public offering* and is responsible for both client relations and putting together the *underwriting syndicate*. As compensation, the managing underwriter receives 20 percent of the *underwriting spread*, as well as what it earns by participating in the underwriting syndicate and having its *brokers* sell *shares*. There are often multiple managing underwriters, in which case one will be the lead manager and "run the books" for the syndicate.

Market capitalization – The number of *shares* a company has issued, multiplied by its market price per share.

Market maker – A *securities firm* which quotes *bid prices* and *asked prices* for particular *shares* in the *over-the-counter* market. A market maker must generally be willing to buy at least 100 shares at its quoted bid price and sell at least 100 shares at its quoted asked price.

Market out also known as "catastrophe out" – Conditions in an *underwriting agreement* giving the *underwriters* the right not to go through with an *underwritten public offering*. They are generally limited to such events as a suspension of the securities *trading markets*, a general banking moratorium, or a "material change in general economic, political, or financial condition." As a practical matter, the underwriting agreement is not signed until hours before the *effective date* and orders for more than all the *shares* have been taken. As a result, the market out conditions only apply to events during the six days or so before the *closing*.

Market research – This is the work done to determine whether a *direct public offering* is feasible, to select the best markets, and to suggest the most effective message and *media*. It is akin to "alpha testing" a new product before the *test marketing* or "beta testing" stage. Tools of market research include studying the case histories of other companies, *demographics*, interviews, questionnaires, and *focus groups*.

Market segmentation – This is an effort to make marketing more cost-effective. In mass marketing, a message is delivered through a medium that includes far more people than those who are likely *prospects* for the product or service being offered. Most print and electronic *media* are priced on the basis of the number of people they reach without regard to their *demographic* or other characteristics. Screening for such factors as income level and age will often suggest media which are directed to the logical prospects.

Market timing – *Shares* of each corporation have their individual price trends depending upon investors' estimates of the corporation's future profitability and growth. Their prices are also likely to fluctuate with the overall market for corporate shares or the market for their industry. Market timing is the effort to buy when the market is at a low point of a cycle and sell when it is at its high point. *Money managers* who practice market timing have generally had a worse record than those who use a random selection method.

Media – The means by which a message is delivered. Popular *direct public offering* media include *direct mail*, the Internet, radio, newspapers, magazines, and seminars.

Merge and purge – A *database management* tool. Computer programs will combine two or more lists of *prospects*, reorder them and eliminate duplications. The process is called merge and purge.

Merit state – A state with *blue sky laws* requiring that an offering of *securities* must meet a quality standard, such as *fair, just and equitable*.

Minimum/maximum offering – In a *best efforts underwriting* or a *direct public offering*, there may be a minimum and a maximum number of *shares* offered for sale. If orders are received for less than the minimum during the offering period, then the offering is cancelled and any money received is returned (funds are usually required to be deposited in escrow). If offers are received for more than the maximum, then shares may be prorated among investors.

Money manager or investment advisor – For *individual investors*, a *financial planner* may be considered their money manager. If they have given discretionary authority to their financial planner or *broker*, then decisions about when and how much to buy, sell, and even borrow, can be made by them without any consultation. Most institutions give this discretionary authority to their *investment advisors* who are usually referred to as money managers.

Narrowcasting – In contrast to broadcasting, this is use of *media* that primarily reaches only certain *target markets*. It most often refers to the use of cable TV. Through *market segmentation*, a *proposition* can be communicated through a cable channel that *market research* shows is watched by a significant number of the likely *prospects* for a *direct public offering*.

NAqcess – The small order handling system installed by the *NASDAQ* to meet objections that persons making relatively small transactions in *over-the-counter shares* were not being treated as fairly in the pricing as those making large transactions.

NASAA (North American Securities Administrators Association).- State agencies administering *blue sky laws* belong to *NASAA*, where efforts are made to coordinate enforcement against fraud and to achieve some uniformity in the rules governing the sale of *securities*.

NASD (National Association of Securities Dealers) – All securities firms included in underwriting syndicates belong to the NASD, which is a *self-regulatory organization*. The *SEC* recognizes regulation by the NASD as a substitute for what the government would otherwise have to police. Tests for *registered representatives*, *broker-dealer* principals, and other securities professionals are administered by the NASD.

NASDAQ (National Association of Securities Dealers' Automated Quotation System) – This is an electronic display system but not a *stock exchange*. It allows subscribers to see the *bid prices* and *asked prices* quoted by each *market maker* for a company's *shares*, as well as certain trading history. Any orders are then placed by a separate communication.

National Market System – The *NASDAQ* reporting system for trading in *over-the-counter shares* that meet similar numerical size standards to *Tier 1* or *Amex shares*.

National Quotation Bureau, Inc. – Now owned by the NASD and formerly a subsidiary of Commerce Clearing House Inc., it has been the publisher since 1913 of the *Pink Sheets*, the daily printed lists of 10,000 to 12,000 *over-the-counter* market *shares* and the most recent bid and asked quotations announced by their *market makers*. Before *NASDAQ* and the *OTC Bulletin Board*, this was the only source of information about *shares* which are not listed for trading on a *stock exchange*.

Net worth – The *shareowners' equity* in a corporation. Through double entry bookkeeping, it equals assets less liabilities. It results primarily from money invested by *shareowners* and the earnings (or losses) not paid out in *dividends*.

New issue – Any security being sold by the company issuing it. A *primary market* transaction rather than a sale by an investor-owner into the *secondary market*.

New York Stock Exchange – The largest *stock exchange*, with numerical size standards for listing only the largest *publicly traded shares*.

Niche marketing – Directing a marketing program at a particular group of *prospects* who fit defined characteristics and are seen as neglected by competitors. A niche is selected and described through m*arket segmentation*. It is a step beyond selecting *target markets*, because the search is for prospects that are in an overlooked niche.

No-action letter – This is a letter from the staff of the *SEC* saying that it will not recommend enforcement action. A no-action letter is issued in response to a request by lawyers for the company, prepared because they are uncertain whether some proposed steps are in violation of the securities laws. The no-action letter is limited to the facts presented in the letter request. However, the SEC releases most no-action letters for publication and lawyers often use them to support their own opinion to clients. As a matter of published policy, the SEC will not issue no-action letters on certain types of questions.

Offering circular – The information or disclosure document by which an offer of *securities* is made to *prospects*. It is the same type of document as a *prospectus*—the different name results from the term used in the applicable securities laws. For instance, a security registered under the federal *Securities Act of 1933* would be offered by a prospectus, while one filed under the *Regulation A* exemption from that act would use an offering circular.

Offering expenses – Costs incurred by the company for the purpose of the *public offering*. Major offering expenses include legal and accounting fees. Internal costs, such as an allocation of compensation and overhead for employees' time, are generally not shown in the filings under the securities laws. For an *underwritten public offering*, more than half the total offering expenses will be the *underwriting spread*, which may be subject to a maximum under *NASD* rules. The *SEC* requires disclosure of the underwriting spread and total offering expenses in the *prospectus*, with an itemization in the nonprospectus portion of the *registration statement*. Some *blue sky laws* in *merit states* set maximums on offering expenses, such as a percentage of the total *proceeds* of the offering.

Offering price – The price at which *securities* are offered for sale in a *public offering*. Because it is offered to the public, it is not practical to negotiate the price with *prospects*. In an *underwritten public offering*, the offering price is fixed by the *underwriting agreement* between the company and the *managing underwriter*, typically after orders have been taken for all the *shares* (at an estimated price or range). In a *direct public offering*, the price will have been set by the company's *board of directors* before the offering begins.

Officers and directors' questionnaire – As part of the *underwriters'* and lawyers' *due diligence*, a lengthy list of questions is required to be answered in writing by the company's officers and *directors*.

Options – Contracts allowing the owners to buy or sell *securities* at an agreed price and within an agreed time. In an *underwritten public offering*, the company will often grant options (also called *underwriters' warrants*), giving the *underwriters* the right to buy a *new issue* of the company's *shares* at any time within five years after the offering. The price is set at the minimum permitted by the *NASD* and *blue sky laws*—usually from 100 percent to 140 percent of the *offering price*.

OTC Bulletin Board – An electronic information system started in June 1990. Initially available only to *NASD dealer* members who are *market makers* in *over-the-counter shares*, it displays names and telephone numbers of market makers in a company's *shares*. The dealers may or may not list firm or "unfirm" *bid price and asked price* quotations. Rules for use of the OTC Bulletin Board are expected to evolve to make it similar to *NAS-DAQ*, with more firm quotations and much broader access.

OTC companies – Corporations which have *over-the-counter shares* traded by *market makers*, rather than *exchange traded shares*.

OTC market – The "inter-dealer" trading of *shares*, where a *brokerage firm* quotes a *bid price* and an *asked price* at which it will buy or sell shares.

Overallotment – In an *underwriting syndicate*, the *managing underwriter* allots *shares* to be sold among the participating *securities firms*. The total number will initially be considerably more than shown in the *prospectus*, as the *underwriters* create a short position (selling more shares than they have agreed to purchase from the company). The reason for selling short is to cover *indications of interest* which become reneges after the *confirmations* are sent out to investors, as well as shares repurchased by the underwriters from *flippers* under a *stabilization bid*. If the amount of overallotment were to exceed the amount of reneges and stabilization bid repurchases, the *underwriting syndicate* would be forced to buy shares in the *aftermarket* in order to deliver shares sold in the *underwriting*. This could cause a *short loss*. That risk gave rise to the *green shoe* option which allows the underwriters to buy more shares at the *offering price* "to cover overallotments."

Over-the-counter shares – Corporate *shares* that are not listed for trading on a *stock exchange*. There are an estimated 47,000 different issues of shares traded over the counter in the United States, according to the *NASD*. Of these, approximately 4,300 meet standards for quotation on

NASDAQ. Bid *prices* and *asked prices* quoted by *market makers* for 10,000 to 12,000 issues are printed daily in the *Pink Sheets*. An increasing number of these are also available through computer terminals to subscribers of the *OTC Bulletin Board*.

Par value – When *shares* are issued, they may be assigned a par value. This number no longer has any practical meaning, except that it must be less than the *offering price*. Many corporations now issue "no par" shares, assigning them instead a "stated value" for accounting purposes.

Partial public offering – Selling *shares* in part of a business by having a subsidiary corporation *go public*. This is currently being done with subsidiaries operating in foreign countries, so that the *shares* can be marketed to residents there and traded on local *stock exchanges*. It could be especially appropriate for a *direct public offering*, where part of a business can be matched to *target markets* in another country.

Penny stocks – Low-price *shares*, trading at anywhere from a fraction of $.01 to $5. A price movement that is very small in amount can represent a large percentage change. Penny stocks are the specialty of some *securities firms*, many of which have defrauded investors by manipulating the market and misrepresenting the facts.

Pink Sheets – A 300-plus page book or electronic listing of about 10,000 to 12,000 corporate *shares* traded in the *over-the-counter* market. The name comes from the non-glare color of their original form. It's published once each business day. There are about 2,000 subscribers to the Pink Sheets, which has been published by the *National Quotation Bureau Inc.* since 1913. The National Quotation Bureau Inc. is now owned by the *NASD*, which also uses the information to display prices for some shares through its *OTC Bulletin Board*.

Poison pill – A *shark repellent* device to discourage a hostile *takeover* of a controlling number of the company's *shares*. A poison pill is a right to buy *securities* of the corporation at a bargain price, with the right being triggered by a hostile takeover. It is intended to make the takeover too costly to be profitable.

Positioning – A marketing strategy. It considers the frame of reference in the *prospects'* mind, then conveys an image to fit a particular mental position. The classic positioning is in contrast to a dominant competitor's product: "the Uncola," "We're No. 2," "IBM compatible." In a *direct public offering* it may be necessary to position corporate *shares* in reference to other investments (savings, real estate) or other ways to spend discretionary funds (automobiles, gambling). Then the particular company's distinguishing facts can be positioned within the prospects' understanding of the market, product, management, and competition. Positioning often comes after initial *market research* and *market segmentation*, but before planning the marketing program.

Posteffective period – The period after the *effective date* and before the *public offering* is considered to be over. During this time, any material changes in the information contained in the *prospectus* need to be disclosed, usually by *stickering the prospectus*.

Preferred shares – A separate class of corporate *shares* having some preferential feature over *common shares*. Preferences often include a right to receive a percentage rate of *dividends*, to be repaid first if the corporation liquidates, or to elect a majority of the *board of directors* if performance standards are not met. Preferred shares may be voting or nonvoting and may or may not participate in dividends on common shares.

Prefiling conference – A meeting with staff members of the *SEC* or state *blue sky laws* administrators, held before the filing of a *registration statement* for the proposed *public offering*. There may be a question as to whether the offering would meet the standards required by the laws, or whether some variation from usual practice may be used. Resolving these issues in a prefiling conference can prevent later delay or the receipt of a *bedbug letter* in response to a filing.

Prefiling period – The time between a decision to make a *public offering* and the initial filing under the securities laws. Care must be taken not to do something inadvertently that could be considered *gun-jumping* during the prefiling period.

Price/book ratio – The market price of a company divided by its *book value*, either in total or on a per *share* basis. For a company in the business of investing in marketable *securities*, which are frequently "marked to market" on the company's accounting records, book value can be a measure of real or market value; for most companies, however, it is not that useful.

Price/cash flow ratio – The market price of a company divided by the annual cash flow generated by the company. This is used by sophisticated analysts and investors, with varying interpretations and methodologies. "Cash flow" is the excess of cash received by a company during an accounting period over the amount paid out. It will differ from net earnings because nearly every company with *publicly traded shares* uses the accrual method of accounting, rather than the cash method. Some who use this ratio apply it to "free cash flow," meaning cash not required for debt retirement or asset replacement. Since there is no generally accepted definition or usage, comparisons can be misleading.

Price/earnings ratio – The market price of a company divided by its annual earnings, either on an historical or projected basis. This information is readily available in published tables of *publicly traded shares* and has become the most common means of comparing one corporation's *share* price with another's, as well as comparing stages in the *stock market* for *market timing*.

Price/revenue ratio – The market price of a company divided by its annual revenues, either on an historical or projected basis. Earnings may be thought of as unreliable for comparison, because they are so affected by the stage of a corporation's growth, by management policy, and by accounting methods. Some investors prefer using total revenue for comparison.

Primary market – The sale of a *new issue* of its *securities* by a corporation, in contrast to the sale of outstanding securities by their owner in the *secondary market*.

Private placement – In the language of the federal securities laws, a sale of *securities* "not involving a *public offering*." Generally, a negotiated sale between a corporation and one or a few investors. An *investment banker* or other agent may be involved for a fee. There is a web of regulations and decisions about what is legally a private placement, since the securities laws dictating use of a *prospectus* do not apply.

Privatization – When a government-owned business is transferred to nongovernment owners or operators. This can happen by contracting out a service formerly provided by government employees, or by negotiated sale of an operation. Privatizations through *initial public offerings* are occurring in nearly every part of the world, except North America. England and other countries have used consumer marketing campaigns to motivate the broadest individual purchase of *shares*.

Proceeds – The amount received by the *issuer* from a *public offering* of *securities* (after the *underwriting spread* in an *underwritten public offering*). Net proceeds is the amount after payment of all other *offering expenses*. Securities laws require that the *prospectus* have a "Use of Proceeds" section explaining what the issuer is going to do with the money received from investors.

Projections – Estimates of the future operations and conditions for a business. They have been permitted and encouraged for many years but almost never used in *prospectuses* for *underwritten public offerings* of *shares*. Projections are generally used in *private placements* of shares and in *public offerings* of *junk bonds*.

Promoter – The founder or organizer of a corporate business. Securities law administrators often require the identity and background of promoters to be described in the *prospectus*.

Promotional shares – *Shares* issued in return for services or ideas, usually when a business is first incorporated. Securities regulators look for full disclosure about promotional shares in the *prospectus*. Shares issued to founders or promoters at a nominal price within three years before filing the *registration statement*, will often be considered *cheap stock*, and it may be necessary for those shares to be kept in escrow for a period after the *public offering*.

Proposition – In *direct marketing* parlance, this is the first stage—the offer to *prospects* of something they can request through a *response*.

Prospects – Potential investors in the company's shares. In an *underwritten public offering*, they will be customers of *registered representatives* and those on lists used for *cold calling*. In a *direct public offering*, prospects may be people known to the company's employees and *directors*, names obtained through *market research* and *list brokers*. They may also be self-selected through their *response* to a *proposition* made in the *media*.

Prospectus – The disclosure document by which *public offering* of *securities* is made (sometimes known as an *offering circular*). The prospectus will be the major part of any filing with the *SEC* and with any state securities regulators under the *blue sky laws*. Its contents are prescribed by rules, forms, and instructions. In *underwritten public offerings*, a *prospect* does not see the prospectus until after placing an order to buy *shares*. It has often been said that only three kinds of people ever read the prospectus: the lawyers and accountants who prepare it, the SEC and blue sky laws staff assigned to review it, and the securities litigation attorneys hired to recover money lost from buying the shares. As a result of this view of the prospectus as a "liability document," it is generally very long and very difficult to read. In a *direct public offering*, the prospectus is the *fulfillment* of the prospect's *response* to the company's *proposition*. It is the principal selling tool, intended to be read before a decision is made to buy shares. To be effective it must be readable and interesting. This requires some change in the habits of securities lawyers and regulators.

Public offering – When *securities* are offered for sale to the public rather than in a negotiated *private placement*. The basic rule of the *Securities Act of 1933* is that no public offering may be made (unless an exemption applies) until delivery of a *prospectus*—and then only after the *effective date* of the *registration statement*, which includes the prospectus. There is a gray area into which companies may inadvertently stumble, where private becomes public in violation of the securities laws. This may be uncovered during the *corporate cleanup*, *due diligence*, or *regulatory review*, and can require a *recission offer*.

Public relations – Communications to the public in *media* that are not directly paid for, as opposed to advertising. It includes being mentioned in articles written by journalists, being featured on radio, TV news or feature programs, and other more subtle ways of having "independent" third parties convey facts or images which originated with the company. It can be done in ways that are entirely legal and ethical. While the cost may be much lower than purchasing media usage, the company probably has little control over the content of the message and the market to which it is distributed. The use of public relations in a *public offering* is made particularly sensitive by the risk of *gun-jumping*, that is, influencing *prospects* before they have received a copy of the *prospectus*.

Publicly traded shares – *Shares* that are available in the *secondary market* through a *securities firm*. Trading may occur through listing on a *stock exchange* or price quotation in the *over-the-counter market*. When few trades occur, shares are considered to be "thinly traded." Where it is necessary for a *broker* to make calls in order to find a match for a prospective buyer or seller, there is a "work out market," or a "market by appointment." There are numerical standards for *publicly traded shares* set by the stock exchanges, *NASDAQ*, and the *Securities Exchange Act of 1934*. They include having a minimum number of *shareowners* and a required *float*.

Qualify – This has two different meanings in *public offerings*. To qualify shares under a state's *blue sky laws* means to meet the requirements for a public offering to that state's residents. To qualify the *prospects* for a share offering means to determine that they then have the interest and the *suitability* to invest in the shares.

Quiet period – A period of up to 90 days after the *effective date* of an *IPO* during which a *prospectus* may have to be delivered to buyers in the *secondary market*. Special care is necessary for any other written communications, especially if they are not preceded or accompanied by a *prospectus*.

Recirculation – Providing another *prospectus* to persons who received an earlier version. This may be required for people who were provided a *red herring*. It may become necessary as a result of *stickering the prospectus* or having to print an amended prospectus.

Recission offer – An offer to existing *shareowners* to exchange their *shares* for return of the price they paid. A recission offer is usually made only because the shares are considered to have been originally sold in violation of the *securities* laws. Most often this is discovered by the securities lawyers during the *corporate cleanup* or *due diligence*. A typical case is a series of share sales to small groups of investors without following the filing and *prospectus* deliver requirements for a *public offering*.

Red herring – A preliminary *prospectus* that has been filed with the *SEC* but is used before its *effective date*. The name comes from the legend required to be printed on the cover, in red ink, to the effect that it is not a final prospectus. *Shares* can not be offered by the red herring and anyone receiving the red herring must later be given a final prospectus.

Regional exchange – One of the five remaining *stock exchanges* in the United States, other than the New York and the American. They include the Boston, Chicago (formerly Midwest), Cincinnati, Pacific, and Philadelphia. The Cincinnati does not currently trade *shares* for the public market. The other four primarily trade "dually listed" shares, ones which are also traded on the *New York Stock Exchange* or another market. The "exclusive listings" are either *"Tier 1"* or *"Tier 2"* based upon numerical size standards. The principal difference is the number of states in which listing results in treatment as *exempt securities*.

Registered representative – An individual licensed to act as agent for a *broker-dealer* in buying and selling *securities* for the account of others. Also known as *"brokers,"* "stockbrokers," "account executives," *"financial planners,"* "financial consultants," and "investment representatives." At most *securities firms*, the registered representatives keep from 35 percent to 75 percent of the commissions generated on their transactions. Discount brokers pay their registered representatives a salary to process orders from customers without giving advice or participating in the investment decision.

Registered shares – Corporate *shares* covered by a registration statement filed with the *SEC*. When shares are registered for a *public offering* under the *Securities Act of 1933*, it is only for the purposes of that offering. When a corporation's shares meet the standards for being considered as *publicly traded*, they must be registered under the *Securities Exchange Act of 1934*.

Registrar – The keeper of the records showing the ownership of *shares*. it is now a combined function with the *transfer agent*, which records transfer of shares from one owner to another. A company may act as its own registrar and transfer agent or may contract the service to a bank corporate trust department, or a data services company.

Registration statement – A filing required by the *SEC* for a *public offering* under the *Securities Act of 1933* or for *publicly traded shares* under the *Securities Exchange Act of 1934*.

Regulation A – An exemption made by the *SEC* from filing a registration statement under the *Securities Act of 1933*. It applies to offerings below a certain dollar amount, which has changed over the years. It still requires much of the same filing material and process as a registration statement, but is processed through regional SEC offices, rather than Washington, D.C. (except for any number of interpretations for which the regional officials may have to send to Washington).

Regulatory review – Review of the registration statement by the staff of the *SEC* and state *blue sky laws* administrators.

Reneges – Cancellations by investors who have placed orders in an *underwritten public offering*. They will have expressed their *indication of interest* to a *registered representative* for a member of the *underwriting syndicate* or *selling group* before the effective date. They will then receive a *confirmation* with the *prospectus*. Within five days the investor must pay for the *shares*. Those who do not are reneges and the shares allotted to them come back to the underwriting syndicate.

Response – The object of a *direct marketing proposition* is to get a response, which occurs when the *prospects* request the *prospectus*.

Restricted shares – Sale of restricted shares is limited, either because of who owns them (such as an *insider*), or because of the way they were acquired (such as in a *private placement*). The restriction may be imposed by the securities laws or by an agreement. When *shares* are used as incentive compensation to employees, they are often subject to a restriction that they can only be sold back to the company until a certain date or event.

Results/cost ratio – Dividing the cost of a *direct marketing* program into the sales or other dollar measurement of results. This is often done with *test marketing*, the use of selected *media*, or lists of *prospects*.

Rights offering – An offering of *securities* made only to persons who are already owners of the company's securities. The name comes from the day when it was common for a company's charter to give current holders the first right to acquire *new issues*. That provision is rare today, but many corporations find they can raise all the capital they need by asking their existing *shareowners* if they would like to buy more.

Risk factors – A section near the front of a *prospectus*, calling attention to the most significant risks of loss from an investment in the company's *shares*. Usually required in *IPOs*.

Road show – Also known as *dog and pony show*. In the last week or so before the *effective date* of an *underwritten public offering*, there is usually a road show. Top officers of the company, *investment bankers*, and perhaps lawyers and *auditors*, travel to meetings with *money managers* and representatives of the *underwriting syndicate*. These are usually conducted over the days' three meals, with smaller sessions for major *prospects*. Preparation for road shows is often very elaborate, with speech training, mock session rehearsals, video, and slide presentations. *Shares* can legally be offered only by the *prospectus*; however, that document is not yet available in required final form at the time of the road show. While the road show cannot lawfully provide any information that is not available to the entire public, it is typically the only marketing effort in which the company participates.

Safe harbor rules – The *SEC* has issued interpretations for some of its rules, giving numerical and other objective standards. They are not the exclusive answers. However, if the facts of a particular situation fall within those standards, then the rules provide a "safe harbor" and the company does not need to get a *no-action letter* or other assurance that it will not violate the securities laws. There are, for instance, safe harbor rules with respect to the use of financial forecasts in a *prospectus*.

SCOR (Small Corporate Offering Registration) – Also known as *ULOR*, the Uniform Limited Offering Registration. It is a procedure for *public offerings* of *securities* in amounts of up to $1 million every 12 months. These "small offerings" are exempt from *SEC* registration but must still *qualify* under state *blue sky laws* that require delivery of a *prospectus* or offering circular to *prospects*. The form used by corporations has been approved by a committee of the American Bar Association and by *NASAA*. The SCOR rules had been adopted in 18 states through 1990. (42 states by 1997.)

SEC The United States Securities and Exchange Commission – administers the federal *securities* laws.

Secondary market – The *trading market* for *securities* that have been previously issued by a corporation. (The original issuance would have been an offering in the *primary market.*)

Secondary offering – An offering, generally through an *underwriting*, of *securities* already issued and owned by a *selling shareowner*. This occurs when the number of *shares* to be sold is considered too large for the *trading market* to absorb without harmful effects on the market price. A secondary offering is often included with a primary offering made at the same time by the company. When there is a secondary offering included in the *initial public offering*, some investors believe it shows a lack of faith and an effort by the selling shareowners to bail out. The term secondary offering is frequently misused to apply when a company makes its second *public offering*.

Securities – There has been considerable litigation over what securities are, especially in the areas of real estate transactions, borrowings, and joint ventures. Corporate *shares* are clearly within the definitions of securities.

Securities Act of 1933 – Amended from time to time, this law is the federal structure governing *public offerings* of *securities*, the *primary market*. It is administered by the *SEC*.

Securities Exchange Act of 1934 – (There is no "and" in the title, as there is in the "Securities and Exchange Commission.") Amended from time to time, this law is the federal structure governing the trading of *securities*, the *secondary market*. It defines and governs *stock exchanges*, *securities firms*, and other participants in the securities markets.

Securities firm – A business which acts as a *broker*, *dealer*, or *investment banker*.

Securities fraud – Transactions in *securities* are subject to the same laws concerning fraud as other types of commerce. In addition, the securities laws make certain specific actions subject to criminal prosecution, to *SEC* "cease and desist" enforcement, and to actions for damages by persons claiming loss. These are referred to as securities fraud.

Selected dealer agreement – Large *public offerings* often require a broader *telemarketing* network than all the *registered representatives* employed by members of all the *underwriting syndicate*. Other *securities firms* will be invited to sell a specific number of *shares* in return for the selling concession portion of the *underwriting spread*. They sign a selected dealer agreement, which becomes effective when the *underwriting agreement* is signed.

Selling concession – The portion of the *underwriting spread* paid to the *securities firm* employing the *registered representative* who actually sells shares in an *underwritten public offering*. The selling concession is typically 60 percent of the underwriting spread.

Selling group – The *securities firms* who sell shares in an *underwritten public offering*, but not as members of the *underwriting syndicate*. They sign a *selected dealer agreement* and receive a *selling concession* for *shares* they sell.

Selling materials – Any written, filmed, recorded, or broadcast materials used in selling the *shares* other than the *prospectus*. Except for a very limited announcement of the proposed *public offering*, no selling materials may be communicated to *prospects* until after the *effective date*, and then only if they are preceded or accompanied by a final prospectus. During this *free writing period*, the *fulfillment* package will include selling materials along with the prospectus. Additional selling materials will be used in the follow-up efforts for *conversion*.

Selling shareowners – In a *secondary offering*, the persons selling their *shares* in the company.

Selling short – Selling *shares* without delivering them by the *settlement date*. The seller borrows shares from another owner to meet the delivery requirement. The purpose is to eventually replace the borrowed shares by buying later, at a lower price. If the seller owns the shares, but still chooses not to deliver them, it is called "selling short against the box," a practice used for income tax purposes.

Settlement date – When payment for *securities* is due and certificates are to be delivered, generally three (five before 1996) business days after the *confirmations* of sale are dated and mailed.

Shareowners – Persons owning *shares* in a corporation. Also known as shareholders or stockholders.

Shareowners' equity – The dollar amount of the *shareowners'* interest in the corporation, as shown on its accounting records. Also known as *net worth* or *book value.*

Shares – Fractional ownership interests in a corporation. Shares are also called *stock.* There are *common shares* and *preferred shares.* They generally have the right to vote for the election of *directors* and on certain policy issues. Shares receive whatever *dividends* the *board of directors* decides should be paid. If the company is sold or liquidated, *shareowners* receive whatever is left over after payment to all creditors.

Shark repellents – Legal devices used to prevent a *takeover* of a controlling number of a company's *shares.* They are intended to make the acquisition too costly for the outsider, thereby protecting the *insiders.*

Shelf offering – A *public offering* of *securities* which have been through the *effective date* of a *registration statement* and then held "on the shelf" until the company decides to offer them. This allows management to indulge in *market timing,* trying to sell securities when the terms are most favorable to the company. It also encourages *bought deals,* where *underwriters* come to the company after they have already arranged for the buy side of a transaction.

Shell corporation – A corporation with *publicly traded shares* but no operating business. This can happen when the business has been sold or discontinued without dissolving the corporate form. It also results from a *blind pool IPO.* By placing an operating business into the shell corporation, a business can *go public* by the *back door.*

Short loss – Money lost by the *underwriting syndicate* as a result of selling more shares in the *underwriting* than it agreed to buy from the *issuer* (including shares purchased under the *green shoe* option). Twenty percent of the *underwriting spread* is intended to help defray any short loss (see *flipper, overallotment,* and *reneges*).

Short swing profits – Once a company has *securities* registered under the *Securities Exchange Act of 1934,* officers, *directors,* and owners of more than 10 percent of the *shares* must file reports. They must also pay over to the company all "profits" resulting from any matching of sales and purchases of shares within any six-month period. This rule has nothing to do with intent and is often triggered accidentally.

Small cap stocks – The shares of companies with a *market capitalization* of less than $100 million to over $500 million, depending on the line drawn by a *money manager.* Measurement may also be in terms of the *float.*

Soft dollar deals – Arrangements where goods or services are provided to investors, usually *money managers,* in return for an understanding that the provider will be compensated in commissions from *securities* transactions. For instance, a *securities firm* may provide research services to a money manager. When that money manager buys *shares* in an *underwritten public offering*, it may instruct the *managing underwriter* to treat it as a *directed sale* so that the *selling concession* is paid to the provider of soft dollar services. Before Mayday 1975, when fixed commission rates were deregulated in the *trading market*, money managers used soft dollar deals to get volume discounts for their trades. Now, commissions in the *secondary market* have all been negotiated down by money managers to a fraction of their fixed level, leaving no room for discounts. The *underwriting spreads* on *bonds* have been similarly negotiated down by the large corporate borrowers, especially with the tools of *shelf offerings* and *bought deals*. (Rated bond *public offerings* that paid .875 percent are now sold at .25 percent or less. Unrated *junk bonds* were underwritten at 3.0 percent or more, but very few have recently been issued.) As a result, about the only vestige of pre-Mayday commission rates is in underwritten public offerings of shares, particularly *IPOs*, where the underwriting spread has actually increased from about 6 percent to 7 percent. Money managers are the major buyers of *underwritten initial public offerings* and use them extensively to make payments on soft dollar deals.

Specialist – The *securities firm* assigned to make the market for a company's *shares* on a *stock exchange*. A specialist continuously announces *bid prices* and *asked prices* and generally owns an inventory of the shares. All trades in *listed shares*, by *brokers* or *dealers* who are members of the stock exchange, are required to go through the specialist (with increasing exceptions). The specialist is a dealer, buying and selling shares for the dealers' own account. This serves to maintain an inventory, allowing trades when there are no corresponding bid and asked prices being offered. It also allows the specialist to accumulate positions in the shares for an expected profit on future moves in the market.

Sponsor – A person, group, or company standing behind an offering of *shares*. Investors can reasonably conclude that the sponsor has performed *due diligence* and has an economic stake in the company or its shares. In *underwritten public offerings*, the *managing underwriter* is usually thought of as a sponsor (and is referred to by that term in England). In a *direct public offering* there may be a large corporate *strategic partner* or *venture capitalist* who purchased shares of the company in an earlier *private placement* and whose name conveys endorsement or sponsorship. Arrangements can be made for a recognized name to be a sponsor through a *standby commitment*, by agreeing to buy all shares not purchased by *prospects* in the offering.

Self-Regulatory Organization (SRO) – A trade group recognized by the *SEC* as capable of enforcing rules about fairness of the *securities* markets. Principal SROs are the *stock exchanges* and the *NASD*.

Stabilization bid – A bid for *shares* made shortly after the *underwritten public offering* by a member of the *underwriting syndicate*. There is a specific exemption for this under the antimanipulation provisions of the *securities* laws. The purpose is to keep the market price from falling below the *offering price* until the *underwriting syndicate* has disposed of all the shares it committed to buy in the *underwriting agreement*.

Standby commitment – An agreement to purchase any *shares* left over after completion of a *public offering*. This is commonly done in a *rights offering*, where a standby *underwriter* agrees to purchase all shares not subscribed for by the existing *shareowners*. Initially, the function of an underwriter in a public offering was to insure that all the money would be raised by issuing a standby commitment. It was akin to a performance bond. Today, there is only a *letter of intent* between the underwriter and the company proposing to *go public*. The risk that the public offering will not occur, or that the *offering price* will decline substantially, is borne entirely by the company. It is not until hours before the *effective date*, after all the selling efforts have been completed, that the contemporary underwriters will sign an *underwriting agreement* to buy the shares at an agreed price.

Statutory underwriter – Someone who has become an *underwriter* within the meaning of the securities laws, even if that was not the intended status. The statutory definition of underwriter has sometimes been interpreted very broadly, especially where *securities fraud* has been alleged. Persons who purchased *shares* from the company or an *insider* and then resold them, may find they are a statutory underwriter. So may persons who provide services in a public offering. Since liability can arise solely out of the status of underwriter, often without regard to intent, it is an important area for preventative law.

Stickering the prospectus – Attaching a paper to the cover of a *prospectus* as a means of providing additional information. This is often required when material events occur after the *effective date*, but before the offering is concluded. It is an alternative to printing a new prospectus with amendments. Sometimes, the *SEC* will require *recirculation* of the revision to everyone who received the original prospectus. In rare circumstances, a *recission offer* may be required.

Stock – Another name for corporate *shares*.

Stock exchange – One of the seven national securities exchanges registered with the *SEC* (New York, American, Boston, Chicago, Cincinnati, Pacific, and Philadelphia). *Shares* of U.S. companies may also be traded on the *Vancouver Stock Exchange* or other foreign-based *stock exchanges*.

Stock market – The *trading market* for *shares* including the *stock exchanges* and the *over-the-counter* market (quoted on *NASDAQ*, the *OTC Bulletin Board*, or in the *Pink Sheets*). The stock market for *listed shares* is made by the assigned *specialist* for the stock exchange. For shares traded over-the-counter, one or more *securities firms* act as *market makers*. Beyond the stock exchanges and the over-the-counter markets, there are the so-called "third market" and "fourth market." The "third market" is made by securities firms who trade listed shares among themselves without going through a stock exchange. This *disintermediation* of the specialist is carried one step further in the "fourth market," where *money managers* trade among themselves without even going through a securities firm as *broker* or *dealer*.

Strategic partner – A business which has bought *shares* in the company through a *private placement* for the dual purpose of making an investment return and helping its own business. Large corporations often become strategic partners of companies still in their development stage. This can provide access to new technology that complements the large corporation's products. It may give them access to a market they have not otherwise developed. In addition to investing *capital*, the strategic partner may also provide support services to the smaller business. Some entrepreneurs try to avoid having a strategic partner, feeling that they lose some independence in future policy decisions.

Street name – When certificates for *shares* owned by an investor are issued and held in the name of a nominee. *Securities firms* often own all or part of a nominee corporation, used exclusively as the street name in which *securities* are held for its customers. The reason is to make shares more quickly available for transfer in the event they are sold. Sometimes, a street name is used to conceal the identity of the real owner from corporate management or others.

Suitability – A test for whether someone really should be investing in a particular *security*. Checking suitability goes along with the *know-your-customer rule*. Several *blue sky laws* require that certain investments be offered only to persons meeting a set of suitability standards, usually related to wealth and income. Determining suitability is part of what it means to *qualify* a prospect.

Supermajority – When a vote requires more than a majority of the *shares* owned by the *shareowners*. Provisions of the corporate charter may, in some states, provide that a merger or a recall of the *directors*, for instance, must be approved by 80 percent of the shares. The purpose is usually to create a *shark repellent* in order to prevent a *takeover*.

Takeover – The transfer of a controlling interest in a corporation, usually by a purchase of more than half its outstanding *shares*. Although there can be a friendly takeover, the term usually refers to a hostile takeover. The best protection against a takeover is having a broad base of individual shareownership and a share price in the *trading market* that does not represent a bargain when compared to the company's "real value." *Shark* *repellents* are used as defenses against takeovers, but they are generally perceived as being for the benefit of management rather than *shareowners*.

Tangible book value – The *book value* (also known as *shareowners' equity* and *net worth*) after adjustment by subtracting the recorded amount for such intangibles as good will. It is intended to represent the "hard assets" of the company less its liabilities.

Target markets – *Prospects* for buying the company's *shares* organized into groups with similar characteristics, such as place of residence, occupation, or other *demographics*. The target markets are defined through *market segmentation*.

Telemarketing – Using the telephone as a means of marketing. This has been virtually the only medium employed in *underwritten public offerings*, where *securities firms* have their *registered representatives* telephone *prospects* to announce the offering, make a sales presentation, and take an order—preferably all in one call. In a *direct public offering*, telemarketing is one component of the marketing program. It may be passive (limited to answering incoming *responses* from prospects to the *proposition*) or active (initiating follow-up calls to prospects, after the *fulfillment* for their *conversion* into a sale). Careful procedures must be prepared and supervised to avoid violation of the securities laws, especially if the telemarketing staff are not registered representatives under the supervision of a registered *broker-dealer*.

Test marketing – A limited offering of *shares* to a *target market*, using particular *media* or copy or graphic presentation. The purpose is to refine the marketing program as quickly and cost-effectively as possible.

Tier 1 or Tier 2 stocks – The Chicago, Pacific, and Philadelphia Stock Exchanges each has two classes of listings for companies' stocks, based upon numerical size standards. Those companies qualifying for Tier 1 will be exempt from *blue sky filings* in all states. Tier 2 companies are exempt in about 25 to 30 states.

Time and responsibility schedule – A listing of all the steps to be accomplished in preparing and completing a *public offering*, together with the time by which the step is to be accomplished and the name of the person responsible for seeing that it is done.

Tombstone ad – A formal announcement of a proposed or completed *public offering*. In an *underwritten public offering*, the tombstone ad typically appears only after the sale is completed. It advertises the names of the *underwriting syndicate* and shows that the *managing underwriter* has originated and completed a deal. The name tombstone ad comes from the sparse copy and the layered format. In a *direct public offering*, a tombstone ad can be used to announce a forthcoming offering. After the *effective date*, a tombstone ad can be used as the *proposition* stage of a direct public offering, promising to deliver a copy of the *prospectus* to the reader. It will contain a coupon, address, and a telephone and facsimile number for the *response*. In a *broker-assisted* offering, the tombstone ad may suggest calling any of the participating *securities firms* or *financial planners*.

Trading market – Where *publicly traded shares* are bought and sold. The *secondary market*, which is made either by a *specialist* for *shares* listed on a *stock exchange* or by *market makers* for *over-the-counter shares*.

Transfer agent – The keeper of records showing transfers of the record ownership of *shares*. This is generally combined with the *registrar* and may be performed by the company or an independent contractor.

ULOR (Uniform Limited Offering Registration) – Also known as *SCOR*. Available under some state *blue sky laws* for *public offerings* of not more than $1 million, which are then exempt from *SEC* registration.

Unbundling – Separating services that were formerly sold as a package. In *securities firms*, this has meant having businesses that only act as a *broker* and not as a *dealer* or *investment banker*. Many *financial planners* sell only financial advice, unbundled from any other services.

Underwriter – A *securities firm* that sells securities in an *underwritten public offering* and then purchases those securities from the *issuer*. The name came from the former practice, where the underwriter became legally obligated to buy the securities at a fixed price, well in advance of selling them to the public. In insurance terms, it underwrote the risk that the securities would not be sold to the public at a price higher than the underwriter agreed to pay the company.

Underwriters' warrants – Also known as *options*. They are rights to buy *shares* of the *issuer* in the future at prices based upon the *offering price* in an *underwritten public offering*. They represent additional compensation to the *underwriters* beyond the *underwriting spread*. Their terms are usually for five years, with the option price starting at 100 percent of the offering price and increasing by 10 percent each year. These terms are limited by *blue sky laws* and the *NASD*, which also permit the warrants to cover no more than 10 percent of the number of shares in the *underwriting*.

Underwriting – The process of doing an *underwritten public offering*.

Underwriting agreement – The legal document which commits the *underwriters* to buy *securities* in an *underwritten public offering*. Typically signed just hours before the *effective date*—after orders for more than the entire offering have been obtained—it fixes the *offering price* and the *underwriting spread*, usually within a range stated in the *letter of intent*.

Underwriting spread – The commission paid to the *underwriters* in an *underwritten public offering*. It is called "the spread" because it equals the difference between the *offering price* and the *proceeds* of the offering paid to the *issuer* before *offering expenses*. An underwriting spread is generally divided in these proportions: A 60 percent *selling concession* to the *securities firm* employing the *registered representative* who sold the *shares*; a 20 percent "management fee" to the *managing underwriter*; and 20 percent for the "syndicate account," which pays the underwriters' expenses and applies toward any *short loss*.

Underwriting syndicate – The group of *securities firms* that have signed an *agreement among underwriters* to sell a specified amount of an *underwritten public offering* and to bear a proportion of the *underwriters'* risks and expenses. Most of the selling is done through *telemarketing* by employees of syndicate members.

Underwritten initial public offering – A company's first *public offering* of its *shares*, which it has chosen to do through an *underwriting*.

Underwritten public offering – An offering of *securities* to the public, using a *securities firm* as an *underwriter*. The securities are sold by *registered representatives* of the underwriters to *prospects* they have selected. Selling occurs through *telemarketing*. If sufficient orders are collected for the securities, an *underwriting agreement* is signed. A week later there is a *closing*, where the underwriters pay the company the *offering price* for the *shares* less their *underwriting spread* and expenses.

Vancouver Stock Exchange – A *stock exchange* based in Vancouver, British Columbia, Canada, which has often been the trading mechanism for U.S. and Canadian companies conducting their *initial public offering* of *emerging growth stocks*.

Venture capital – Money invested in a business in its early stages, when the risk of loss is generally greater and there is usually no *trading market* into which *securities* can be sold. There are stages of *venture capital* investment, from start-up or seed *capital* to second-round or sprout capital, mezzanine financing, and on to succeeding rounds. A venture capitalist—the investor—needs a potential exit from the investment, usually either a *public offering* or a sale of the entire business. Venture capitalists may be friends and relatives of the entrepreneur, venture capital firms, individual *angel investors* (*informal investors*), or other corporations as *strategic partners*.

Videotex – Use of a video monitor for the *direct marketing* of products and services. Information may be transmitted by cable TV installations to the *prospects'* television receivers, through telephone installations to the prospects' computers, or by the prospects' operation of the keyboard at a retail site. Most videotex only delivers the *proposition*; a prospect's *response* comes through telephone, personal appearance, or other *media*. *Interactive marketing* through videotex will be particularly useful for *direct public offerings*, with the *prospectus* instantly accessible to prospects. The proposition, response, *fulfillment*, and *conversion* could take place during a single online interaction. New "multi-media" cards for personal computers allow the user to combine digital transmission from a computer with images from television, videodisk, or VCR. This will allow a completely electronic fulfillment package of the textual prospectus and graphic *selling materials*.

Waiting period – The time between the filing of a *registration statement* with the *SEC* (or application to *qualify shares* under *blue sky laws*) and the *effective date* of that filing. Because there is no final *prospectus* available, no sales of shares can be made. Care must be taken to avoid *gun-jumping*, although the rules are somewhat different from the *prefiling period*. For instance, oral statements are permitted, even if they would be considered offers to sell shares. Video and slide presentations of company officers talking may be allowed, especially if the officers are available in person for questioning.

When-as-and-if-issued market (WAII market) – When a *public offering* of *securities* is expected, a *trading market* will sometimes develop in advance. In periods when there have been many *hot new issues*, speculators have bought and sold *shares* with payment and delivery to be made when, as, and if the shares are actually issued. This is a form of risk *arbitrage*, where the participants are predicting the *offering price* and the subsequent price in the trading market.

Wire house - A large *securities firm* with multiple offices serving retail (*individual investor*) customers. The name is from the days when orders for trading *securities* were transmitted to New York headquarters by a proprietary telegraph or telephone wire.

INDEX

A

B

E

F

J

L

About the Author

Drew Field has provided direct share marketing advisory services since 1976, helping clients raise over $100 million in Direct Public Offerings of corporate shares to individual investors. As a securities lawyer and CPA, Field has not only advised companies on DPOs, but also provided consultation on private financings, acquisitions, and restructurings. Field's expertise is widely syndicated, with columns appearing in *Management Review*, *Business Horizons*, *San Francisco Business Times*, as well as more than 10 banking journals nationwide. He has also appeared in many business publications and major newspapers, including *Inc.*, *U.S. News & World Report*, *The Wall Street Journal*, *The Los Angeles Times*, and *The San Francisco Chronicle*.

Field has been a member of the California State Bar since 1960 and Certified Public Accountant in California since 1961.